Body and Soul

Body and Soul

*Jazz and Blues
in American Film,
1927–63*

Peter Stanfield

University of Illinois Press

Urbana and Chicago

© 2005 by Peter Francis Stanfield
All rights reserved
Manufactured in the United States of America

♾ This book is printed on acid-free paper.

1 2 3 4 5 C P 5 4 3 2 1
Library of Congress Cataloging-in-Publication Data
Stanfield, Peter, 1958–
Body and soul : jazz and blues in American film,
1927–63 / Peter Stanfield.
p. cm.
Includes bibliographical references and index.
ISBN 0-252-02994-1 (cloth : alk. paper)
ISBN 0-252-07235-9 (pbk. : alk. paper)
1. Jazz in motion pictures.
2. Blues (Music) in motion pictures.
3. Race in motion pictures.
I. Title.
PN1995.9.J37S72   2005
791.43'657—dc22   2004029989

In memory of Lee Brilleaux and Joe Strummer,
rockers supreme

Contents

Acknowledgments

This book was written with the aid of many, but most is owed to Esther Sonnet. Esther, without you this would be worth no more than a nickel and a nail.

I also want to acknowledge the help of Ron Sonnet, who was the first to read the manuscript and whose love and knowledge of jazz music inspired many of this book's more interesting digressions and footnotes—Jelly Roll Morton always sounds better in his company.

Frank Krutnik provided videos and CDs galore. His critical reading of parts of this book was greatly appreciated. Frank's work is an inspiration, as is Steve Neale's, Richard Maltby's, Ed Buscombe's, and Lee Grieveson's; all generously gave time and encouragement to this project. Thanks also to Corin Willis for tapes and ideas and Andy Forbes, librarian at Southampton Institute, who located numerous obscure titles. Thanks as well to John Paddy Browne, who provided an essential recorded version of "Frankie and Johnny."

This project was supported by a research leave grant from the Arts and Humanities Research Board and a sabbatical provided by Southampton Institute. Special thanks to Anne Massey, whose tour of duty at Southampton Institute ensured that academic research was both encouraged and supported.

Though much revised, parts of this book were previously published:

"'An Octoroon in the Kindling': American Vernacular and Blackface Minstrelsy in 1930s Hollywood." *Journal of American Studies* 31, no. 3 (1997): 407–38.

Acknowledgments

"'Extremely Dangerous Material': Hollywood and the Ballad of Frankie and Johnny." In *Classic Hollywood, Classic Whiteness,* ed. Daniel Bernardi, 442–66. Minneapolis: University of Minnesota Press, 2001.

"An Excursion into the Lower Depths: Hollywood, St. Louis Blues, and Urban Primitivism." *Cinema Journal* 41, no. 2 (Winter 2002): 84–108.

Body and Soul

Introduction

What do you think were the tunes they danced to?
What were the figures they advanced to,
Up and down as they chanced to?
Tails they were too long!
"Duck in the kitchen," "Old Aunt Sally,"
Plain cotillion, "Who keeps Tally?"
Up and down they charge and rally!
—"The Monkey's Wedding"

"America was born in the streets."
—*Gangs of New York* (2002)

Though *Gangs of New York* gives its own particular gloss on an American street culture, it is but an echo of a story told many times before by Hollywood and others. In Bill the Butcher's hangout of the 1860s, Satan's Circus, a young black man "wearing a pair of scuffed shoes hammers out a syncopated rhythm on broken glass—an early version of tap dancing." "Look at that," says Bill. "What is that? Rhythms of the Dark Continent tapped out in a fine American mess . . . a jig doing a jig."[1] To give weight to this small unspectacular moment in the film's unfolding, Bill's question, dramatic pause, and answer attempt to momentarily still the narrative. The dance is significant because it symbolizes America's becoming. The subterranean Satan's Circus is the meeting place for the Atlantic diaspora: Europeans and Africans cross paths here and in that moment share, borrow, or steal the other's culture. The fair or unfair exchange produces a distinctive American accent: African and Irish rhythms ("a jig doing a jig") recast as an American tap dance.

With its historical setting in the early years of the American Civil War, riots against the draft providing the backdrop to its climax, its motley cast of first-generation Americans and Irish immigrants, and the dramatization of an emerging modern political system, *Gangs of New York* is "about" America. As the nation undergoes its first true test, a civil war which has at its center the figure of the slave, the film reflects upon the conflict by reenacting *Uncle Tom's Cabin* in a Bowery theater. The play's concern with an America divided over race is carried into the audience, which launches a barrage of rotten fruit against the angelic image of Abraham Lincoln hanging on a wire above the tableau of death played out on the stage below. The violence escalates when an Irish assassin shoots Butcher Bill, the leader of the Nativists. Given the wider context of the Civil War, the image of Americans fighting over representations of themselves is apt. But the film's turn away from Uncle Tom and to Bill, from black to white as the victim of violence, is symptomatic of a wider elision of historical fact confirmed by the role given to African Americans as "innocent bystanders" caught up in the maelstrom of the draft riots, rather than one of the key targets of the rioters' wrath.

The film's use of black characters, one suspects, serves only as an authenticating presence demanded by a concern for historical verisimilitude. Like the tap dancer, blacks in this version of American history are left to dance in the shadows cast by the light the filmmakers chose to shine on the humdrum toil of the film's stars. Yet if the film evacuates any real historical sense of the symbolic power that such a dancing figure might hold as the lived embodiment of cultural crossing—an "American mess"—it nonetheless gestures toward a complex and rich historical narrative that, as I want to explore here, has defined American popular culture.

In *Impossible Purities,* Jennifer DeVere Brody provides a paradigm for understanding English and American national identity. She argues that, in counterpoint to an Englishness constituted as white, masculine, and pure, Victorian culture produced an American identity figured as black, feminine, and impure. The selections from American culture that I have chosen to present here are all marked, to use Brody's turns of phrase, as "impure," "muddied," "muddled and mixed"—an American mess.[2] In the films I discuss, American cultural identity is presented as a miscegenated product defined in terms of hybridization rather than as an essential, pure essence. Placed alongside the "impossible purity" of the white, highborn Englishman, the American offers a mirror opposite. Of low estate and mixed origin, American culture emerges from the gutters and streets of the metropolitan New World. Hollywood routinely dramatized this process, producing, at its best, a poeticized version of burgeoning American identity that resisted and opposed an Old World value system.

Marking some of the earliest documented instances of American minstrelsy, cultural historian W. T. Lhamon Jr. records the "overlay" of identities, the "joinings" and "mergers" that accompanied the dancers in New York's Catherine Market during the nineteenth century's formative years:

> At Catherine Market and other early spots for the performances of American culture there was an eagerness to combine, share, join, draw from opposites, play on opposition. An enthusiasm for the underlying possibilities in difference continually reappears in the popular-folk culture of the Atlantic diaspora. People in the market at Catherine Slip articulated these possibilities early. The market at Catherine Slip was a relay in the conduction of that culture, a relay that stamped what it passed on.[3]

The imprint embossed by all this stamping, all the dancing for eels, and all the jumping for Jim Crow, was carried forward by professional performers whose livelihood depended on their ability to make a fine American mess out of black and white, creating an indisputable American art form—blackface minstrelsy. By the time Hollywood attached synchronized sound and music to the minstrel's stamping feet, the streets of Catherine Market had long acceded to the stages of vaudeville and the banjo's clatter had been harnessed to jazz, adding its all to the American dance hall whirl of cacophony and melody. The products of miscegenated culture, minstrelsy, jazz, and blues were America's gutter music.

For a hundred years, discourses on national identity, race, European ethnic assimilation, and the problem of class division within the United States had been principally addressed in the popular arts through the agency of the black mask of minstrelsy. Although blackface was waning as a form of mass entertainment by the late 1920s, its influence on successive musical and theatrical forms would never entirely disappear. The most obvious legacy of blackface was its location at the center of America's theatrical history, and, as such, its use in American films was primarily determined by its value as a nostalgic symbol. This theatrical legacy of

3

minstrelsy corresponded well with the excesses of lurid folk songs with a black cultural provenance, such as "Frankie and Johnny" and its commercial counterparts like "St. Louis Blues." What both the commercial and folk forms shared with minstrelsy was a concern with the figuration of "blackness" in their production of an American vernacular. Outside of its nostalgic evocation of minstrelsy, Hollywood made greater use of the legacy of blackface performance through the manner in which it presented black musical forms. This enabled the development of more insinuated representational practices that removed the black greasepaint while continuing a tradition of performance plays with race, sexuality, and class.

With its suggested promotion of illicit acts of sexual, racial, gender, and class communion, jazz undermines not only the pieties and moral certainties of bourgeois sentimental popular music, but its discordant nature also made it an insolent provocateur of highbrow, European-born culture. Cultural historian Lawrence W. Levine writes:

> I am convinced that we should know ourselves better if we understood our past more firmly as the history of a people who attained political and economic independence long before we attained cultural independence. Culturally we remained, to a much larger extent than we have yet recognized, a colonized people attempting to define itself in the shadow of the former imperial power. Jazz was an expression of that other side of ourselves that strove to recognize the positive aspects of our newness and our heterogeneity; that learned to be comfortable with the fact that a significant part of our heritage derived from Africa and other non-European sources; and that recognized in the various syncretized cultures that became so characteristic of the United States not an embarrassing weakness but a dynamic source of strength.[4]

As American music, jazz and blues are defined as black, but they are not purely black and American any more than a true-born Englishman is purely white and English. As Brody writes, "The visibility of perfect whiteness (or blackness) may be merely the suppression and denial of blackness (or whiteness) . . . purity as a concept-metaphor is not pure. It is defined always through negation." Whiteness can only exist, therefore, in a relationship with blackness; the separation between black and white is constantly breached in order to reveal a difference that would otherwise not be recognized. Brody continues, "the very concept of hybridity presupposes pure forms that can be mixed, and the reproduction of purity requires the erasure of hybridity . . . Purity and hybridity are therefore mutually constitutive rather than mutually exclusive. Pure purity is an impossibility."[5] At their best, jazz and American culture are liminal, anarchic, and miscegenated.

Writing in the late 1930s, New York journalist Joseph Mitchell observed, "Except for the minstrel show, the strip act is probably America's only original contribution to the theater."[6] Like blackface minstrelsy, the striptease has a particular American history. It was born of the hootchy-kootch, an exotic dance of specious oriental origin, that drew audiences of thousands down the midways, the main drags, of the turn-of-the-century world trade fairs and expositions. Despite their exotic stage names, cootch dancers Fatima and Little Egypt—the forbears of strippers Gypsy Rose Lee, Lili St. Cyr, and Tempest Storm—were actually pure products of the American imagination.[7] The Middle East evoked by their names, costumes, and dances drew from the same cultural pool that made white men in blackface promote themselves as Ethiopian delineators. Blackface and striptease mirror one another with the former putting on (and covering) identity while the latter reveals (and elides) it. The figures of the blackface minstrel and the burlesque stripper provide the extremes from which the median of American culture is produced. The structure of this book echoes Mitchell's observation. It begins by exploring how Hollywood used blackface minstrelsy to help represent an emerging urban American theatrical history, and ends with a look at how American film at the close of the studio era represented urban decay through the trope of the burlesque dancer and stripper. In between, the book considers the representation of American urban life in jazz, blues, ballads, and sin songs and the manner in which the film studios exploited this music.

My thesis, then, is that popular music in general, and jazz and blues in particular, with the transition to sound, provided Hollywood with a newly resonant resource that would be exploited to construct and negotiate the boundaries of American cultural identity. The book is primarily concerned with the manner in which a specific type of popular song, one that articulates an excess of yearning and emotional turbulence—"Frankie and Johnny," "St. Louis Blues," "The Man I Love," "Blues in the Night," and "Body and Soul"—is invoked across a significant number of Hollywood films in the period from 1927 to 1963. Outside of film, these songs have their own histories, and considering what these represented and how the studios made them conform to their own representational practices will enable a better understanding of American cinema and its construction of a national identity. In particular, I ask how Hollywood exploited the prior meaning of these songs, which often dealt explicitly with issues of class, gender, race, and sexuality. And how did the songs contribute to Hollywood's strategies for articulating American cultural identity?

The economic and social transformations of American modernization had a pressing effect on the historical organization of discourses of sexuality, race, gender, and class fashioned through popular culture. The repercussions of modernization were so great that, as literary historian Marcus Klein writes, "approximately . . . at the turn of the new century . . . an America which had definitions in myth and idea—variable definitions but nevertheless antique and accepted ones—all but disappeared . . . What had been a facsimile of culture was chaos within which everybody was a foreigner, including the native-born and the millions of authentic foreigners."[8] With the impact of urbanization, industrialization, immigration, and migration, the period of modernization saw a unified American identity visibly decentered. What replaced the consensus? And how did these earlier transformations in gender, race, and class identity continue to resonate in American culture in general, and through Hollywood in particular? How did Hollywood use the culture of America's marginalized people, and what image of American national identity did it produce out of this heterogeneous material? What legacy did blackface minstrelsy, the dominant nineteenth-century popular discourse on American identity, leave with the equally iconic twentieth-century musical forms of jazz and blues?

As part of an *industrialized* popular culture, the songs and the films exemplify modern production and consumption practices, but they can also be understood as manifestations of an authentic or vernacular American culture. The blues and jazz songs are performed on film in the urban spaces of nightclubs or played on modern technologies of radio and phonograph. But they belong simultaneously to a modern present and a primitive American past. These representations of America's past invoke the culture of black Americans or, rather, the white-sponsored fantasy world of blackness. The processes by which "black" songs were circulated took a more refined turn with Hollywood's departure from its representation of the concert-saloon of the late 1800s to the modern spaces of the nightclub, from a focus on vaudeville "coon shouters" to urbane torch singers of the 1920s and 1930s, and finally, for this study, to the polished informality of night club singers in the 1940s and 1950s, for whom the relative sophistication of "The Man I Love," "Body and Soul," and "Blues in the Night," all written by professional songsmiths, were more suited. The commercial exploitation of blues and jazz idioms in the 1930s was paralleled by an increased awareness and politicization on the part of young white fans and performers of the music's racial provenance. Certain Hollywood films of the 1940s—*Blues in the Night* (Warner Bros., 1941), *Crossfire* (RKO, 1947), *Body and Soul* (Enterprise Productions, 1947), for example—were in part responses to this process of politicizing black American music. But despite this progressive image, the book ends where it began: back in the gutter, with an "examination" of burlesque dancers and strippers who appear with some regularity as the key object of investigation in police procedural films of the 1950s.

Before undergoing numerous revisions, the title of my book was originally a straight cop from the title of an Art Hodes tune, "A Selection from the Gutter," that was recorded in New York in 1940. It is a solo piano blues that, given its title, sounds exactly as you would expect, or hope, it to sound like. Hodes played an important and central role in the Chicago jazz scene of the 1930s and later in New York; he became a great proselytizer for blues and jazz on radio and in print. He was not native to either Chicago or New York but was born in Russia, although, as jazz historian Dan Morgenstern notes, "he played with no trace of a Russian accent—strictly South Side Chicago."[9] His biography and his music provide a good cover for any of the stories told in this book.[10]

An Octoroon in the Kindling:
A Black and White Minstrel Show

Way down on the levee in old Alabamy
There's daddy and mammy there's Ephraim and Sammy,
On a moonlight night you can find them all,
While they are waitin' the banjos are syncopatin'

—L. Wolfe Gilbert and Lewis F. Muir,
   "Waitin' for the Robert E. Lee" (1912)

The films discussed in this chapter were produced during the first ten years of synchronized sound cinema, representing some of the most commercially successful pictures released in this period, and featuring some of the biggest stars of the day. For my purposes, these films—*The Jazz Singer* (Warner Bros., 1927), *Matinee Idol* (Columbia, 1928), *She Done Him Wrong* (Paramount, 1933), *The Bowery* (Twentieth Century Pictures, 1933), *Barbary Coast* (Goldwyn/UA, 1935), *Show Boat* (Universal, 1936), and *San Francisco* (MGM, 1936)—suggest that the Hollywood studios had something approaching a unified understanding of what constituted an American vernacular culture. These films are dramatizations of America's formative years as an industrial urban nation; the coarse, vulgar, bawdy culture of an undifferentiated underclass initially defines their understanding of an American vernacular. However, the films are not simply displays of a nostalgic vision of American culture: more precisely they suggest how far removed contemporary America is from such humble origins. The process of cultural refinement is dramatized through an initial depiction of blackface minstrelsy as the key to America's theatrical and musical heritage, but which, by the end of the film, is safely contained within the past. The focus on minstrelsy is not only a recognition of its historical role in the development of American theater but also of its role in dramatizing racial crossings—the cross-pollination *and* contamination of black and white cultures—that are central to any realization of an American vernacular culture. Whites wearing blackface makeup are present in most of these films, but even in their absence, minstrelsy's legacy is evident. Hollywood's evocation of a vernacular tradition, then, is formed out of the conventions of blackface minstrelsy, conceived as a defining symbol of America's theatrical and musical past.

The decline in the popularity of the discrete minstrel show in the urban north of the United States during the latter part of the nineteenth century paralleled its diffusion into other forms such as burlesque and vaudeville. Individual white blackface performers found spots in the growing vaudeville circuit where minstrelsy maintained popularity through its ability to influence and be adapted into new musical forms such as ragtime and later blues and jazz.[1] By placing the blackface performer in a variety setting, vaudeville had the effect of containing and isolating the performance. Rather than the whole show, minstrelsy now became an attraction among many others and a familiar sight given back its novelty value. But the novelty value was limited. While individual minstrel performers such as George Jessel, Al Jolson, and Eddie Cantor could still become major stars, minstrelsy as a performance style could no longer escape from its own history. Locked into the past, it was now primarily a signifier of an American theatrical tradition. Although the popularity of theatrical blackface performances decreased during the 1930s (alongside the patronage of live vaudeville), it maintained a limited role in Hollywood's films. It was partly on account of the industry's recruitment of Broadway stars following the transition to synchronized sound production that minstrelsy remained visible in film, but it was also due to the dramatic need to represent a recognizable American theatrical history.[2]

The meaning produced in the performance of blackface in Hollywood movies is the particular focus of Michael Rogin's *Blackface, White Noise* (1996), but the emphasis on the form's latent connotations leaves little space for an assessment of blackface's performance legacy in Hollywood, a subject demanding a more historically grounded reading of its accents and disguises.[3] Rogin's assertion, however, that American cinema is obsessed with race is indisputable. David Roediger claims, as does Rogin, that the blackface mask was a device for assimilation that enabled marginalized groups, such as Jewish and Irish immigrants, to claim both a symbolic and literal whiteness defined against the black "other" of minstrelsy and the black bodies minstrelsy purports to represent.[4] But, as Dale Cockrell has counterargued, minstrelsy's play with fluid identities in the nineteenth century subverted "'knowing' gained through image—the eye is drawn to representation, which might not be the real—just as a Western mask is not really as it appears: it conceals and promises reordering," which suggests there could be no certain route via minstrelsy to an authentic American identity.[5] W. T. Lhamon Jr. argues that while blackface carries its "inevitable quotient of demeaning attributes" and its "opposing urge to authenticity" in its "radical portion" it highlights "contamination, literal overlap, and identification with [the] muddier process" of self-generating identities.[6] By arguing that the mask of blackface minstrelsy does not fix identity but instead puts it into continuous play so that liminality is its defining characteristic, Cockrell and Lhamon challenge the argument put forward by Rogin and Roediger that the blackness of minstrelsy is about "eager replacement of ethnicity or Jewishness with whiteness."[7] Rather, as Lhamon claims, blackface stages "continual transactions of assimilation."[8] It should also be noted that blackface minstrelsy, as Chip Rhodes argues, was "a *performance* that foregrounded the fact that it was an act and not reality—hence it is cynical: audiences 'did not care much if the discourse of blackness coincided with black Americans.'"[9] This cynicism is most apparent in the work of Al Jolson.

Despite its centrality to debates on Hollywood and blackface, *The Jazz Singer* is an anomaly. Rather than being an isolated performance moment, Jolson's character defines himself as an American and as a star through blackface: his performances in blackface are intrinsic to the narrative. In contrast, Eddie Cantor's discrete blackface acts operate within a different set of dramatic imperatives, as another avenue by which he celebrates his star persona. In *Palmy Days* (Goldwyn, 1931), blackface is used in a musical scene that is given narrative causality as a ruse to attract more customers to the restaurant in the bakery where Cantor's character works. Blackface signifies nothing beyond its own status as a showpiece for Cantor, whose star persona was based on his presentation of a fey, spectacle-wearing minstrel. In *The Kid from Spain* (Goldwyn, 1932), Cantor's character is on the run from gangsters; having applied a cover of burnt cork (literally, in this case) to his face, he momentarily evades their notice (like Edgar Allen

Poe's purloined letter) by presenting himself front and center for a song and dance number. Blackface is used here as part of a comedy sketch; the humor is dependent upon the adversary's inability to see through that which is transparent—the blackface mask. Other films which employ blackface in a similar manner include *Round Up Time in Texas* (Republic, 1937), where Gene Autry's sidekick, Smiley Burnette, blacks up to impersonate an African chief, and *A Day at the Races* (MGM, 1937), where the Marx brothers perform in blackface in front of African American characters. In these examples, the antagonists are the only ones fooled by the disguise. The blackface mask does not hide the "performer"; instead the mask highlights and draws the audience's attention to the irrepressible nature of the protagonists. The transparency of the disguise is made particularly notable in *Round Up* and *Races* by having the principal characters perform in blackface alongside African Americans. There is no attempt on the part of the white characters to strive for an authenticity in their performance of blackness; the goal is, in fact, the reverse—it is the act of fabrication that is important. As a functional disguise, blackface is patently inadequate, however. In these examples, it justifies a theatrical performance that is achieved outside of a legitimate theatrical space. In such films, there are no theater stages upon which to enact the protagonists' recital of racial crossings (as occurs in *The Jazz Singer*). Instead Cantor, Burnette, and the Marx brothers present their turns at, respectively, a restaurant, an African village, and a racetrack. In complete contrast to those in *The Jazz Singer,* these routines are conceived and presented as solipsistic.

The backstage story of the Jolson character Jack Robin's striving for theatrical and material success and the conflicting desire for reconciliation with his family and religion govern the use of blackface in *The Jazz Singer*. Unlike blackface performance in Cantor's films, in *The Jazz Singer* blackface reaches out beyond its immediate location to inform all aspects of the narrative and the film's production. This distinction is important, because blackface in *The Jazz Singer* also differs significantly from its use elsewhere in Hollywood's films during the 1930s, where it is used as the predominate signifier of America's theatrical past. *The Jazz Singer* is set in the present; *Show Boat,* a similarly canonical backstage musical, begins in the past, with the heroine performing in blackface, and ends in the present: the film's heroine has become a grand old lady of the American theater, and blackface is safely located in history. Jolson in blackface fades into black at the end of *The Jazz Singer,* not into the theatrical spotlight that illuminates, and further whitens, the heroine at the end of *Show Boat.*

The Jazz Singer's project is to reconcile Jakie Rabinowitz's (Jolson) movement from his parents' Jewish culture into his adopted American Jack
Robin identity, a process that is mediated through the mask of blackface. Though the film suggests a resolving of the cultural conflicts at its
closure—with Jolson assuming the dual role of Jewish cantor and blackface entertainer—it is a resolution achieved at the cost of creating an
oxymoron. Jolson may have gained an American identity, but it is an
identity formed in the likeness of the most oppressed of all Americans,
despite the film's attempt to evade such a conclusion. To shake off his
Old World identity he must embrace its opposite, the secular world of
vulgarity represented by the figure of the black man. The money, fame,
and the enduring love of his mother are small compensations for his
descent into blackness and cannot disguise the conflicted nature of his
identity as Jew and secular American. When in the latter stages of the film
Jolson's character applies his black greasepaint, we do not see the exuber-
ant and dynamic persona of earlier scenes but rather a cowed and pathetic
figure. The emphasis on a sexually charged performance witnessed (out
of blackface) with "Toot Toot Tootsie" is replaced by the sentimentality
(in blackface) of "My Mammy"—a half man–half child's appeal to his
mother to mediate and resolve the crushing dilemma that makes him
so powerless: behind the black mask he is American *and* Jewish, yet he is
neither. Rather, he is caught in a state of limbo between the two competing worlds. By ending the film with Jolson in blackface, the question—is
he Jewish Jakie Rabinowitz, Americanized Jack Robin, or a cowed black
man?—becomes momentarily mute. He is all of these identities and he
is none of them.

In the most engaging analysis of the film published in recent years,
W. T. Lhamon Jr. writes of the film's finale:

> The final gesture appeals to the mother, of course. By its copping of
> the abolitionist pose, however, it appeals also to his peers and pals. It
> compresses the various anxieties of the film in one tableau. The last fad-
> ing on the screen as the scene and film go dark is the tight white collar
> round Jolson's neck. It is brilliant bricolage of success and failure, of
> blackness championed and choked. The image continues unto darkness
> the anxieties and irresolution in Jolson's fable of membership that must
> extend so long as heterogeneous groups and classes try to meld in the
> Atlantic and, now, global economies. We will continue to require the
> sorts of transactions which *The Jazz Singer* brazenly supplies.[10]

Earlier in his analysis, Lhamon examines in detail the scene set in the San Francisco restaurant Coffee Dan's. Its significance is that it is "the first Vitaphone sequence they used in the movie. It was also the first scene in which Jolson appears in the film, its first California scene, its first in which Jews do not predominate, its first scene where women appear independent."[11] Lhamon then provides a compelling account of the scene based on the understanding that Jolson's work is "nakedly earnest and poignant." The two-song sequence—"Dirty Hands, Dirty Face" and "Toot Toot Tootsie"—is examined in some detail, but what overrides his analysis is the placing of the performance within the spaces provided by an American modernity. Significantly, this is a modernity that does not represent a marked break with the past but rather "connects to it and pulls it along."[12] Writing in 1916, a vaudeville critic encapsulated Jolson's mediating role: "he is the old-time minstrel man turned to modern account."[13] The key motif in this connectivity between past and present is Jolson's explosive whistle solo during "Toot Toot Tootsie," which Lhamon likens to the "sign of the train" and links to the whistle at the beginning of Jelly Roll Morton's "Sidewalk Blues," a jazz recording that functions as a "pedestrian's reproof to those who administer technology. Part of the pride in popular music, white and black, is to keep up with and democratize all the whistles of technology. If one cannot ride, then one can face them down, as Morton's sidewalk star does."[14] In a similar context, biographer and novelist Nick Tosches offered the supportive pronouncement that whistling was, indeed, a "supremely democratic art." Tosches' practitioner of the common art was George Washington Johnson, "the Whistling Coon who became America's first recording star."[15] This is one of the links to the past—the heritage of blackface minstrelsy—that is made by Jolson's whistle. But Lhamon takes the link even further back, away from the modernity of America and phonograph recordings, across the Atlantic to Europe when he likens its sound to the European blackbird: "Jack Robin's whistle is an Atlantic crowing—a record of minstrel performers crossing and recrossing the Atlantic [that] visually and orally documents the European origins of so many blackface performers, including Jolson."[16]

In the preface to the stage play upon which *The Jazz Singer*'s screenplay was based, author Samson Raphaelson writes:

> He who wishes to picture today's America must do it kaleidoscopically. . . . In seeking a symbol of the vital chaos of America's soul, I find no more adequate one than jazz. Here you have the rhythm of frenzy

staggering against a symphonic background—a background composed of lewdness, heart's delight, soul-racked madness, monumental; boldness, exquisite humility, but principally prayer.

I hear jazz, and I am given a vision of cathedrals and temples collapsing and, silhouetted against the setting sun, a solitary figure, a lost soul, dancing grotesquely on the ruins. . . . Thus do I see the jazz singer.[17]

"The singer of jazz" Raphaelson suggests "is what Matthew Arnold said of the Jew, 'lost between two worlds, one dead, the other powerless to be born.'" Jolson's performance in blackface at the end of *The Jazz Singer* represents the indeterminate space between these two worlds. For Raphaelson, the two worlds are explicitly defined as spiritual and secular, but the vision of the jazz singer dancing on the ruins of temples is also a profoundly *modern* image. "Take up your pickaxes, your axes and hammers and wreck, wreck the venerable cities, pitilessly," wrote the Italian futurist Marinetti, "Erect on the summit of the world, once again we hurl defiance to the stars!" The terms of engagement with the modern are remarkably similar, even if the polemical attack of Marinetti far outstrips Raphaelson; however, where the European and American visions of the modern part company is with who dances, and to what rhythm, over the ruins of the city.

"We had stayed up all night, my friends and I, under hanging mosque lamps. . . . For hours we had trampled our atavistic ennui into rich oriental rugs, arguing up to the last confines of logic and blackening many reams of paper with our frenzied scribbling . . . we felt ourselves alone at that hour. . . . Alone with stokers feeding the hellish fires of great ships, alone with the black specters who grope in the red-hot bellies of locomotives launched down their crazy courses." Suddenly, Marinetti's and friends' reverie, their groping in the primitive blackness of the Orient, is broken by the intrusion of the "mighty noise of the huge double-decker trams that rumbled outside." The friends rush outside and climb aboard their automobiles. "'Let's go!' I said. 'Friends, away! Let's go! Mythology and the Mystic Ideal are defeated at last.'"[18] In their headlong rush into the modern promised by the white-hot thrill of technology, the futurists left the ruins of the past behind. This is the European modernist ideal. The modern American, however, does not leave mythology and mysticism behind. In the figure of the jazz singer dancing between the fallen columns of civilization, modern Americans brought their version of Oriental primitivism into the present (which in turn would become available for European modernist appropriation). In the years following the Great War, cultural historian

Anne Douglas writes, "America entered its own post-colonial phase. . . . Newly fascinated with their own cultural resources, the American moderns repudiated the long ascendant English and European traditions and their genteel American custodians as emblems of cultural cowardice. . . . Americans, black and white, discovered their African-American heritage of folk and popular art; the deepest roots of American culture."[19] In this vision, the liberating impulse behind American modernity is not only claimed by technology but also by the vital white fantasy of a primitive, unspoilt, black American culture. Early jazz with its "thick and explosive collective improvisation," writes musicologist Robert Cantwell, "fuelled by the sounds of barrelhouse, brothels, and bandwagon, was a tribal bonfire in which all the sordid piety and vulgar sentimentality of bourgeois popular culture went up in smoke."[20]

While certain modernist artists in Europe before the Great War had become fixated with African objects, they did not yet, as Bernard Gendron argues, "exemplify the phenomenon of negrophilia that materialized in the waning years of the war and peaked in the mid-twenties." This was because an essential characteristic of negrophilia, according to Gendron, was a complete conflation of "African and African American cultural production."[21] Noting Jean Cocteau's fascination for jazz in the early 1920s, Gendron writes:

> As the "soul of all these [urban] forces," jazz was for Cocteau the proper signifier of modern life in its postwar embodiments, and thus the proper object of the *flâneur*'s gaze. It combined speed, noise, vulgarity, aggression, America, the inner city, danger, transgression, the exotic, the Negro—all stock images celebrating the mystique of modernity. In effect, jazz became the paradigmatic object of the avant-garde slummer, the new signifier for bohemian life. The concepts of jazz and *flâneur,* in their European setting, became for a period inextricably interlocked.[22]

With its dual identity formed in the mirror images of low-down black primitivism and high-rise white urban modernity, jazz, as noun and adjective, was the preeminent symbol of modern America. In the Coffee Dan sequence, *The Jazz Singer* perfectly encapsulates this duality. This is the scene, as Lhamon notes, that represents Jack Robin's "rise in a denatured modern future, but also a longing to return to his Mammy."[23] The fact that, as one jazz historian after another has pointed out, the film is devoid of any "jazz" music is immaterial. On the same basis that Paul Whiteman could claim the title "King of Jazz" when he played a sweet, schmaltzy, sentimental symphonic pop music, Jolson could claim he sang "jazz." Jazz was whatever was of the moment: even if a jazz dancer's leg was placed in the past, the other was sure to be straddling the present and stretching into the future. Behind Jolson's whistle was a blast of steam from an American locomotive *and* the trill of a European blackbird . . . toot, toot . . . machine and nature . . . modern and premodern . . . the songs may have been vaudeville pop but Jolson's performance was pure jazz.[24] Warner Bros. evidently thought "Toot Toot Tootsie" represented jazz because they repeated it as part of the sound track to accompany a different, but complementary, "rising in the underground" (to coin Lhamon's description of Jolson in Coffee Dan's) in *Public Enemy* (1930). With new suits ("plenty of room in here, see") and automobile, Tom Powers (James Cagney) and his sidekick display their newfound wealth and reputation as rising stars of gangland by visiting a black-and-tan joint where the mixed-race customers are entertained by a black band playing "Toot Toot Tootsie."

The complexity of *The Jazz Singer*'s engagement with contemporary concerns can be gauged by comparing its conception of modernity with Frank Capra's silent romantic comedy *The Matinee Idol.* That film's leading protagonists are two young lovers from seemingly opposed theatrical worlds: Don Wilson (Johnnie Walker) is a blackface Broadway star and Ginger Bolivar (Bessie Love) is the ingénue in a traveling tent show owned and managed by her father. The Wilson character is based on Jolson, suggested by mimicking his supplicating style of performance—down on one knee, head back, arms outstretched to the heavens—and its opposite—arms wide to embrace the audience and torso switching from side to side on the groin's axis. Wilson is billed as the "king of the blackface comedians," echoing Jolson's "The World's Greatest Entertainer" (it was not until the late 1920s that Jolson became primarily identified as a singer—before that he was considered a comedian.)[25] The two theatrical worlds meet when, during a weekend's excursion into the countryside, Wilson and his managers attend a show by the Bolivar Players. In the opinion of the city sophisticates, the Players are "so terrible, they're great," and so the troupe is invited to appear in Wilson's Broadway revue. The Bolivar Players are a band of third-rate actors who specialize in the production of Civil War melodramas of the old school, which are warmly appreciated by their rural audience. However, the urbane metropolitan Broadway crowd cynically receive the plays as burlesque. The Players' lack of critical reflection on the quality of their act carries the obvious implication that they are rubes, too stupid to recognize the inanity and anachronistic nature of their drama and performance. Superficially, the gulf between Don Wilson's Broadway and Ginger Bolivar's tent show appears unbridgeable; however, with her bobbed hair and modish sportswear, Ginger is the very image of feminine modernity while Don's blackface routine, particularly when it is interpolated into the Bolivar's Civil War stage show, is a direct link back to the Old South and the premodern form of American entertainment represented by the Players. In this context, blackface is little more than a symbolic bridge that links the two theatrical worlds and, unlike its use in *The Jazz Singer,* it has little to say about American identity.

For Roediger, blackface acted as a syncretic form where ethnic markers such as Irish dance, Alpine yodeling, Shakespeare, Polish polkas, and Italian opera would be performed through the Americanizing mask of burnt cork. He considers whites' use of blackface as creating a dependency on those it exploits similar to that which exists between the master and servant in Hegel's celebrated essay "Lordship and Bondage": "blackfaced whites derived their consciousness by measuring themselves against a group they defined as largely worthless and ineffectual . . . the trajectory of minstrelsy was to create an ersatz whiteness and then to succumb to a mere emphasis on the vulgarity, grotesqueness and stupidity of the black characters it created."[26] In *The Jazz Singer,* blackface produces an ersatz whiteness that does, indeed, invite European immigrants to measure their recently acquired status as Americans and citizens of the United States against the black American Other. Yet, as a mask for pathos, Jolson's blackface act attempts to transcend the limits of minstrelsy as a pantomime of vulgarity. In its attempt to find a resonance and relevance for blackface performance in a contemporary setting, *The Jazz Singer* proffered a complex and problematic image of American identity. It was, however, an image that proved to be unsustainable both in Jolson's later films and in Hollywood's productions as a whole. By the beginning of the twentieth century, minstrelsy had so ossified into a performance style that it is difficult to imagine the mask of black greasepaint being read as anything other than an overdetermined and abstracted performance style. Moreover, the post–Civil War emergence on stages before white audiences of African American performers who performed in blackface—like Bert Williams, the first African American star of Broadway—could only have furthered the process of staging racial artifice at the cost of performing racial authenticity. If the evidence of the movies is anything to go by, blackface minstrelsy by the second quarter of the twentieth century was incapable of dealing with the nuance of contemporary racial concerns and the increasing visibility of African Americans within the body politic and culture at large.

This withering of effect is particularly apparent in Jolson's *Big Boy* (Warner Bros., 1930). As in the *Matinee Idol, Big Boy* seeks to resolve the conflict between the old and the new, between the rural and the urban, between premodernity and modernity, and, uniquely, between theater and film. The setting for Jolson's blackface performance is a Kentucky stable in the final stages of preparing for the Kentucky Derby. Jolson plays Gus, a black stable hand and jockey. The film is little more than a series of "plantation"-based vignettes and tableaus in which Jolson performs familiar songs and engages in typical blackface comedy routines (drawn wholesale from his years in vaudeville and the stage show upon which the film was based) that are effortlessly self-reflexive on his star persona—full of knowing jokes, winks, and smiles to the audience. But this "ragging" or self-revelation in front of the camera carries no more meaning than Wilson's homage to Jolson in *Matinee Idol*—it simply confirms his status as star performer. There are, however, two scenes that reveal more about the role of blackface in Jolson's filmic oeuvre and of his place within a film aesthetic.

The first scene is in the Brown Hotel; Gus has taken employment as a waiter, which gives Jolson's character ample room to undermine customers' pretensions. While attempting to serve a large plate of oysters to a table occupied by a middle-aged gray-haired man and his cigarette-smoking androgynous companion who sports very short oiled hair and masculine eveningwear, Gus mistakenly assumes she is a he. "Can't you tell the difference?" asks the gray-haired man. "Not lately," replies Gus. In a world of dissembling identities, represented predominantly by Jolson's masquerade as a black man, this momentary pause to comment on the period's blurring of gender boundaries seems almost unremarkable, except that where Jolson's play with identity represents a conservative and reactionary expropriation of another's identity, the young woman's dissembling of identity is radical and truly, for the time, transgressive. Just as Wilson's blackface balanced Ginger's modish appearance in *Matinee Idol*, Jolson's primitive black mask provides a counterforce to the role subversion implied in the modern masquerade of androgyny. Safe and familiar, the use of blackface in *Big Boy* is conservative and reactionary rather than, as suggested by its use in *The Jazz Singer*, radical and provocative; it enables the crossing of cultural, ethnic, gender, and racial boundaries.

The second scene of interest is the film's coda. Gus has won the Derby.

Body and Soul

Breaking off from his winner's speech, he turns his back to the camera and the microphone he has been talking through and rubs his hands over his face; turning back to the camera, his black mask has vanished and filmic space has given way to the props of a stage setting. Gus is revealed to be Jolson and the film is revealed to have been artifice. Jolson's blackface alter ego Gus appears within the diegesis of the film but not in the stage show with which it ends; the coda is the space needed for Jolson to proclaim (once again) himself as the film's star. The blackface mask acts as the mediating link between theater and film, between the modernity represented by the latter and the premodern world represented by the former. During the coda, Jolson noticeably dispenses with the microphone and, leaning over the lip of the stage, appeals directly to the theater audience. The attempt to collapse the distance between performer and audience suggests that the "real" Jolson works in a theatrical environment unmediated by modern technology—"The World's Greatest Entertainer" did not need to use a microphone to put his act across. A downbeat review of one of his Kraft Music Hall radio shows in early 1933 made a similar point:

> We should prefer to have Mr. Jolson sing, and it is not because we are inordinately enamored of his singing. His voice is at its best when he has both knees in the footlight trough, but the microphone has no footlights. If there could only be an occasional light moment in his acting, or at least a moment that is not so highly overwrought. There is a tear in Mr. Jolson's every word. We find his broadcasts growing too humid for comfort long before he has worked himself up to sobbing into the microphone.[27]

His biographer Herbert Goldman concurred: "Jolson in a theatre was electricity personified—thrilling, immediate, memorable, and, unfortunately, unrecordable. He was never captured on film."[28] By 1933 Jolson's claim to the title of the "greatest" was no longer unchallenged. Through working *with* the microphone, Bing Crosby would revolutionized male singing. Bing would sometimes appear in blackface and sing in black dialect, but it would be a sideline, an occasional turn, and he would do it in an entertainment context that was defined through the new mediating technologies of phonograph recording, radio, film, and stagecraft built on broadcast technology and amplification. By avoiding the microphone, Jolson avoided the modern and wrote himself into the past.

Jolson made a decreasing number of film appearances as the decade of the 1930s wore on; indeed, there was a three-year break between his last starring performance in the *The Singing Kid* (Warner Bros., 1936), a weak attempt to team him up with one of the studio's answers to Shirley Temple, and *The Rose of Washington Square* (Twentieth Century Fox, 1939) where he played an old-style song and dance man, *Hollywood Cavalcade* (Twentieth Century Fox, 1939) where he played himself, and *Swanee River* (Twentieth Century Fox, 1939), a Stephen Foster biopic in which he played the minstrel E. P. Christy. All of these film appearances traded on Jolson's persona as a star from a bygone theatrical age. By 1946 he was himself the subject of the biopic *The Jolson Story* (Columbia). His appearance in *Washington Square* was advertised as "the man who sings the past the way you want to remember it." Biographer Herbert Goldman writes: "At fifty-three, Al had become 'nostalgia.'"[29] This was, I think, already foreshadowed in *Big Boy* and in his preceding film *Mammy* (Warner Bros., 1930), the story of an old-time minstrel show that *Variety* reviewed as a "glimpse of a dying earlier day."[30] This, increasingly, was how blackface minstrelsy came to be portrayed in Hollywood films. If blackface was dead or dying, it could yet be revived as part of America's cultural legacy if contained and distanced as *history;* in films such as *Mammy* and *Show Boat,* the white characters escape the blackface mask and thus chart their cultural passage from vulgarity to refinement by positioning blackface as historical, as an outmoded and "primitive" cultural form. Yet *The Jazz Singer* complicates the use of blackface as retrospective invocation of past history and uses its "antiquated" performance traditions in significantly more complex ideological play around notions of ethnic, sexual, and national self-identity.

Despite *The Jazz Singer*'s attempt to maintain a relevance and currency for blackface, by the 1920s it was no more than an empty racial signifier. In *Dante's Inferno* (Twentieth Century Fox, 1935), blackface's emblematic function is to mark a character's low social and moral status. Having been sacked as chief stoker in the merchant navy and unable to find any other form of employment, Spencer Tracy's character accepts a job as the target in a "Hit the Nigger" carnival sideshow. The film unambiguously offers his appearance in blackface as a sign of absolute destitution: he has all but left the white world of respectability behind. His blackface performance in the carnival marks and measures his fall, rise, fall, and eventual redemption. His initial rise is witnessed through the control he exerts over the carnival, which he turns into a huge pleasure park built around roller coaster rides. His fall occurs when he refuses to fund the necessary safety measures; his hubris and greed lead to disaster. His fall from grace, however, does not descend to the social, moral, and economic level that was earlier implied by his work in blackface. Blackface was used to signpost the gutter from which he begins his career and is then promptly forgotten. On the journey Tracy's character undertakes, the film never again raises the image of racial difference.

In *Show Boat,* blackface is similarly used as a sign of a low past and as a marker against which to judge social progress. By presenting African American actors as themselves, the film gives a different meaning to the performance of blackface by white characters than that found in *The Jazz Singer.* The black characters in the film all conform to the various racial and gender stereotypes found in minstrelsy: Joe (Paul Robeson) is a lazy and childlike Sambo figure and Hattie McDaniel plays the Mammy role. In blackface, white characters confirm and reinforce these representations, but, unlike the African American performers, they are not contained by minstrelsy's stereotypes because, out of blackface, they are able to distance themselves from the degrading image associated with blackness that they have helped produce. In *The Jazz Singer,* the signified of blackface, the African American, is absent, but rather than simplify matters this lack enables competing identities to be contained, none dominating, because blackness operates in the world of the imaginary rather than the real. In a film such as *Show Boat,* African Americans enable a display of essential-ized racial identities. This is why the key event in the first half of the film is the exposure of Julie's (Helen Morgan) racial crossings. The subject of miscegenation reinforces the idea of essential racial types by proffering the moral and social cost paid when racial borders are transgressed. Julie, however, will be summarily expelled from the narrative and her heritage of racial crossings will be forgotten at the narrative's end, maintaining an image of a racial order rather than its confusion (as suggested by the ending of *The Jazz Singer*).

The anxiety around racial mixing was present not only in *Show Boat*'s narrative but also in its production. The film's producers had hoped to cast white actress Tess Gardella in the role of Queenie, the Mammy fig-ure, alongside the black actor Paul Robeson. Gardella was best known by her stage name Aunt Jemima, and she had previously played Queenie in the New York productions of the play in 1927 and 1932. Working on the assumption that this pairing of a black actor and a white actress would prove controversial with some cinemagoers, Universal asked Joseph Breen, head of the Production Code Administration, for his advice. He wrote back, "I think you should be extremely careful, however, not to indicate any physical contact between a white woman and a Negro man for the reason that many people will know that Aunt Jemima is a white woman and might be repulsed by the sight of her being fondled by a man who is a Negro."[31] In light of this observation, Universal cast the black actress Hattie McDaniel in the part. What did not change were the character's traits, which would remain firmly in the tradition of minstrelsy, regardless of whether a white (in blackface) or black woman played the part.[32]

In any event, both the earlier theatrical production and the 1936 film version of *Show Boat* were alive with the possibility of racial confusion and overlap. A scene that exemplifies this potential for racial crossings is where Magnolia (Irene Dunne) learns the song "Can't Help Lovin' Dat Man." Overhearing Miss Julie singing to Magnolia, Queenie wants to know how she learned that "colored folks' song." In answer to Queenie, Julie shifts the song's register and begins to sing it as a blues. The change encourages communal participation with Queenie and Joe singing it as a duet. Positioned stage front, Magnolia transforms herself into a blackface minstrel (without the burnt cork) by puffing out her cheeks, contorting her torso so her bottom is emphasized, and then sashaying her hips. A chorus of black folk gathers alongside the showboat, and Magnolia leads the troupe in an impromptu cakewalk out onto the boat's deck. The scene establishes a question of doubt over Julie's whiteness because of her knowledge of the blues. However, questions regarding Magnolia's whiteness, raised when she spontaneously breaks into a dance associated with blacks, are contained by the conventions and heightened artifice of minstrelsy. Conversely, the authenticity of Julie's performance of the blues is later confirmed when she is exposed as being "black." In her studious analysis of *Show Boat* and the performance of this song in particular, Linda Williams writes:

> The performance of this song thus takes on special resonance in a double display of posing as black *and* passing as white. Where whites who pose as black intentionally exhibit all the artifice of their performance—exaggerated gestures, blackface make-up—blacks who pass as white suppress the more obvious artifice of performance. Passing is a performance whose success depends on not overacting. Julie has gained the privileges of whiteness—the ability to perform as leading lady opposite a white leading man, the ability to be married to that leading man—by not calling attention to the difference between herself and the role she plays.[33]

At all points in the film, Magnolia's move from humble Southern origins into Northern society is marked through the signs of blackface performance. When Julie and her husband are forced to leave the showboat, their place is taken by Magnolia and Ravenal (Allan Jones), a down-at-his-luck gentleman gambler who needs a job. Provided with a professional performance space, Magnolia confirms the artifice of her earlier masquerade when she performs in blackface. Having married Ravenal and become pregnant, Magnolia discovers Ravenal's shady side as a gambler; following a lucky streak he takes her and their new baby to Chicago. His luck does not hold out, and, almost destitute, Ravenal deserts his family. Without the means to support herself, Magnolia is forced back onto the stage. After being asked at an audition what she does, she replies, "I do Negro songs." "A coon shouter, huh?" the theatrical impresario responds. Nervously, and without a hint of blue notes, she sings "Can't Help Lovin' Dat Man." Unknown to Magnolia, Miss Julie is the star of the show for which she is auditioning. Overhearing Magnolia's performance, and realizing that she must be desperate for a job, Julie creates a vacancy by disappearing from the theater and the narrative—doomed to play out forever the role of the loyal and self-sacrificing friend. Like Queenie and Joe, Julie defers her own needs and desires to help her "little sister," her white "family"—the "family" from which she is excluded by the narrative, minstrelsy, and racism.

The piano "professor" (Harry Barris)[34] transforms Julie's song into a ragtime number and Magnolia gets the job, but she does not perform "Negro" songs or even a raggy rendition of "Can't Help Lovin' Dat Man" in the show. Instead, Magnolia treats the audience to an "old favourite," the Tin Pan Alley warhorse "After the Ball." Years pass and Magnolia's acclaim grows. She retires and her daughter follows in her footsteps; a theatrical dynasty is born. Magnolia has progressed from the vulgar—and from what is now marked as a vernacular and nostalgic tradition of blackface—to the refinement and modernity of the New York stage where, at the end of the film, to rhyme with her changed circumstances, blackface minstrelsy has been transformed into a ballet with a plantation setting, and her daughter is given the role of a Southern belle. As if to deny absolutely any racial contamination, in the final scene both mother and daughter are costumed in resplendent and brilliant white costumes.[35]

The stage play was an adaptation of Edna Ferber's novel, published in 1926, which provides a different but complementary construction of Magnolia's move from vulgarity to refinement, from a world defined by racial crossings to a world that denies the possibility of miscegenation. Because of her Southern background, Magnolia's imitations of black song in the novel are positioned as more authentic than those found in the vaudeville culture emerging in turn-of-the-century America. At Magnolia's Chicago audition, she gives the following performance: "She threw back her head then as Jo had taught her, half closed her eyes, tapped time with the right foot, smartly. Imitative in this, she managed, too, to get into her voice that soft and husky Negro quality which for years she had heard on river boats, bayous, landings. I got wings. You got a wings. All God's chillun got a wings."[36] Magnolia's performance is marked out as an authentic and essential evocation of the South, a vernacular folk music uncorrupted by vulgar commercial imperatives. "'What kind of a coon song do you call that?' inquired the gray derby. 'Why, it's a Negro melody—they sing them in the South.' 'Sounds like a church hymn to me.' He paused. His pale shrewd eyes searched her face. 'You a nigger?'"[37] Irene Dunne's Magnolia is never so racially confused. The novel's reader knows that the only cross in Magnolia's blood comes from the Basque region in France via her father, which gives the fire in her dark eyes and a liking for good food. It is not Magnolia's racial pedigree that is at stake (her whiteness is confirmed by the scarlet color that rises to her cheeks in response to the "gray derby's" question), but her authenticity.

In the novel, the showboat, its inhabitants and audiences, and Magnolia are cast as nostalgic and sentimental constructions of a lost, yet authentic, America. Kim, Magnolia's daughter, carries the burden of modern America. Kim's marriage and acting are shown to lack the authenticity of earlier days. For Magnolia, her daughter's three years at acting school represent a refinement of the profession that is wholly alien to her: "Her performance had been clear-cut, modern, deft, convincing. She was fresh, but finished. She was intelligent, successful, workmanlike, intuitive, vigorous, adaptable. . . . There was about her . . . nothing of genius, of greatness, of the divine fire."[38] This "lifeless" approach to theater is echoed in Kim's marriage. "Her marriage with Kenneth Cameron was successful and happy and very nice. Separate bedrooms. . . . Personal liberty and privacy of thought and action. . . . Magnolia wondered . . . seeing this well-ordered and respectful union, if Kim was not after all, missing something. Wasn't marriage, like life, unstimulating and unprofitable and somewhat empty when too well ordered and protected and guarded? Wasn't it finer, more splendid, more nourishing, when it was, like life itself, a mixture of the sordid and the magnificent?"[39] Through its construction as authentic, the South is made to work in distinction to the refined, sterile, and nice world that Kim inhabits and to the vulgar roots of vaudeville exemplified in the coon song.

Body and Soul

According to Charles Hamm, a leading historian of popular American music, coon songs were the fifth and last stage of the minstrel song. The first stage he calls the antebellum nigger song, which is exemplified by tunes such as "Old Dan Tucker" and "Jump Jim Crow." This stage was followed by the plantation song, of which Stephen Foster is the prime exponent. The third stage was the postwar song styles exemplified by the nostalgic sentiments of "Carry Me Back to Old Virginny" and "The Old Home Ain't What It Used To Be." The fourth stage, the minstrel-spiritual, was popularized by the Fisk Jubilee Singers in the 1870s and speedily appropriated by white performers.[40] Magnolia sings in this latter style in the novel; Kern and Hammerstein's "Ol' Man River" is also based upon the spiritual tradition. The coon song was in some respects a return to the nigger song, eschewing both nostalgia and any notion of spiritual uplift.[41] However, the coon song plumbs the very depths of racial caricature, unseen before or since in American popular culture. This racism needs to be measured against the still fairly widespread understanding of Stephen Foster's work, despite the evidence of the songs themselves, as "stereotyped yet sympathetic approaches to Black song."[42] The full version of "Oh! Susanna," for example, contains the couplet:

> I jumped aboard de telegraph,
> And trabbelled down de ribber,
> De Lectrie fluid magnified,
> And killed five hundred Nigger.[43]

The coon song managed to make even this characterization of African Americans seem polite. The "Bully Song," performed by May Irwin in the 1890s, is one of the better-known examples of coon songs. Irwin sang it in dialect, crossing both racial and gender lines, as is clearly heard on the phonograph recording she made in 1907:

> I was standin' down the Mobile Buck just to cut a shine
> Some coon across my smeller swiped a watermelon rin'
> I drawed my steel dat gemmen to fin'
> I riz up like a black cloud and took a look aroun'
> There was dat new bully standin' on the ground.
> I've been lookin' for you nigger and I've got you found.
>
> Razors 'gun a flyin', niggers 'gun to squawk,
> I lit upon that bully just like a sparrow hawk,
> And dat nigger was just a dyin' to take a walk.

When I got through with bully, a doctor and a nurse
Wa'nt no good to dat nigger, so they put him in a hearse,
A cyclone couldn't have tore him up much worse.[44]

The fad for coon songs lasted almost forty years (between 1880 and 1920) and became synonymous with a number of vaudeville's greatest stars. Among those who carried the epithet "coon" shouter or singer were Sophie Tucker, May Irwin, Norah Bayes, Dolly Connolly, Billy Murray, Bert Williams (the first African American Broadway star), and Al Jolson. For the most part, the songs are delivered as comedies, because without this distancing effect of humor, the listener is confronted with the frightening caricature of an African American as utterly vicious and bestial. The coon song has no saving grace, and many historians of popular song prefer to concentrate their studies of the era on the parallel development of ragtime, which allows a much less problematic transition to discussions on the development of jazz. Yet the coon song entered all walks of American cultural life, and its influence on African American song was profound, not least because African Americans were major contributors who wrote some of the most popular songs of the genre, for example, Ernest Hogan's "All Coons Look Alike to Me." The coon song would also find its way into the most "authentic" of African American musical forms, the blues, a process of assimilation and adaptation that the blues historian Paul Oliver has studiously traced.[45]

Magnolia's Chicago audition in the novel is rhymed with an earlier scene when she first came into contact with her husband's gambling cronies. She plays the banjo and sings the same songs that she would later perform at her audition. The response of these yahoos complements those of the "gray derby": "You call that a coon song and maybe it is. I don't dispute you, mind. But I never heard any song like *that* called a coon song, and I heard a good many coon songs in my day."[46] Magnolia, then, is emphatically not a coon shouter: her "Negro Spirituals" present an authentic, albeit sentimental, mediating ground between the urban lowlife of violence, crime, gambling, and prostitution carried by the coon song and the metropolitan refinement, sterility, and professionalism of modern theater represented by her daughter. The character of Magnolia embodies an American femininity that is sturdy and frail, rough and polished, virginal and sexual, but always true and bold. She personifies a particular image of the pioneer woman that Ferber later illustrated to greater effect in her novel *Cimarron*.[47] The process of refinement that she undergoes, from showboat to Broadway, contains her vulgar (raced) beginnings. Female performers who did not follow a similar path to theatrical legitimacy, such as those played by Mae West, would be defined by the racial crossings that were both explicit and implicit in their vulgar exhibitions for America's lowlifes.

The performance space of the showboat displaced the sentimentality expressed in Magnolia's spirituals from its usual locus within a plantation setting (which the film version tacitly evokes in its closing moments) and instead locates it within more novel surroundings while also representing a recognizable lowbrow context for a theatrical performance. Like the showboat, the concert-saloon offered a historical setting for vulgar musical performances but with the added attractions of sex and alcohol. First appearing along the Bowery in the 1860s, the concert-saloon in films was true to the spirit if not the actuality of these spaces. With their heady mix of low-class patrons, dance, song, liquor, and suggestion of lurid sexuality, the concert-saloons represented in the movies nevertheless proved to be an able substitute for the historical reality. In his study of burlesque, Robert C. Allen notes that what distinguished concert-saloons from other performance spaces where alcohol was consumed was the "incorporation of feminine sexuality as part of the entertainment." The concert-saloon appealed primarily to working-class men, who were served their beverages by women waiters in "what were, for the period, short dresses," with variety acts providing the onstage amusements.[48] In short time, laws were passed driving the concert-saloon underground. The idea of independent, working women in a male environment carried implications of prostitution for the period's middle-class moral guardians. For Hollywood's filmmakers, the implication that the saloon girl was a prostitute continued to resonate, and much play would be made around this ambiguity. The concert-saloon provided a place for musical and other divertissements of a decidedly vulgar turn and provided a milieu in which the kind of characters found in the coon song could feel at home. It was a mise-en-scène most fully and successfully exploited by Mae West in the series of films she made in the early 1930s.

More than any other Hollywood performer in the early 1930s, Mae West represented a low, coarse, bawdy, and vulgar image of early-twentieth-century urban America. In her critical biography, Mary Beth Hamilton writes, "Like burlesque performers, West wriggled her body in dances redolent of 'primitive' cultures: not just the cootch, but the Grizzly Bear and the Turkey Trot, raucous steps that were rooted in African tradition and were all the rage in the urban working class dance hall . . . Mae West performed [these dances] in a fashion that brought lower-class 'indecency' to the foreground."[49] Hamilton then quotes a passage from her subject's autobiography where West recounts a defining moment in the construction of her stage persona:

> We went to the Elite Number One and the colored couples on the dance floor were doing the "shimmy-shawobble." Big black men with razor-slashed faces, fancy high yellows and beginners browns—in the smoke of gin-scented tobacco to the music of "Can House Blues." They got up from the tables, got out to the dance floor, and stood in one spot, with hardly any movement of the feet, and just shook their shoulders, torsos and pelvises . . .
>
> The next day on stage at the matinee, the other actors were standing in the wings watching my act. I always did a dance for an encore. Then inspired by the night before, during the dance music I suddenly stood still and started to shake in a kidding way, for the benefit of the actors in the wings backstage, recalling to them what we had seen the night before at the Elite Number One. The theater began to hum.[50]

This anecdote is used to underscore Hamilton's argument that West's vulgarity scared off big-time audiences. But it also resembles other musicians' and minstrels' authenticating accounts of their appropriation and commercialization of vernacular black culture. In the early 1830s, so the apocryphal story is told, the originator of blackface, T. D. Rice, acquired the clothes and mannerisms of a Negro performer who offered his open mouth for boys to pitch pennies into at three paces. Blacked up and wearing the man's wretched clothing, Rice strolled onstage: "the extraordinary apparition produced an instant effect. . . . The effect was electric."[51] W. C. Handy's first encounter with the blues, according to his autobiography, follows similar lines. Waiting for a train, Handy noticed that "a lean, loose-jointed Negro had commenced plunking a guitar beside me . . . his clothes were rags; his feet peeped out of his shoes. His face had on it some of the sadness of the ages." Handy fully recognizes the commercial potential of the blues when, during a scheduled break, he and his orchestra give up the stage to a local "colored band": "The music they made was pretty well in keeping with their looks. They struck up one of those over-and-over strains that seem to have no very clear beginning and certainly no ending at all . . . [The audience went wild and threw money onto the stage.] Then I saw the beauty of primitive music. They had the stuff the people wanted. It touched the spot."[52]

29

In each example, the originator functions to authenticate the appropriating performer: the wide-mouthed and bedraggled Negro for Rice's "Jump Jim Crow," the lone itinerant guitarist for Handy's stature as "Father of the Blues," the razor-slashed faces of black men and high yellow dancers for West's taboo-transgressing tough girl. Each artist takes the raw material that it was their fortune to encounter and turns it into a performance that simultaneously signifies and distances itself from its site of origination. The originators provide the performers with a veneer of authenticity, which in turn is reified by the appropriating artist and transformed into a commodity. Mae West's persona is formed through this play between authenticity and artifice, creating, as Hamilton notes, a style that is "exceedingly hard to pin down. She performed an impersonation at several removes: an authentic tough girl mimicking fairy impersonators mimicking the flamboyance of working-class women. What resulted was a baffling hall of mirrors that fascinated and bewildered nearly all who saw it."[53] Hamilton adds race to the hall of mirrors' emphasis on class, gender, and sexuality: "West's early Broadway exploits earned her the title 'World's Wickedest White Woman,' a phrase that suggested an excess of lewdness rivaled only by legions of lascivious blacks."[54]

When Mae West sang in her movies, she sang the blues: "Mister Deep Blue Sea" and "I'm an Occidental Woman in an Oriental Mood for Love" in *Klondike Annie* (Paramount, 1936); "They Call Me Sister Honky Tonk" and "That Dallas Man" in *I'm No Angel* (Paramount, 1933); "St. Louis Woman" and "Memphis Blues" in *Belle of the Nineties* (Paramount, 1934); and, in *She Done Him Wrong,* "Frankie and Johnny," "Easy Rider," and "I Like a Guy That Takes His Time." The sexual appeal in the latter is obvious, and though "Easy Rider" is ostensibly about a day at the races, in delivery and sentiment it is a blues number about a pimp and his whore. The title *She Done Him Wrong* is a gendered inversion of the refrain from "Frankie and Johnny," a song of no certain origin but performed by black and white vernacular and professional musicians since at least the turn of the century. "Frankie and Johnny"'s lack of authorship gave it an aura of authenticity compared to contemporary Tin Pan Alley–crafted coon songs, and for Mae West, no doubt, the song appealed because of its public display of love, sex, and violence.

In her "hall of mirrors," Mae West in feathers and shimmering dress can, with only a little imagination, be found facing Bessie Smith: "Mae learned from the songs of the Blues Queens," reads yet another formulation of authentication. "She went to Harlem to see them and listened to their race records with more than passing interest. She tried to imitate them."[55] But the imitation only went so far, because however sincere Mae West may have been in her imitations of blues singers, the performance's function was to further her identity as the personification of vulgar female sexuality, not to "articulate a consciousness that takes into account social conditions of class exploitation, racism, and male dominance as seen through the lenses of the complex emotional responses of black female subjects" that feminist Angela Davis argues is central to the expression of female blues.[56] The blues singer Ethel Waters turned the tables on Mae West in her 1934 recording "Come Up and See Me Sometime" when in counterimitation she sang:

> They say they're hot out there on that movie lot
> Now really that's a crime.
> Please wire Mae West, say "stay west."
> She's an Eskimo
> Come up and see Waters sometime.[57]

In this version, West is just a poor approximation of the real thing. She may not have worn burnt cork, but West's racial crossings were pure minstrelsy.

The first film produced by Twentieth Century Pictures, formed by Darryl F. Zanuck and Joseph M. Schenck after the former left Warner Bros., was *The Bowery* (1933), and it was clearly intended to ride the success and celebrity of *She Done Him Wrong.* Released in October, seven months after the Mae West vehicle, the film draws its story from the same romanticized locale and time period, the Gay Nineties, but suppresses the transgressive sexuality radiated by Mae West and replaces it with images of an ethnically and racially polyglot urban America that was barely there in *She Done Him Wrong,* and that, with the exclusion of Jewish immigrants, was suppressed in *The Jazz Singer.*

The Bowery begins with a bravura sequence introducing the central characters. Opening with a shot of a saloon called Nigger Joe's, a series of rapidly cut shots introduces the street life and the different ethnicities that inhabit the Bowery: a police raid on Suicide Hall (the setting for Mae West's play *Diamond Lil* that was adapted for the screen as *She Done Him Wrong*), singing waiters, street merchants, drunks, prostitutes, and the Salvation Army are all burlesqued. At the hub of this steaming mass of humanity is the Irishman Chuck Connors (Wallace Beery), a saloon keeper, misogynist, surrogate father to Swipes (Jackie Cooper), and leader of a volunteer fire brigade. His chief rival in work, love, and volunteer fire brigades is his fellow Irishman Steve Brody (George Raft). The two are like little boys in men's bodies, endlessly playing pranks on each other, until the denouement when both become fully assimilated Americans by joining the armed forces and fighting the Spanish in Cuba, by implication leaving behind their childhood and their Irish identity.

The infantilism of the characters is displayed through pleasures of the body, their love of the sensational and the spectacular, their loud and vulgar humor, their misogyny and racism, their lack of any meaningful responsibilities or deference to figures of authority, and their nonproductive and barely legitimate source of employment (both men front saloons for competing breweries, which allows them pretty much to please themselves). These traits, if not exactly a match with contemporaneous representations of African Americans are, nevertheless, a display of masculinity and class analogous to that found within coon songs. Connors and Brody *are* white, however, even if this is qualified by their being Irish, and they *are* given a space within the body politic of the United States at the end of the film; African Americans, though physically absent from the story and represented only in the racist dialogue that calls attention to "those coons down at Nigger Joe's," function as the lowest mark on the social scale that these giants of vulgarity remain only slightly distanced from.[58]

The film's creation of a vulgarity signified as American through its invocation of blackness as a means of authentication is carried through in the dance numbers performed on the stage in the saloon. In front of a chorus line of rather seamy women, Trixie Odbray (Pert Kelton), sings and dances her way through "Ta Ra Ra Boom Der Re," a song made famous by the English music hall star Lottie Collins, which before it made its Atlantic crossings was composed and first performed in a St. Louis brothel run by Babe Connor. Mama Lou sang the song in front of a chorus line of Creole dancing girls who, at the appropriate moments, according Tin Pan Alley historian Ian Whitcomb, lifted their skirts to reveal their lack of underclothes.[59] Clearly Trixie Odbray is not Mama Lou, her supporting dancers are not Creole, and, just as clearly, are fully clothed. But this does not negate the performance's vulgar connotations and its roots in a black imaginary. Overhead shots to show the girls' jiggling breasts are matched with cutaways to the leering faces of male punters who look up at the dancers' high kicks, suggesting a reveling in the performance of a lurid female sexuality. In his history of burlesque, Allen quotes from a contemporary critique that notes how the transgressive quality of many

Pert Kelton in *The Bowery* (courtesy of the British Film Institute)

of the burlesque dances were compared to minstrelsy: burlesque offered only "cheap rhymes, pre-Adamite puns, impudent distortions of grave political and social subjects" and "uncouth and immodest imitations of Negro dances by young women."[60] Yet, despite their overtly sexual content, Trixie Odbray's routines are, nevertheless, infantile, which mitigate the more lewd expressions of sexuality. Her dance steps are significantly similar to Shirley Temple's, which drew heavily on styles developed as part of a blackface repertoire. The tradition is invoked in many of Temple's films when she is "taught" her dance steps by either African Americans, such as Bill Robinson, or by Jimmy Clayton's (Jimmy Durante) Jazz Bandits as in *Little Miss Broadway* (Irving Cummings, Twentieth Century Fox, 1938). Either way, her dance style is usually signaled as having black roots. Even in a film such as *Poor Little Rich Girl* (1936), set in the world of radio advertising where there are no overt references to African American song and dance traditions, Temple injects "hallelujahs" and "hosannas" into a performance, creating a contrast to the more sophisticated and repressed (hence adult) delivery of her coperformers Alice Faye and Jack Haley. The black roots are called upon in this film, as in her other performances, to infer childishness rather than sexuality, though, of course, this does not preclude the latter.

Just as the characters deny any seriousness in the face they show to the world through appropriating a pre-self-conscious childishness, the play with ambivalence over the representation of sexuality in the film was a conscious ploy on the part of the producers to maintain deniability if censors accused them of being licentious with the material. *The Bowery,* perhaps because it was Twentieth Century's first production, was not submitted in script form to the Motion Picture Producers and Distributors Association (MPPDA). Instead the first report was conducted after a preview screening. Two deletions were demanded, an image of Beery stepping into cat excrement and a shot of him mouthing "son of a bitch." It was noted that the dance scenes with Pert Kelton and her chorus girls were "questionable," but deletions were not demanded. When the film played before censor boards both in America and abroad, cuts were asked for to eliminate the shots of the dancers' breasts, and the Australian authorities demanded the removal of all the ribaldry in the opening scenes. On the film's rerelease in 1946, Pennsylvania asked for the word "coon" to be deleted along with the sign "Nigger Joes." It is debatable how much of the film's coarseness would have been cut at the script stage if the screenplay had been submitted for the usual review process under the Production

34

Code, but it is clear from the reports in the film's file that the MPPDA's censors responded very enthusiastically to the performances of George Raft and Wallace Beery. Arguably their comic delivery undercut what on the scripted page would have been unacceptable. By playing their parts in a childishly innocent manner, the actors helped dilute most objections to the film's relentless reveling in vulgarity. As "children" in adult bodies, they find their most ready comparison in the happy and unthreatening caricatures of the plantation darkey of minstrelsy and the comic yet fearful urban figure of the coon; an ambiguity that allows them to be both thuggish bullies and innocent clowns.[61]

The Bowery and *She Done Him Wrong* popularized and helped fix Hollywood's representation of the concert-saloon, making it an essential dramatic space in rowdy portrayals of nineteenth-century America. In films that dramatized America's move from anarchic and vulgar beginnings to ordered civilization, such as *The Frisco Kid, Barbary Coast, San Francisco,* and *In Old Chicago,* the concert-saloon is the site of contestation between the forces of lawlessness and reform. Originally conceived by producer Samuel Goldwyn as a dramatic adaptation of Herbert Asbury's best-selling book *The Barbary Coast* (1933), the second in the author's series of informal histories of America's urban underworlds, Goldwyn had to abandon his initial plans for the book when its subject matter proved too controversial. The PCA's file on the film's production contains numerous letters between various parties recommending caution in dealing with the film's bawdy material. One internal memo noted how Goldwyn appeared to be abandoning his reputation for high-class productions and was now attempting to appeal to the more base instincts of his cinema patrons: "instead of the old-time Goldwyn quality he is going in for the salacious or the near-salacious, thus going the way of others to substitute jazz and questionable material for the old-time Goldwyn art; that he has given up all his old-time artistic supremacy save only when he happens to have a star, like Cantor, who carries the picture by reason of the name of the artist." A further memorandum produced by the PCA sums up their fears for *Barbary Coast*'s reception. It begins by suggesting alternative titles:

A *The Whorehouse District*
B *The Red Light District*
C *The District*

The reason for the substitution is that they mean just the same thing. The title *Barbary Coast* so certainly means "red light district" in this country, that several newspapers took it up as meaning just that. See *Chicago Tribune*. All over the country the words Barbary Coast mean exactly the red light district as generally understood with not only facilities for that profession, but gambling, shanghai-ing, rapine and murder. It especially connotes the red light district.[62]

The producers, however, worked to keep the promotional value of the title while attempting to ensure that there was nothing in the film that could cause offense. In a letter to Will Hays, Joseph Breen noted:

Mr. Goldwyn seems set on using this particular title. As I told you in our conversation the other evening, the story, as we now have it, is thoroughly and completely acceptable under the Code, and I have the thought that even if Mr. Goldwyn does use the title, the film may serve a good purpose in showing just what we are compelled to do on the screen by way of removing from popular literary works those offensive elements which seem to have been accepted by people generally but which, in the development of our principal of self-regulation we withhold from screen presentation.[63]

This ruse did not fool Cincinnati's moral guardians, who wrote to Breen to protest against the film's production. Helen Wilson Oesper of the Cincinnati Better Motion Picture Council argued that:

If Mr. Goldwyn is permitted to put out his adaptation under the title *Barbary Coast,* we can only infer that he wishes to trade on the popularity of the book, which we have examined and which is still going the rounds of the lending libraries. (Our public library significantly does not have a copy.) . . . If he's changing the emphasis from gambling, vice, and the usual concomitance of an historical, wide-open district of entertainment, Mr. Goldwyn is placing himself in the vulnerable position of seeming to misbrand his intended production. The public should not be misled into expecting "lusty" entertainment and be given something else. No, this won't do, Mr. Breen.[64]

Barbary Coast transposed the then popular gangster genre to California at the height of the gold rush. Louis Chamalis (Edward G. Robinson) runs San Francisco and the Bella Donna saloon, where he tricks miners out of their new wealth. Mary Rutledge (Miriam Hopkins), who is absolutely broke, has traveled by ship from New York to marry a man she has never met. On her arrival, she discovers her betrothed has been killed after losing his money to Chamalis. Virtually destitute, the only thing of value that she possesses is her whiteness. Disembarking from the ship, Mary is met by gasps of surprise and desire: "Suffering snakes, a white woman," says Old Atrocity (Walter Brennan), who ferries her to shore. His observation is repeated again and then reinforced by a call from a group of men waiting at the quayside: "What you got there?" they shout to him. "A white woman." "You're lying!" they respond. "No I'm not. A New York, white woman—whiter than a hen's egg."

The scene introduces the main musical themes, a medley of Stephen Foster's minstrel songs interspersed with other nineteenth-century signature tunes such as "Molly Malone." The men, making a great fuss, carry Mary across the muddy streets and walk her past a line of bars, out of which piano renditions of more minstrel tunes are heard; as they pass a group of Chinese men the music changes to an Oriental theme. An American specificity returns to this image of a godless alien hellhole when an off-screen female is heard singing a few lines of "Frankie and Johnny." Mary's presence (her whiteness) causes the cessation of a performance of "De Camptown Races" at the Bella Donna saloon, and, like all the men, Louis Chamalis is instantly smitten with Mary. Mary begins working for him at a crooked roulette wheel, and he changes her name to Swan.

Though the dialogue denies any physical relationship between Chamalis and Mary, her self-loathing and easy manner when drinking hard liquor suggest she is a kept woman. When Chamalis demands that she love him, her reply is that he should be content with what he has: "Do you still think I'm Mary Rutledge?" she asks him. "Do you think I'm still a white woman?" Eventually, she finds redemption through the love of the poet and prospector James Carmichael (Joel McCrea), who takes her away from the saloon, Chamalis, and minstrel songs and gives her instead marriage, self-respect, a book of poems by Shelley, and the return of her whiteness. Old Atrocity, who has conned James Carmichael out of his gold, like Mary Rutledge, reforms midway through the film. He wishes to cleanse his "black soul" by returning some of Carmichael's gold, "the only decent thing I've done in my whole black life, sort of overwhelms me," he tells Carmichael. "I feel like a little white kitten—reborn." Both moral and material progress is measured by the characters' distance from the image of blackness.

In *Barbary Coast,* blackness is equated with the deep mud the characters are shown trudging through—it is the primal element out of which America is formed, but like the mud it is destined to be cleaned away: "Rome wasn't built in a day," says the town's first newspaper man, "the paths of

Miriam Hopkins and Edward G. Robinson in *Barbary Coast* (courtesy of the British Film Institute)

empire have always started in mud and ended in glory." The mud neatly represents the idea of racial hybridity. Neither solid nor liquid it is simply in a permanent state of process moving between the two extremes.

A much less bawdy representation of a concert-saloon is displayed in *The Frisco Kid* (Warner Bros., 1935), which *Variety* characterized as so "similar to the *Barbary Coast* as almost to be its twin." Likewise, *In Old Chicago* (Twentieth Century Fox, 1937) attempted to emulate the success of MGM's *San Francisco* (1936). Both films offered sensational special effects in their representation of their respective city's destruction. Chicago and San

Francisco are America's Sodom and Gomorrah, with the sinful gathered together in concert-saloons awaiting judgment day. "On April 18, 1906, the city of San Francisco met destruction—the old San Francisco—the wicked, ribald, licentious San Francisco—ceased to exist."[65] Just before the earthquake rips San Francisco apart, the great and the mighty are brought together for the Chicken Ball, a yearly talent contest that Blackie Norton (Clark Gable), a saloon owner, has yet to lose. Mary (Jeanette MacDonald), daughter of a country parson, opera sensation, and one-time protégée of Blackie, figuratively descends into the gutter to win the contest for him and finally to provide the vital and vulgar performance of the song "San Francisco" that she has resisted throughout the film.

Echoing Magnolia's first audition in *Show Boat,* Mary is ill equipped for the bawdy song material and lewd performance style demanded in concert-saloons. The published screenplay describes Mary's performance as "naturally failing to give the song its low-down Frisco rhythm." Like the professor who rags "Can't Help Lovin' Dat Man," Blackie tries to cajole a more expressive performance from Mary by "tearing off the song in hot rhythm at the piano." "'That's not it' he disgustedly cuts in. 'Put something into it! *Heat it up!'* Blackie emphasizes the rhythm with his shoulders."[66] The scene also foreshadows Alice Faye's character in *In Old Chicago* whose performance denies the vulgar provenance (and blackface heritage) of her material when she sings "Carry Me Back to Old Virginny" with great reverence. Earlier in *San Francisco,* a performance of "Ta Ra Ra Boom Der Re" is heard but not seen, which suggests the shift in representing the vulgar that has occurred between *The Bowery* and this film. The debauchery of some of San Francisco's aristocracy is similarly not seen but referred to through dialogue and a distantly heard rendition of "Hot Time in the Old Town Tonight," a standard in the coon singer's repertoire. Popular song derived from black culture is still the signifier of vulgarity, but here it is being pushed to the margins by the apparently divinely sanctioned operatic style of Jeanette MacDonald's singing. What the film wishes to achieve through its evoking of low- and highbrow musical cultures—coon songs and opera—is an eventual reconciliation that will form a uniquely American culture that is neither low- nor highbrow, but one that transcends hierarchy.

Listening to the coon songs emanating from a party at the aristocratic McDonough mansion ("There isn't a rougher joint on the whole Barbary Coast than that 'home' right here on Nob Hill"), Mary becomes involved in a conversation with a more sedate representative of the city's ruling class:

it's a bitter shame—it is—for deep down underneath all our evil and sin we've got right here in San Francisco *the greatest set of human bein's ever rounded up in one spot!* . . . Sure—they had to have *wild adventure* in their *hearts* and *dynamite* in their *blood* to start out for here in the first place. And they had to laugh at death and danger the whole way—in order to get through! That's why they're so full of untamed deviltry today. But we mustn't go on like we're doin'—blasphemous and sinful and with no feelin' for God in our hearts . . . I want my boy to have a good woman, Mary, and raise fine, beautiful kids for the *glory* of our heritage.[67]

This speech by Mrs. Burley suggests how culturally and historically close the San Francisco aristocrats are to the vulgar hordes that inhabit the concert-saloons. This sanctions Mary's love for the lowlife Blackie Norton *and* legitimates her desire to sing opera. The earthquake that destroys old San Francisco will, it is assumed, give birth to a new San Francisco without divisive hierarchy, symbolized by Blackie and Mary's reconciliation at the end of the film. Opera and coon song are united just as minstrelsy and ballet were at the end of *Show Boat.* But while this may lead to the safe containment in history of a low, vulgar, and black form of American entertainment, its ability to transcend class hierarchy is less certain, because what is produced will lack the dynamic interplay between the high and the low that creates a distinctive American self-image and will instead manifest a faceless homogenization—middle-brow conformity. This is why these films always end at the point of rapprochement between the low and the high: what follows can only be banal caricature of a vital and energizing American culture. This is certainly what happened in the production of *Barbary Coast* where the immediate inspiration for the story, Herbert Asbury's delirious examination of San Francisco's history of vice, was dropped and in its place, as Breen gleefully noted in a letter to Hays, Goldwyn produced:

a very fine love story between a fine, clean girl and a sentimental character who is a poet. This, of course, is played against the background—low, hardy and boisterous—of the Barbary Coast, but there is no sex, no unpleasant details of prostitution, questionable dance-halls, etcetera, in this picture. The heavy who runs the crooked gambling joint is a ruthless cruel character imposing upon the ignorance and stupidity of the miners who dig for gold.

There is a full, and completely compensating, value in the picture, and the whole thing is really quite attractive. Indeed, it is my thought . . . that the picture was so good from an entertainment and artistic standpoint, that it is not unlikely that it might receive the Academy prize for the Best Picture of the Year. It is really a magnificent production, well worthy of the industry.[68]

The "low, hardy and boisterous" are reduced to "background" and all potentially disruptive "unpleasant" elements have been expunged. This process of refinement was paralleled in the manner by which Hollywood used blackface in films at the end of the 1930s and on into the 1940s. The decreasing numbers of examples of blackface minstrelsy were almost exclusively confined to elegiac tributes to America's theatrical past in films such as *Babes in Arms* (MGM, 1939), where showbiz kids hope to revive vaudeville, or *Dixie* (Paramount, 1943), a musical biography of the nineteenth-century blackface star Dan Emmett that made full use of burnt cork. *My Gal Sal* (Twentieth Century Fox, 1942), a biopic of the minstrel tunesmith Paul Dresser, however, substituted the truncated "Lisa Jane" for "I'se Your Nigger If You Wants Me, Liza Jane," and kept the banjo-strumming star of the movie (Victor Mature) out of blackface. By the early forties, with the success of Westerns like *Dodge City* (Warner Bros., 1939) and *Destry Rides Again* (Universal, 1939), the concert-saloon had become part of the iconography of the Western.[69] In its transition to the West, the concert-saloon loses much of its urban specificity, but it remains a sign of America's primitive beginnings. The dances on stage are often little more than variations on "Ta Ra Ra Boom Der Re" in *The Bowery,* and the incidental music in the Western is almost without exception based on the most immediately recognizable minstrel tunes of the nineteenth century, "Oh Dem Golden Slippers," "Oh! Susanna," "De Camptown Races," and "Buffalo Gals." The Western's play with minstrelsy is iconically configured in John Wayne's appearance in blackface in *The Spoilers* (Universal, 1942). Hollywood's representation of blackface as a signifier of nostalgia helped to undercut whatever relevance the form still had for a contemporary audience, but in doing so it also made blackface an essential element in the evocation of an American vernacular, a cultural miscegenation at once recognized and denied.

As film historian Thomas Cripps has noted, Hollywood was profoundly conservative in its representation of African Americans. In part this was dictated by what he calls the "myth of the Southern box office," but also by an inability to envision a role for African Americans that did not draw upon images of the Old South, a subject of only marginal interest within Hollywood's trends and cycles during most of the 1930s.[70] When *Gone*

Body and Soul

With the Wind (MGM, 1939) made stories of the antebellum South popular again, the role of African Americans in the film (despite being drawn from the pool of minstrel types) represented, according to Cripps, "a shift in racial arrangements."[71] Hollywood had became more sensitive during the latter part of the 1930s to how it represented black characters, and the more overtly derogatory racist representations used in early to mid-1930s films, such as that implied in the occasional use of racial epithets like "nigger" and "coon," became less common.[72] The movement towards more positive portrayals of blacks was confirmed in 1942 when senior Hollywood executives met delegates of the National Association for the Advancement of Colored People. At this meeting an agreement was reached whereby the studios agreed to "abandon pejorative racial roles."[73] "March 1942," writes Cripps, "became a date by which to measure the future against the past."[74]

Nevertheless, popular song derived from black American culture would continue to be a significant element in American cinema's representation of a vulgar, yet vital, American culture. When the donning of the black mask of minstrelsy became less visible within popular arts, it did not mean the end to the racial crossings blackface had helped mediate, rather, to appropriate the common vernacular of the 1930s, blackface in American films shifted from the idea implied in the racial slur "nigger in the woodpile" to the rather less visible, but no less derogatory, "octoroon in the kindling." I first encountered this phrase in *Her Man* (Pathé, 1930), where it was used to suggest that something is amiss, but I am using the phrase to suggest the cultural miscegenation that informs much of the material discussed here. American cinema found itself in the paradoxical position of needing to evoke traditions of blackface minstrelsy so that a given film could bring vernacular discourses into play while simultaneously attempting to efface the influence of blackface as the racial crossings implied in its use became ever more difficult to contain, a type of play that oscillates between revelation and concealment of its racial signifiers. It is of some significance that while blackface minstrelsy became less visible on professional stages and in the movies, it gained remarkable popularity in radio *(The Amos and Andy Show)* and with phonograph recordings (particularly Mack and Moran's "Two Black Crows" skits). In the new aural media, minstrelsy was present but invisible.

In an early scene in *Show Boat,* two hillbillies attend their first theatrical performance. They have paid for their tickets with Confederate currency:

42

the money is worthless, but it is still in circulation. Blackface is like that worthless currency; its time had passed, yet it refused to disappear, staying in circulation, returning whenever American culture needed to express a vernacular tradition.

2

This Extremely Dangerous Material: Frankie and Johnny Go to the Movies

Johnny grabbed off his Stetson, "Oh, good Lord,
Frankie, don't shoot!"
But Frankie pulled the trigger and the gun went
root-a-toot-toot.
He was her man, but she shot him down.
—"Frankie and Johnny"

The encoding of blackface minstrelsy as a key trope in Hollywood's representation of America's theatrical past compounded a diminishing of the form's vitality that at other times had enabled it to engage meaningfully with contemporary issues of identity. That engagement was now far better effected through the type of song that emerged out of the popular trends of ragtime and coon songs that could be performed either inside or outside the racial masquerade of blackface. The ballad of "Frankie and Johnny" was the preeminent example of a song form that emphasized identification with female subjectivity: during the late 1920s to mid-1930s, "Frankie and Johnny," which recites the tale of a betrayed lover who exacts violent revenge on the man "who done her wrong," sustained remarkable popularity. It was disseminated through commercial phonograph recordings, in folk song collections, as stage and puppet plays, in literature, and in newspaper articles. Poems were written extolling the couple's virtues and vices, paintings were commissioned that depicted them in all their infamy, Oscar of the Waldorf popularized a Frankie and Johnny cocktail, comedian Joe Cook fashioned a vaudeville sketch built around his rendition of the song, and in 1938 a ballet based on their exploits was performed. Inevitably, given its commercial and artistic profile, the ballad was used as the basis for two Hollywood screenplays, and appeared either as a discrete performance or as part of the sound track in a number of films.

Music publishers Shapiro and Bernstein copyrighted "Frankie and Johnny" in 1912. Words and music were credited to Ren Shields, a writer of comedy sketches for vaudeville, and the Leighton Brothers, a popular blackface vaudeville team.[1] But they were no more the song's authors than Hughie Cannon, the writer of the coon song "Bill Bailey, Won't You Please Come Home," who published the first commercial version of the "Frankie and Johnny" ballad in 1904 under the title "He Done Me Wrong." Nor was Frank Crumit its proprietor, despite his claim of "complete authorship." A singer of novelty numbers ("Abdul Abulbul Amir"), Crumit had the biggest "hit" recording of the song in 1927. In counterpoint to its commercial exploitation, the folk song collectors Alan and John Lomax noted in the early 1930s that over 300 variants of the ballad had been documented.[2] But the ballad was neither a folk song nor a strictly commercial property.[3]

It is certain that the ballad was already well known across the continent in 1912 when the Leighton Brothers changed the male protagonist's name from Albert to Johnny in their bid to secure copyright. The popularity of this version ensured that the man who did Frankie wrong would be henceforth known as Johnny, though Albert would never entirely disappear from recorded versions. The song's melody has been traced back to a Scottish folk song "Tattie Jock" and other variants, and its subject matter to the murder in December 1831 in the Blue Ridge Mountains of western North Carolina of Charlie Silver by his wife Frankie. But song collectors and folklorists contest even these claims. Some say the song was first sung by Federal troops besieging Vicksburg in 1863. Carl Sandburg claimed the song "was common along the Mississippi River and among railroad men as early as 1888."[4] Others have argued that it was first performed in Tennessee, or Arkansas, or Texas, or California, or anywhere else where good songs are sung. The most often repeated origin, and the one that has substantial supporting evidence, is that the song documents the killing of Allen Britt by Frankie Baker, a black couple who resided at 212 Targee Street, St. Louis in 1899—a contemporary newspaper account of the slaying described her as "an ebony hued cake-walker."[5] Frankie Baker would aid her claim to immortality by taking Republic Pictures to court in 1939 for defamation of character and invasion of privacy brought about by their distribution of the film *Frankie and Johnnie.* Baker would eventually lose her suit, but the case for the song being based upon her actions is not so easily dismissed. The small section of St. Louis where she and Britt plied their respective trades has an extraordinary musical heritage. Writing in 1930 about the social world the ballad was formed in and depicted, a young John Huston noted how "St. Louis became known as the toughest town in the west. Boogie-joints and bucket-shops opened on Twelfth, Carr, Targee, and Pine Streets. The fast colored men and women lived up to their necks. Stack-o-lee stepped out and made a legend of his Stetson hat. The girls wore red for Billy Lyons. Duncan killed Brady. The ten pimps that bore the dead were kept on parade between the infirmary and the graveyard."[6]

St. Louis's geographic location placed it at the center of America's entertainment map: the Mississippi carried songs and performers up and down its length and the railroads connected the east and west. In his dissertation "Tragedy in Ragtime: Black Folktales from St. Louis," John Russell David creates a vivid portrait of the turn-of-the-century city that produced two of the most enduring popular songs of the twentieth century, "Stack O'Lee" and "Frankie and Johnny."[7] David uncovers the city's rich contribution to ragtime and the events that influenced some of the key ballads of a coon song subgenre, the "bully" song, which was responsible in turn for the "bad man"/"bad nigger" genre of which "Stack O'Lee" is the best-known example. The black urban culture David discusses was centered on the saloon and bawdy houses, both homosocial spaces and political power bases for the city's not insubstantial black electorate. The more up-market houses of pleasure also secured the patronage of white male adventurers who sought thrills in "Tamale Town" that could not be found in white neighborhoods.

Babe Connor's Castle Club, a saloon, brothel, and concert hall, was the greatest attraction. It was here, apparently, that the European classical composer Ignacy Paderewski first encountered black vernacular American music. "Ta Ra Ra Boom Der Re" was said to be first performed here, sung by Mama Lou as "Creole" girls dressed only in stockings high-kicked, twirled, and danced to the tune. David argues convincingly that it was here that "Stack O'Lee" had its first performance. Shelton Lee, otherwise known as Stack Lee, had killed William Lyons in Bill Curtis's saloon on Christmas night 1895 in a fight started over the ownership of a hat. The slaying took place ten blocks south of where Frankie Baker shot Allen Britt, which in turn was one block south of Charles Starkes's saloon where the white police officer Brady was killed by the black man Harry Duncan in 1890, an event immortalized in another "bad man"/"bad nigger" folk song, "Brady and Duncan":

> Brady fell down on the barroom floor
> Cried, "Please, Mr. Duncan, don't you shoot me no more."
> The women all cried, "Oh, ain't it a shame,
> He's shot King Brady—gonna shoot him again."

Stack Lee was sentenced to serve time in prison for the killing of Billy Lyons; among those who petitioned for his early release was Thomas Turpin, St. Louis's leading ragtime pianist who played at Babe Connors's club before he opened his own hostelry, the Rosebud Saloon. Babe Connors had given up on the saloon business and had converted to Catholicism by the time Frankie Baker shot Allen Britt, but her successors would have provided ample space and opportunity to develop the ballad.[8] Whatever the ballad's place of origin, it carried connotations of a low and vulgar view of American life; it was, as the historian of popular song Sigmund Spaeth wrote in 1948, "as American as anything in our archives, musical or literary."[9]

The low and raced origin of the ballad is echoed in the preface for John Held Jr.'s exquisite series of woodcuts *The Saga of Frankie and Johnny* (1930). The celebrated illustrator records that he first learned of the song as a youth "from a colored piano player, who was called 'Professor' in a parlor house . . . owned and run by a lady who was called Madam Helen Blazes"[10] (this, no doubt, was not the name on her birth certificate). Held's version follows the basic outline of the ballad—"the eternal triangle" as he describes it. The setting is an unidentified American city around the turn of the century, and Frankie and Johnny's professions are unambiguously stated: she worked "down in a crib house, / Worked there without any drawers" while Johnny spends all her money "on parlor-house whores" and the dreamier pleasures provided in "hop-joints." Held's work was privately published.

More readily available to public scrutiny was Thomas Hart Benton's mural "Typical Scenes of Missouri" (1936), which included Frankie and

Johnny alongside images of slave blocks and a portrait of Jesse James. The mural "produced an immediate uproar" in the media, which deemed it "offensive" and an affront to Missouri's "growing refinement and nobility." The low nature of the subject matter was compounded by depicting Frankie and Johnny as a black couple and by showing Frankie shooting Johnny in his posterior, an image that had earlier been seen in Held's woodcuts; Frankie says, "I didn't shoot him in the third degree / I shot him in the ass." Benton was a leading proponent of American regionalism in the arts and had chosen to use Frankie and Johnny because he understood them to be quintessentially American, and therefore an aid in his confrontation with European artistic and "aesthetic colonialism" in America.[11] The poet Louis Untermeyer similarly felt the ballad was quintessentially American and included it in his anthology *Modern American Poetry* (1919). The American specificity of the ballad also attracted the Popular Front composer and protégé of Aaron Copland, Jerome Moross, who wrote *Frankie and Johnny* for the Chicago Ballet, choreographed by Ruth Page and first performed in 1938.[12] Duke Ellington similarly essayed a more highbrow version of "Frankie and Johnny" when he composed and produced it as a concerto in 1941.[13]

The ballad's attraction is its aestheticized (and highly romanticized) portrayal of the vulgate: the common speech within which "Frankie and Johnny" is couched represents a set of material and sexual desires that appear unhampered by mundane concerns and repressive forces, but which are offered at the cost of offending those for whom desire in themselves and in others must be tamed. John (Jack) M. Kirkland's play *Frankie and Johnnie* opened at the Republic Theater in New York in September 1930. The police, who raided the play during its tryout, were "offended" according to theater historian Gerald Bordman "by its story, its characters, and lines such as the one defending prostitution as 'the only profession for which women are exclusively equipped.'"[14] Reviewing the play for the Studio Relations Committee (the precursor to the Production Code Administration), Lamar Trotti wrote, "This is unbelievable cheap melodrama and I can't conceive of any company being interested in it. It is of course entirely out so far as the Code is concerned as is censurable from beginning to end."[15] On reading Trotti's comments, another staff member wrote back to him, noting "that Pathé has already produced a picture based on this property. When you see *Her Man* you will hardly recognize it as the child of such a parent."

Her Man had begun life as *Frankie and Johnny* and was in fact an original screenplay by Tay Garnett and Howard Higgin, not based on Kirkland's stage play. Nevertheless, the proximity of play dates between the drama and the film caused *Variety* to note, "Plenty of 'Frankie and Johnny' publicity around New York of late with the dirty play of that title pinched. The picture here [*Her Man*] merely basing [*sic*] that verse is not dirty."[16] In the same year Frank Held Jr. had published his woodcuts of the ballad, Milt Gross published his "graphic" novel *He Done Her Wrong* (the title exploited the refrain from the ballad but otherwise the novel had little or nothing else in common). Meyer Levin's novel *Frankie and Johnnie* gave the story a contemporary twist by playing the lovers as juvenile delinquents, and John Huston gained some success with a puppet show, *Frankie and Johnny*, which played New York and was published alongside thirteen versions of the ballad and some agreeably evocative illustrations by Miguel Covarrubias.[17] Commercial phonograph recordings also figured highly in the ballad's increasing profile in the public's consciousness.

Commercial sound recordings of the ballad have to rely on innuendo, suggestion and prior knowledge of other versions if the song's vulgar and lewd subject is to be acknowledged. The details of Frankie's relationship to Johnny tend to be carried by the lyrics:

> Frankie and Johnny were lovers
> Lawdy, how they did love
> Swore to be true to each other
> True as the stars above . . .
> Frankie was a good girl everybody knows
> Paid about a hundred dollars
> For Johnny's suit of clothes.

The couple appear to be in love, but Frankie is doing all the giving and Johnny all the taking. More explicit versions reveal that Johnny is using Frankie to give the money she gives to him to his lover Nelly Bly (or some other woman with a similar name):

> Frankie she shot Albert
> And I'll tell you the reason why,
> Ever' dollar bill she gave Albert,
> He'd give to Alice Blye.

While Frankie's occupation as a prostitute and Johnny's as her pimp is easily surmised by more sophisticated listeners, versions in private folk song collections can dissolve all ambiguity:

> Frankie goes down to the whore house,
> Peeks in at the window so high;
> There she sees her lover, Johnny
> Finger fuckin' Nellie Bly.

Whatever the references to the specifics of Frankie and Johnny's love lives, the wide musical appeal of the ballad is partly explained by its malleability and adaptability to a number of performance styles. Recordings by jazz men such as King Oliver (1929 and 1930) and blues queens Mamie Smith (1923), Bessie Smith (1924), and Ethel Waters (1938) continued to confirm the image of Frankie and Johnny as low class, urban, and black.[18] At the more pop end of the market, best personified by Frank Crumit's 1927 rendition, the instrumentation and arrangement is usually studded with jazz inflections to help emphasize the illicit nature of love and murder in the underworld.[19] Both black and white musicians also represented the ballad in pre-1940s rural blues and "old-time" or hillbilly commercial recordings. Following Frank Crumit's model, "The father of country music" Jimmie Rodgers produced what has since become the best known "white" version of the song in 1929. Rodgers's "Frankie and Johnny" gave rise to a number of imitations, most notably by Gene Autry (1929) who specialized in the late 1920s and early 1930s in covering Rodgers's songs for cut-price record labels (the Marvin brothers, who were Autry's mentors during this period, performed under the name Frankie and Johnny). Well before his first success as a singing cowboy in the movies, Autry also cut an extremely risqué version for private distribution, wherein Frankie accuses Johnnie of giving his "peter" away to another gal, and whores and pimps get called whores and pimps.[20] Charlie Poole, like Autry a challenger to Rodgers's crown, had earlier recorded the ballad under the title "Leaving Home," and Tom Darby and Jimmie Tarlton recorded the song in 1930 under the title "Frankie Dean." Revealing the mixed and contested parentage of the ballad, these title changes were justified as a way of claiming publishing royalties.[21] Black songsters such as Mississippi John Hurt (1928) and Leadbelly (1939) produced equally "traditional" yet unique versions while Delta bluesman Charlie Patton recorded one of the most confused, confusing, and beautifully surreal of all recorded versions (1929). In his telling, Patton misses the central incident of Frankie shooting Albert, and Albert stands trial for the crime of killing himself, or so it seems: "Oh Albert was convicted, Frankie hung her head and cry." In 1928 the white Kentuckian Emry Arthur recorded a two-part, six-minute version, entitled "Frankie

Baker" (it is unknown whether he was also sued by the song's namesake). In the same year, the black Dallas songster Nick Nichols recorded another two-part version of the ballad. There is little discernible difference in the plot lines between the black and white vernacular recordings.

In all, Frankie and Johnny profess their love for one another, but Johnny is fickle and finds comfort in another woman's arms until Frankie discovers his betrayal and guns him down. Arrested by the police, she is taken before the judge. If there are significant differences between black and white versions, they tend to be concentrated towards the end of the ballad and revolve around whether Frankie is freed or executed. In Nick Nichols' version, Frankie, after getting drunk on gin and dancing the "shim-shim" to celebrate Johnny's murder, seduces the judge by dancing in the courtroom:

> Frankie she start to shimmy,
> And the judge begin to smile,
> Says "My golly, she's a pippin,
> Oh, she's my angel chile,
> I'll be her man and I won't do her wrong."

Blues historian Paul Oliver has noted that Nichols' "tongue-in-cheek amorality would have appealed at a time when blacks believed that they had little justice in the courts and had often found that pretending naiveté, or repentance . . . was as likely to turn the case in their favor, as any attorney's pleading."[22] But there is no direct reference to the race of the characters.

Published versions do exist where the characters' race is alluded to—"'Listen here, Mr. Bartender, don't tell me no lies. / Have you seen that Nigger Albert? With the girl they call Katy Fly?'"[23] Commercial recordings, however, tend to forsake any overt racial signifiers. The presumption is that the characters in the song belong to the same race as the singer. The African American poet and Howard University professor Sterling A. Brown, who produced other reworkings of black folklore, drew upon the racial instability of the two protagonists across versions of the ballad in a poem he published in 1932. Frankie is the white "halfwit" daughter of a "red-faced cracker, with a cracker's thirst," Johnny is a black field hand. Frankie flirts, teases, and tempts Johnny, giving no more thought to her actions than she does when pulling "wings off of living butterflies," whipping dogs, and throwing "stones at the brindle calf." Johnny eventually succumbs to her temptations but before long Frankie's father catches the "lovers" and Johnny is lynched:

> Frankie, she was spindly limbed with corn silk on her head,
> Johnny was a nigger, who never had much fun—
> They swung up Johnny on a tree, and filled his swinging hide with
>   lead,
> And Frankie yowled hilariously when the thing was done.[24]

Brown politicizes the ballad; uniquely for an African American version of the tale, he takes it out of the city and into the countryside, which denies the characters' attempts to assert their individuality against the claims of the urban and modernity. Brown takes the characters back to the root of American racism—the rural South—making the relationship between blacks and whites recognizable. What, in part, gives urban versions of the tale their power is that the racial world of the turn-of-the-century American city is in some ways unknown and unrecognizable; where are the borders and boundaries in a city defined by a polyglot citizenship? Nevertheless, Brown saw in the song's dual appeal to black and white audiences a politics of race that otherwise remains, as in Nick Nichols' version, at best latent. The ballad had multiple commonly recognized racial roots: from the stories of its origin, its early dissemination as part of blackface routines (one of its first recordings was in 1922 by the blackface minstrel Al Bernard, who billed himself as "The Boy from Dixie"), its emergence into a popular public arena during the widespread fad for ragtime and coon songs, to the continued mimicry, through jazz, of black culture by white performers. "Frankie and Johnnie"'s presence in all of these cultural sites consolidated the connotation that the ballad offered a privileged view of the new urban black population.[25] This privileged view, moreover, was identified as feminine.

John Huston's puppet play is book-ended by Frankie's execution. In between, Huston revels in a highly stylized vulgarity epitomized by the secondary character Lila, a bedraggled and broken-down old chippie (prostitute) who enters and exits scenes singing "Ki-yi, whoops! I'm fulla alkali." Suffering from delirium tremens, she is stopped by a policeman:

> LILA: They's a whole menagerie a rodents inside my skirts.
> SHERIFF (lifting Lila's dresses): How's that?
> LILA: They've et my legs away.
> SHERIFF: What has? I don't see nothing.[26]

Despite the comedy, Huston's is a tragic version. As Frankie stands on the scaffold getting ready to teach her friends a new dance, she tells a weeping sheriff to dry his eyes: "Wipe the water from your eye, Sheriff. It may hinder ye in your job. We mustn't welch now, we got somepin to do together,—not thinkin' on ourselves, but on what it'll come to. Without it endin' thisaway, they'd be no point to the story."[27] Where other ballads of the period that emerged out of the same locale and culture, such as "Stack O'Lee," have a male protagonist as the central point of identification, "Frankie and Johnny" focuses on an active female sexuality that operates outside of the domestic sphere, and, while in some versions Frankie is punished for her misdeeds, the audience's sympathies are exclusively with her (excepting Sterling A. Brown's version, which has Johnny as the victim). Jimmie Rodgers completes his telling of the tale by taking an amoral stance:

> This story has no moral
> This story has no end
> The only thing it goes to show
> Is there ain't no good in men.

The tragic figure is the woman, and with only one or two exceptions Hollywood's use of the ballad would be to aid identification with and the character development of the female principal.

In a memorable and early scene from MGM's *Three Godfathers* (1936), Bob (Chester Morris), a cowboy Johnny in search of his Frankie, fails to seduce Molly, a blonde paragon of virginal purity. Bob revives his spirits in the saloon and turns his attention to Blackie, the town's resident chippie. To the piano accompaniment of "Frankie and Johnny," Bob and Blackie dance into the fadeout as Bob tells her, "I danced at the social, but it didn't get me anywhere." The fadeout, demanded by the PCA, eliminated the tag line "wonder how I'll do with you." However, the instantly recognizable refrain from "Frankie and Johnny" carries enough lustful significance to compensate for the lost dialogue. Bob's motives are transparent: having failed with the good girl, he seeks comfort with someone from his own moral level. Though Blackie's occupation is not overtly announced, she is the only female in the saloon and her dress, hairstyle, makeup and body posture are strongly contrasted to the good girl. Blackie's name, dark hair, sexually revealing black dress, heavy makeup, and slovenly physicality imply an almost explicit racial distinction between her and Molly (a Protestant Mary).

Body and Soul

The ballad of "Frankie and Johnny" signifies a world defined by the promises and limits of the saloon, whether it is located on the Western frontier or the frontier between urban black and white neighborhoods. The song plays out a series of conflicts that are posed as operating on the frontiers of modernity. For white characters, this is most ably signified through the shift from rural to urban lifestyles; for black characters, it is through defining individual agency within an urban space. Either way, the saloon is where these conflicts are most profoundly located and realized. Specifically, the conflicts are between the opposing calls of the homosocial space of the public house and the heterosocial space of the domestic home. The saloon is the site where progressive civilizing impulses clash with the primitive instincts of its habitués.

The saloon holds out the promise of a world divorced from work, home, and church—liquor, gambling, male companionship, and the erotic pleasures figured in the songs and dances performed by women and in the company offered by prostitutes. This is the world portrayed in Mae West's first major film, *She Done Him Wrong* (1933). The title is drawn from the refrain of "Frankie and Johnny," though the gender of the antagonist is switched. West also sings the song in the film. The film was an adaptation of West's stage play *Diamond Lil* (1927), which she also turned into a novel. The setting is a concert-saloon on the Bowery in the 1890s. Lou (West) is the saloon's hostess and main attraction. The plot revolves around the procuring and traffic of white girls to Latin America. Valued for their whiteness, the naive young women are contrasted with the exotic otherness of the characters who threaten their sanctity and with Lou's weary worldliness that is reinforced through her performance of blues songs that further diminish her whiteness.

The performance of "Frankie and Johnny" is one of the film's big numbers. West had sung the song in the stage play, an event that Robert Garland reviewed in the New York *Evening Telegram*: "It is worth swimming to Brooklyn to see her descend those dance hall stairs, to be present when she lolls in a golden bed reading the *Police Gazette*, murders her girlfriend, wrecks the Salvation Army, and sings as much of 'Frankie and Johnnie' as the mean old laws allow."[28] Garland was obviously aware of more salacious versions of the song, confirming the idea of the real and imaginary excessive signification that the song could carry, particularly when contextualized by the appropriate racial, sexual, and social setting.

If *She Done Him Wrong* represents the urban frontier of the later part of the nineteenth century when physical pleasures appeared less heavily policed—the film's source play was written during, and as a reaction to, Prohibition—then *Barbary Coast* (1935), which transposes the gangster genre to California at the height of the gold rush, represents a more familiar frontier milieu where the racial identity of Americans is more clearly an issue. As discussed in the previous chapter, the film's introduction suggests San Francisco is a godless sinkhole devoid of white women and populated by a polyglot citizenship, but the city is given an American specificity through the use of minstrel tunes and, emanating from a dingy gin palace, by a few lines of "Frankie and Johnny."

Outside of the saloon but linked to it through drink, the song becomes an ally in Hollywood's representation of an abject or, at least a troubling, femininity in *Life Begins* (Warner Bros., 1932). Wrapped around the central story of a pregnant female murderer who is transferred from prison to a maternity hospital, this film includes a number of vignettes that depict a "variety of maternal reactions." Florette (Glenda Farrell) is a "good-time girl" who has given birth to twins, but she rejects motherhood and takes comfort in the gin she has hidden in her hot water bottle. Her babies are put up for adoption, but when she overhears a prospective foster parent discussing the separation of the twins she becomes possessive and discovers her maternal instincts. The fact that she is a potentially unsuitable mother is underscored when she sings "Frankie and Johnny" as a lullaby to one of her babies.[29] The PCA advised Jack Warner of a number of censorable scenes, noting "Florette's drunken singing of 'Frankie and Johnny' (which is maudlin, and objectionable from a comedy point of view)." It may well have been objectionable, but being in one's cups and emoting along with Frankie was somewhat in vogue in 1932.

Another of Hollywood's fallen woman films, *Red Headed Woman* (MGM, 1932) caused considerable controversy on its release. The film is concerned with the exploits of "a hardboiled stenographer" (Jean Harlow) who is described in the PCA files on the film as "uncouth, uncultured, only partially educated and quite unmoral in her decisions as to the ethical right and wrong thing to do." As production code operative and later screenwriter Lamar Trotti wrote:

> Briefly, the story is that of a girl who virtually forces a married man to have an affair with her; who pursues the man with the promise of further sex relations in spite of his efforts to avoid her; who creates a scene in his house which leads to his separation from his wife; who takes the man's beating only to force him to end his attack by sleeping with her; who marries him after his divorce; who then sleeps with another and

older man in order to break into society; who creates another scene in the street in her underclothes; who goes to New York and presumably continues her affair with the older man until, through detectives, the latter discovers that she meanwhile is having an affair with his chauffeur; who plans to "keep" the chauffeur after her second divorce and remarriage to the older man; who tries to rebuild her fences when she is found out; and who, after shooting her husband, goes to Paris and is shown at the end living in luxury provided by a Marquis; and receiving the Grand Prix award for the President of France while apparently still carrying on her affair with her chauffeur.

You may comment that the girl is not presented in a sympathetic light, that she is just what she is, a common little tart using her body to gain her ends, and that the sympathy is with the wife. You may also comment that because of the almost hysterical nature of some of the situations there is an element of farce in them. But this does not remove the objectionable qualities of the story. And in our minds, both the theme and the treatment would make the picture a violation of the Code.[30]

When her boss (Chester Morris) stays home with his wife rather than making love to her, Lillian (Harlow) consoles herself by drinking cheap liquor and getting sloppy drunk while "Frankie and Johnny" plays on her phonograph. The song confirms her illicit desires and debased and corrupt femininity. As the PCA became more effective in predicting censors' prejudices and providing the studios with examples of how costly it would be for them if they did not follow their advice, the image of the drunken woman, brilliantly portrayed here by Harlow, would momentarily disappear from Hollywood's productions and so would songs like "Frankie and Johnny" that too overtly signified "obscenities."

By 1936, the public notoriety gained by "Frankie and Johnny" ensured that when Twentieth Century Fox wanted to use the song in *Banjo on My Knee,* Joe Breen at the PCA was strongly advising against its inclusion: "use of the song Frankie and Johnnie is generally deleted by political censor boards. The music alone may be acceptable. We suggest, however, that this be changed."[31] The producers replaced "Frankie and Johnny" with "St. Louis Blues." The change made no discernible difference to the film since both songs carried the same basic images of wanton women and irresponsible men. The usefulness of "Frankie and Johnny" to producers was the fact that it was instantly recognizable, but its notoriety that helped produce this public recognition was increasingly problematic as it was clearly used to signify a set of desires and values inimical to censor boards.

Jean Harlow and Chester Morris in *Red Headed Woman* (courtesy of the British Film Institute)

Body and Soul

Lea Jacobs has argued that self-regulation in the 1930s, rather than quasi-legally enforcing producers to cower to censor boards' demands, was "above all a way of figuring out how stories deemed potentially offensive could be rewritten to make them acceptable." Controversial subject matter was not outlawed by the industry and its censors but "treated as problems of narrative and form."[32] Filmmakers intentionally sought to protect key dramatic moments that potentially violated the Production Code with what Jacobs has called an "instability of meaning," the intentional creation of ambivalence.[33] However, this had to be set against an equal need on the part of the filmmakers to reduce ambiguity, so that a film remained both accessible and comprehensible to as wide an audience as possible. This, as Richard Maltby has argued, meant the studios had to develop a system of representational conventions that allowed films to play to a heterogeneous audience without alienating any particular segment. Quoting Colonel Jason S. Joy (the director of the Studio Relations Committee), Maltby suggests these representational conventions enabled conclusions to be "drawn by the sophisticated mind, but [that] would mean nothing to the unsophisticated and inexperienced."[34] Initially "Frankie and Johnny" was used as a sign, for example, of the abject woman (specifically, of the prostitute) without ever having to refer directly to the character's profession, the musical refrain making the character's trade known to the "sophisticated mind" while remaining indistinct or unproblematic to the "unsophisticated or inexperienced." Certainly this was why "Frankie and Johnny" was used on the sound track of the Barbara Stanwyck film *Ladies of Leisure* (Columbia, 1930), underlining without fully confirming her profession as a prostitute. While "Frankie and Johnny" enabled Hollywood to deal with all sorts of potentially controversial material, films based on or that used the ballad eventually proved resistant to the procedures of what Jacobs has called the industry's "indirect modes of representation."[35]

The first film based on the ballad, *Her Man* secured very positive reviews and box office when it played the large first-run metropolitan theaters. The film had its New York premier on October 3, 1930, and, with only the occasional exception—the *New York Times* claimed it was "a hodge-podge of sentimentality"—it was widely celebrated by film critics.[36] *Motion Picture* magazine countered the *Times* critic: "Tay Garnett's deft hand lifts what might be a maudlin theme into a guaranteed entertainment and makes barroom sentimentality convincing, even sophisticated."[37] Another fan magazine, *Picture Play*, called it a "rattling good picture" that they recommended "without reservation," and, like many other reviews, it praised the fact that "dialogue is subordinate to action." The film reaches a climax in the free-for-all bar fight between Dan and Johnny and their respective cronies: "For a more terrific fight I never have witnessed, nor one that conveys less restraint or calculated fury."[38] The *Exhibitors Herald World* concurred: "To my mind Garnett's fight sequence outdoes any heretofore."[39] Other trade journals were also generally positive; *Film Daily* called the film the "best drama of its kind to come along in quite a while."[40] *Motion Picture News* and *Variety* noted the quality of the acting and direction and gave wholly laudatory reviews.[41] If the New York dailies are a guide, then the picture, echoing the sentiments of the trade and fan press, also enthralled the tabloid papers. Pathé reproduced eight positive film reviews from the New York press as an advertisement for the film in *Exhibitors Herald World*.[42]

In its review, *Variety* deemed the film to be free of the ballad's "dirty" elements and a cautionary and salutary tale for innocent girls.[43] But when the picture moved to small town, rural, and neighborhood cinemas, it attracted damaging criticism from newspaper editors and concerned citizens. The chair of the Motion Pictures Advisors in the Massachusetts State Federation of Women's Clubs wrote to the AMPP complaining that *Her Man* had been screened to a Saturday afternoon matinee audience of five hundred children on a double bill with *Santa Fe Trail;* she denounced the film as "a degrading picture from every standpoint and the *most* drinking picture we have ever seen."[44] In other circumstances the industry could have evoked what Ruth Vasey has called the "transparent principle of 'deniability,'"[45] but the equally transparent premises on which the story is based would have made any denial of the low moral gravity of the characters a clear act of sophistry. The popularity of "Frankie and Johnny," in all it various forms, meant that it was always likely that Hollywood would attempt to exploit the story, but in doing so it had to attempt to contain the more risqué elements that made it so attractive. This is what Maltby has called a "strategy of representation, by which a transgressive spectacle could be contained within a repressive narrative structure."[46] How Hollywood negotiated between the materials, the censor, and its audiences is part of the story told here.

In order to establish the underworld of Frankie and Johnny, the filmmakers used racial signifiers that announced the characters' debased state. Reviewing the first complete script of *Her Man,* a Studio Relations Committee employee asked the filmmakers to be "careful" with the "atmospheric shots of the Barbary Coast showing whites, blacks and yellows, houses of prostitution . . . pimps in the crowd, [and] the 'mad music and madder dancing.'" The more fixed a character's "whiteness," the higher the standing of their moral value. The drive of the story of *Her Man* is to move Frankie out of the "darkness" of saloon culture and into the light and whiteness of the world outside. The SRC reviewer found the whole project objectionable: "the story in its self is pretty bad, with no apparent reason for making it. There is no moral in it . . . in short it is a bunch of apple strudel with a lot of hooey poured over it." Without major changes, the only way it can be saved, he writes, is to make a burlesque of it: "It would be great in the way 'Ten Nights in a Barroom' [a classic nineteenth-century temperance novel] would be and they would have good comedy." Jacobs has noted the regular use of comedy by producers as a ploy to get around censor's prohibitions; writer and director Tay Garnett kept the central romance between Frankie and Dan, the man who saves her from Johnny, relatively po-faced, but he did introduce a series of running gags performed by Dan's drunken sailor friends (played by James Gleason and Harry Sweet) as respite.[47] The *Exhibitors Herald World*'s review of the film suggests how important comedy was in the positive reception of the film: "Even in the climax, when a life or two is in danger, the [comedy] stops the tears, and the belly laughs reissue."[48]

The greatest difficulty in getting the script to the point where it would satisfy the SRC was how to maintain the story of Frankie and Johnny and not make it obvious that he is her pimp and she his prostitute. As the SRC reviewer concluded, "to treat this story, which has to do with a kept man and his ladylove, with anything but levity seems out of the question." It was a problem that was still not solved in the second draft of the script.

> Johnny is one of the most despicable types of men. He is nothing less than a worm. . . . There is as much moral value in this picture as there is in a five week old kippered herring. . . . There is so much drinking, carousing and scenes of bawdy houses that I do not see how this picture can get by as it is now. You are simply dragged through six or eight reels of filth; you wallow in it neck-high, and scream for the whole business to end. All this babble about reformed prostitutes and the creating of sympathy for harlots in general is a lot of tripe, made worse by the inclusion of songs about a vine-covered cottage.

The following month's rewrites offered little improvement: "we look upon the present story as comparatively unattractive, sordid and weak." Most significantly Frankie could not just be saved but must be shown to

Phillips Holmes and Helen Twelvetrees in *Her Man* (courtesy of the British Film Institute)

have been a "good girl" from "the beginning." This meant downplaying Frankie's relationship with Johnny and emphasizing the love story between her and Dan. However, Frankie, in some respect, had to be shown to be living an illicit life that was tied to her relationship with Johnny so that Dan could rescue and redeem her:

> We can assume for the sake of argument that every prostitute would like to marry a good man and have some of the good things of life but it is

not safe to let an admitted prostitute find it possible to succeed in this desire in a picture when it would be hardly possible, or at least probable, that she could do so in real life. However, it is acceptable to necessary standards that a man might be willing to marry a good girl under the circumstances described in this story, and society would agree that it is right that such a girl should be saved from such a life.

The SRC reviewers were unhappy with Johnny's relationship with Frankie because it was based on exploitation and he was shown to be unfaithful to her. However, as Tay Garnett pointed out, to "make the relationship between Frankie and Johnny one of sincere attachment, and to eliminate any indication that Johnny was unfaithful to Frankie, would cause Frankie and Dan to lose sympathy the instant they planned for Frankie to leave Johnny."[49] Frankie's illicit acts would be limited to getting barflies to buy her drinks and the suggestion of pickpocketing. The eventual compromise between the filmmakers and Hollywood's self-censors was based on what was becoming a fixed set of parameters within which negotiations were contained. Discussing the desire to reconcile "morality and fun," "business and art," and, I might add, vernacular and "legitimate" culture, film historian Giuliana Muscio quotes Will Hays: "When you show a woman crossing her legs in a film, you don't have to show how far up she can cross them and still be 'interesting.' . . . This was the challenge," writes Muscio, "to play with the limits, constructing a metaphoric system that allowed film production the stimulating ingredients Hollywood had always used, but dosed more rigorously, according to precise recipes and with the availability of conventional substitutes."[50] Eventually the script for *Her Man* was passed and the finished film given a certificate. It then immediately ran into controversy.

The original script had set the story in San Francisco's Barbary Coast at the turn of the century, which circumvented prohibition and gave the producers an historical angle to exploit. However, during rewrites the story became set in the present and the locale became Havana, then an unidentified island off the coast of America, and, finally, in postrelease publicity, a Parisian dive. Unfortunately for the producers, stock footage of Cuba's best-known landmark, Morro Castle, was left in the release prints and the image of the castle was used in posters and other publicity material. The copy that accompanied the Morro Castle poster read "scarlet streets of the wickedest pleasure mad city of the Universe." The Cuban embassy protested, and there was fear that other Latin American countries would close their markets to the film.[51] Pathé's attempts to protect the film from being censured or banned by Latin American governments eventually led to what were evidently studio-sponsored reviews that attempted to relocate the film, as if by an act of will, in France and to recast Johnny as a Parisian dancer. *Variety* wrote: "*Her Man* carries a new angle for an underworld, that of a French knife throwing Apache in modern dress, with girls under his control. Nearly the entire picture is located in a Paris dive."[52]

In the film, if not in all the reviews, the shifting of the story's location from the United States to a "mythical island" off its coast allowed *Her Man* to constitute the States as a moral alternative to the island city's dens of iniquity. The island's inhabitants are represented as low class, itinerant, lawless, polyglot in character and racially diverse. The United States, on the other hand, is represented as classless, domesticated, policed, and white. The film opens with a worn-out chippie, Annie, trying to disembark from a ship; recognized by the American police she is sent back to the island. As she tries to gain entry into the United States, "No Place Like Home" plays quietly in the background. On her return to the island, Annie enters the Thalia (the Greek muse of comedy) bar, where most of the action will take place. Later, when Dan makes his play for the attentions of Frankie, this déclassé environment will be contrasted with the sentiments expressed in the song Dan sings to Frankie, "Somehow I Know," which calls up the image of the "vine-covered cottage" that the SRC reviewer found so unappealing. The idyll that the song alludes to is to be read as America, and the miseries and travails of the two lovers will not be over until they have successfully made their way back "home." Annie's failure to gain entry into the United States will be Frankie's fate unless she can leave this polyglot world behind.

The film met with some local censorship difficulties, as noted earlier, but these incurred only minor cuts.[53] However, as with the Latin American censors, the British and Canadian film boards were much more active, particularly in Canada where Pathé pulled the film rather than submit to demands for cuts that would have wrecked continuity. These censors seem to have been echoing William Blake's fears in *Auguries of Innocence,* that a society built on a compromise with corruption would inevitably end up corrupt: "The Whore & Gambler, by the State Licenc'd, build that Nation's Fate." Despite the industry's gatekeeping exercises and the thorough attempt to prejudge local and international censors, the film's reception by those political bodies suggested the SRC had not been strict enough in policing the film's subject matter. These reactions meant that the SRC, followed by the PCA, were much more conscious of the potential censorship problems in the use of and with any story based upon the ballad.

All Star and Select Productions' picture *Frankie and Johnnie* was released at the beginning of May 1936. The production had started over two years earlier. What had then seemed to be a novel idea that would also exploit the image of the Gay Nineties made popular in films such as *She Done Him Wrong* and *The Bowery* now seemed old hat and rather tired. The *Motion Picture Herald* critic reviewed the film "with an audience composed of newspapermen and fluffy dowagers, all of whom remained silent throughout the entire film and continually fidgeted in their seats, perhaps from the heat."[54] The reviewer cites two extremes of gendered audiences to suggest the film will not find a specific audience, never mind a heterogeneous one. Frank S. Nugent in the *New York Times* thought the film "slightly more lachrymose and off-key than a whiskey tenor."[55] *Variety* considered it to be "unusually slovenly entertainment."[56] The film's distributor (Republic) tried to boost interest through publicity stunts such as organizing a "cycle excursion" that would leave from New York, initially by train, on which "prizes for the most original gay-nineties costumes were given to members of the bicycling party."[57] But it was to little effect, and the film appears to have met *Variety*'s prediction that it would be "lucky to make dual bookings in most localities." Both the *New York Times* and *Variety* note the difficulties the film had meeting the "Hays code office" and speculated whether this "dehydrating" process ruined a good film or whether it was "pretty bad" from the beginning.

A script was sent to the PCA in February 1934. The response noted the "questionable nature" of the material and that the story was "most certainly open to serious question, both from the standpoint of the industry standards contained in the Production Code and from the standpoint of official censorship." But by then production was already underway. Post-production was completed in September, but a certificate from the PCA was withheld on the grounds that the film was little more than "a sordid sex drama." In October the PCA asked the producers to remove all uses of the song "Frankie and Johnnie" from the film, although it remains in the release print as an occasional instrumental piece.[58] The PCA made a long list of recommended eliminations to help bring the film within the bounds of the code; however, the problem for the producers was not bits of dialogue, overexposure of female anatomy, drinking and gambling, and so on but the picture's overall "philosophy." Earlier in the decade, it would have been possible to "fix" the transgressive elements by interposing "compensating moral values," but as Lea Jacobs argues:

> One of the greatest contrasts between the films of the early thirties and those of the later period lies in the form of what industry censors called the "voice of morality." Prior to 1934, this device was a relatively isolated component of the narrative—a single character would chastize the heroine in one or possibly two scenes. After 1934, the function of criticizing the heroine was no longer limited to the speech of a character but was figured as a more abstract and impersonal level through the mechanisms of narration . . . the values affirmed by individual characters are . . . reinforced at a structural level, through the way in which the story is told.[59]

It was precisely the lack of any compensating moral values at a structural level that bedeviled the producers in their discussions with the PCA. Breen characterized the film as virtually unsalvageable but managed to suggest the following revisions:

> You should determine if it is possible to remove from the present version all objectionable material, this having been successfully accomplished you should prepare a written outline for this office of new scenes and dialogue which will introduce and present the necessary and correct moral values. This will include a "voice for morality" which makes clear that Frankie's illicit love for Johnnie is wrong and sinful in a manner which will not be sympathetic and will also point out the inevitable unhappy consequences of such a life. . . . The means by which those purposes may be accomplished are various and not immediately presentable. The dangerous elements in the story and the changes necessary are interrelated and confused . . .[60]

The release print was a much reduced version and certainly differed greatly from its source material, Jack Kirkland's stage play (which was still sufficiently controversial in 1934 for the PCA to advise that the film's source be removed from the credits). In its abridged form, the film was eventually granted a certificate.

This is what is left. *Frankie and Johnnie* was conceived as an American version of Shakespeare's romantic tragedy *Romeo and Juliet.* Towards the end of the story of these star-crossed lovers, Frankie (Helen Morgan) takes Johnnie (Chester Morris) to a performance of the Shakespeare play. "They're kind of like us," she tells Johnnie. Like the film's producers in their negotiations with the PCA and subsequent script rewrites, Frankie tries to escape the vulgar world she is made to inhabit, St. Louis in the 1870s. Frankie is a singer at the Mansion House, a saloon, concert hall, and, presumably, a brothel, but through costume, dialogue, deportment, composition within the frame, and contrast with her fellow performers and habitués of her place of employment, she is given a cultural refinement at odds with her situation. Her act follows a male performer who is dressed in a jockey's outfit and sings "De Camptown Races." Stephen Foster's blackface minstrel tune plays against Frankie's sentimental rendition of "Give Me a Heart to Sing To"; it is to be Frankie's last performance at the Mansion House. She is engaged to marry Curly, a good man who wants to take her West to new beginnings. As the song moves towards its climax, Nelly Bly wakens her drunken companion, and he interrupts the performance. Nelly, who smokes cheroots, is Frankie's nemesis, and she ensures that it becomes impossible for Frankie to leave the vulgar culture of the saloon behind—this entrapment is Frankie's tragedy.

Later that night, Frankie meets Johnnie, who, by acting the innocent rube, has just taken a group of hardened riverboat gamblers for $13,000; he continues to play the role for Frankie and Nelly. Mistaking guile for innocence, Frankie becomes trapped in Johnnie's web of deceit when she decides to become his protector. Months pass and Johnnie is now a man about town, and dressed up to the nines he and Frankie make a swell couple. Invited to a "colored" wedding, Frankie and Johnnie position themselves as spectators: "They're so simple and sincere. So carefree and happy. They're not afraid of themselves," says Frankie. "What do you mean by that, Frankie?" asks Johnnie. "I mean you, Johnnie." But Johnnie is none of these things.

Variety speculated that the wedding scene was "dragged in bodily presumably to introduce a song number." The scene begins with a close-up on the grinning mouth of the bridegroom. The preacher declares the couple man and wife, and the outdoor congregation breaks for the food—close-ups of black faces pulling the cooked flesh off chicken legs follows. Then the congregation bursts into song and dance to "Get Rhythm in Your Feet." Beyond its use to introduce a song-and-dance number, the colored wedding exists to distance Frankie and Johnnie from the image of blackness that has begun to accrue around their personae. Theirs is a barely legitimate existence, but Frankie and Johnnie are not yet wholly like these "darkies," however far outside the white middle-class ideal the couple might appear.

Towards the end of the wedding scene, Frankie sings a romantic song to

Helen Morgan and Chester Morris in *Frankie and Johnnie* (courtesy of the British Film Institute)

Johnnie. At first the black voices from the wedding are in conflict with the melody she carries, but soon the voices fall into line and offer support and depth to her performance. This is part of an ongoing conflict throughout the film between vulgarity and refinement, with the former defined as black and the latter as white. This time Frankie has suppressed the vulgar, and her refined sensibility has won out. In the following scene Frankie and Johnnie are wed, but their romance is short lived, and Frankie's dominion over the vulgar has proved illusory: she and Johnnie slip back into an underworld defined as black.

In the script rewrites of *Her Man,* the character of Johnny all but fades out of the scenario. The fundamental events in the ballad—Frankie's love for Johnny, his betrayal and death—no longer structure the narrative. Johnny now exists as a foil and a contrast to Frankie's first true love, Dan. Dan, played by Phillips Holmes, is a tall, muscular man with curly blonde hair, a soft voice, and a winning smile. His height, physique, and hair make him stand out from the crowd. His costume is a sailor's jacket, bell-bottom trousers, and a torn, striped T-shirt—the holes in his shirt become enlarged through the course of the film, offering ever more revealing glimpses of his body. In contrast, Johnny (Ricardo Cortez) is marked as being abnormally narcissistic. He is small and dark, with neat, well-oiled hair, and his clothes are tailored. Key scenes show him preening himself in the mirror, and at the point of his death his last action is to adjust his tie, but it is his continual play with a little phallic penknife that confirms the suggestion of his moral degradation and gender deviance.

Johnny's Latin appearance, dandy persona, and immoral actions—his first act in the film is to throw a knife in the back of a rival for Frankie's services—effeminizes this archetypal badman. Cortez's Johnny, like Chester Morris's Bob in *Three Godfathers,* personifies the figure of the "bad man": of Bob, it is said he will "kill anything from a baby to an old woman," but, unlike the figure of Stack O'Lee, he is also a lady's man, someone of suspect masculine traits. Film portrayals of Johnny, then, will visually and aurally represent him as nonwhite, an effect partially achieved by contrasting him with a paragon of white masculinity. The character of Dan performs this task in *Her Man*; Curly in *Frankie and Johnnie.* The contrast is signaled not just in terms of physical differences but also through the sound track; Dan sings a sickly sweet sentimental parlor song; Johnny and the band he plays with, or commands, play hot jazz, and it is Johnny's presence rather than Frankie's that keys in the refrain from the ballad.

The growth in the popularity of the ballad "Frankie and Johnny" parallels the rise in interest not only in indigenous black culture expressed most profoundly in the performance of jazz but also the fad for explicitly sexualized and "foreign" dances such as the tango. In her study of stardom and masculinity in the Jazz Age, Gaylyn Studlar noted how the figure of Rudolph Valentino complemented and developed a masculinity that "defied normative standards of robust, ebulliently childish American masculinity," and how this "deviant" persona was commonly coded as "darkly foreign" and therefore "dangerous."[61] In *Frankie and Johnnie,* Johnnie begins the film masquerading as a stout innocent country boy, but he is really a city boy. His effeminate traits become increasingly marked as the narrative develops. His suits are cut tight into the waist and his sideburns are as fanciful as a Latin lover's, and when he is not out promenading he spends his time lounging around his rooms in a silk dressing gown. Tellingly, he no longer supports himself, instead relying on Frankie. Johnnie loses his money at the gambling tables and is looking to leave town with Nelly Bly, but she will not accompany him unless he can provide a substantial grubstake. While the refrain from "Frankie and Johnny" plays on the sound track, Johnnie lies to Frankie and gets her to borrow money from Lou, the Mansion House madam. Frankie gives Johnnie the money at the evening's performance of *Romeo and Juliet,* which is also attended by the town's prostitutes who cry throughout the show, much to the disgust of the town's better class of theater-goers. As the fate of Romeo and Juliet is sealed, Frankie is left sitting next to an empty seat. With a gun in her hand she goes after Johnnie: the refined culture of Shakespeare is left behind and the degraded world of Johnnie lies in front of her.

Frankie's first, and still true, love is Curly, whose masculinity and race (like Dan's in *Her Man*) is never questioned. Before Johnnie arrived on the scene, Curly had planned to take Frankie to California. Johnnie, though, never looked towards the west as a way to improve his fortune, but south to New Orleans—there he believed he could turn the tables on his streak of bad luck. Johnnie's decadent counter to the American image of progress (going South instead of West) is paralleled by the incremental dissolution of his whiteness and by his ever more feminized dress. In the final scenes, he is made to look pathetic and hopelessly inadequate as he attempts to seduce Nelly Bly. Like Frankie's, his fate is sealed. At the point the shots that will kill Johnnie are fired, the scene cuts to a falling handkerchief, leaving the audience unsure whether Frankie has shot him, or whether it was one of Lou's henchmen. Frankie is then put on board a riverboat with Curly's promise to wait for her still ringing in her ears. Frankie in *Frankie and Johnnie* is given the possibility, but not the promise, of future happiness. In contrast, in *Her Man,* Frankie will shed her barroom gladrags as the film progresses, she will visit church for the first time, be figuratively reborn through the agency of Dan (she does not know her birth date and he gives her one), the shoes that signified her and Annie's life on the streets will be symbolically washed into the gutter, and her selfless actions to protect her first true love from Johnny's murderous plans enable her final redemption. This "moral compensation" enables the formation of the couple and a home in the United States—the given reward for a life lived cleanly.

Body and Soul

The lack of such a neat closure in *Frankie and Johnnie* was due to the difficulty involved in reworking the film to conform to the PCA's edicts. Unable to achieve this end, *Frankie and Johnnie* developed moments of narrative incoherence. The screenplay attempted to "rescue" Frankie from the corrupting influence of the habitués of the Mansion House, and her implied trade, by constructing a facade of refined culture around her, which the producers hoped would help positively define the character. Frankie's principle act of transgression was that she had fallen for a no-account scoundrel, a man who lives off a woman's immoral earnings. The filmmakers hoped to exploit and contain this censorable scenario by suggesting that Frankie was not fully of this diseased world: her fall from the white world of high culture comes to mark her as a tragic figure, and the Code's prohibition against rewarding her through the formation of a couple had the effect of compounding the sense of tragedy—no happy ending. That, at least, must have been the hoped-for effect.

The marks of the censor's scissors are readily apparent on the release print, particularly as the film moves towards its denouement where jump cuts disrupt spatial continuity. The film's production values were never going to match those of the larger studios: the sets and actors are poorly dressed (*Variety:* "it resembles an ordinary costume westerner only that it lacks few of an outdoor film's redeeming features."), musical numbers are unimaginatively choreographed, and the dialogue as written and delivered is leaden. Given the pedigrees of Chester Morris (Johnnie) and Helen Morgan (Frankie), and the notoriety of Kirkland's play, the producers originally must have felt they could make capital out of the ballad of "Frankie and Johnny." Morris in many ways is the perfect Johnny—*Screen Romances Album* described him in 1931 as "a young man who made good by being bad."[62] His earlier appearances in urban crime and gangster movies—*The Big House* (1930), *The Alibi* (1929), *The Bat Whispers* (1931)—revealed an actor with a consummate gift for playing sadistic, narcissistic ladies' men. Helen Morgan had a substantial reputation as a torch singer and had had four film appearances by the end of 1934. Like the more famous role of the mulatto Miss Julie that she played on Broadway and in the later film version of *Show Boat* (1936), Morgan's Frankie is a woman looking at middle age while trying to hold on to the illusion of youth's innocence. Morgan was thirty-four when production on *Frankie and Johnnie* began, only a year older than Morris, but he is made to play a much younger man. Using this perceived age difference, the producers hoped to impart a further sense of the tragic into a story that the PCA felt rarely if at all escaped the realm of the vulgar.

The racially inflected vulgarity that runs through all versions of the ballad was what made it, for the poet and folk song collector Carl Sandburg, America's quintessential anthem. Writing in 1927, Sandburg noted that "if America has a classical gutter song, it is the one that tells of Frankie and her man."[63] The ballad maintained a decidedly déclassé outlook on life, and it told a definitively American tale. The specific appeal of the song was its ability to invoke a lewd, violent, vital, and racially confused vision of American life—Sandburg's "gutter"—that in turn brought the song, when used by Hollywood, within the remit of the Production Code Administration where it was eventually deemed to be censurable. Writing to Louis B. Mayer in 1944, Joe Breen brought to the producer's attention the difficultly Mayer would encounter with local and international censor boards if he proceeded with the planned song-and-dance number built around the ballad of "Frankie and Johnny" in his film *Ziegfeld Follies:*

> Dear Mr. Mayer
>
> We have read the Frankie and Johnnie number for your proposed picture "Ziegfeld Follies." We regret to report that we feel this subject matter would be unacceptable from the standpoint of the Production Code, on account of its flavor of prostitution and excessive sex suggestiveness.
>
> Furthermore, it has been the practice of censor boards generally to delete even the mention of this song, whenever any attempt has been made to inject it into pictures.
>
> We strongly urge, therefore, that you steer away entirely from this extremely dangerous material and substitute something else.
>
> Cordially yours
> Joseph I. Breen[64]

The instantly recognizable melody of "Frankie and Johnny" had enabled filmmakers to use the song to signify desires, impulses, and moral values that could not be relayed to an audience in an unadulterated and unambivalent manner for fear of the censor's scissors. But the song became overworked as a motif, and the set of concerns it was meant to suggest became fixed and direct—ambiguity dissolved. Used originally to mask offensive material, the song itself became censurable. What made the song "American" was the central ambiguity around the characters' racial status. What made it censurable was the ambivalence over racial identity when linked to illicit lifestyles—prostitution, excessive drinking, drugs, gambling, and violence: the very things that made the story so enticing to filmmakers.

In *American Songbag,* Sandburg writes:

> As our American culture advances, it may be that classes will take up the Frankie songs as seriously as a play by Moliere or a Restoration comedy or the *Provencale* ballads of France. It may be said that the Frankie songs, at best, are an American parallel of certain European ballads of low life, that are rendered by important musical artists from the Continent for enthusiastic audiences in Carnegie Hall, New York, or Orchestra Hall, Chicago. Some day, perhaps, we may arrive at a better common understanding of our own art resources and how to use them.[65]

Sandburg's plea for American vernacular arts to receive the same applause as aestheticized European folklore was probably not the intention of the producers of *Her Man* and *Frankie and Johnnie.* More likely both sought to exploit the controversy around the material rather than celebrate a nascent American art form. Nevertheless, it is telling that in the Hollywood versions the story of Frankie and Johnny had to be pitched against an alternative world of refinement and morality. *Her Man* rode the wave of popularity for versions of the song that appeared at the tail end of the 1920s and the beginning of the 1930s; Carl Sandburg's anthology of folk songs that included five versions of the ballad was both a catalyst for and an effect of this popularity. By the time *Frankie and Johnnie* went to market, the fad had waned, and the song's usefulness as a signifier of wanton men and women of dubious moral standing and racial status was played out.

Nevertheless, by 1945 (and despite Joe Breen proscribing its use a year earlier to the producers of *Ziegfeld Follies*), the song was back again as a piano instrumental in a gold rush barroom scene in the Droopy cartoon, *The Shooting of Dan McGoo* (MGM, 1945), four years later in the comedy Westerns *The Beautiful Blonde from Bashful Bend* (Twentieth Century Fox, 1949) and *The Gal Who Took the West* (Universal, 1949), and again in cartoon form in *Rooty Toot Toot* (Columbia, 1952).[66] The song in these films no longer signifies an abject world but now operates as a nostalgic motif of frontier America, its once racialized, lewd, and salacious subject matter contained within the comic field of these films. *The Beautiful Blonde from Bashful Bend* is a Betty Grable vehicle in which she plays a saloon singer who avoids the law by masquerading as a schoolteacher. She had discovered her paramour in the arms of another women, at which point an instrumental refrain from "Frankie and Johnny" kicked in, accompanying her until the end of the film. Like the Frankies in Held's and Hart Benton's art works, Grable shoots her victim in the backside, but here this violent act simply signals childish humor. The charges of obscenity leveled against Benton's work is sublimated in the film, alongside any sexual innuendo, by the absurdity of the scenario: Grable's sexuality is no more threatening than the female saloon singer in the Droopy cartoon. *The Gal Who Took the West,* like *Beautiful Blonde,* is a comedy of manners with a western setting, but this time the song is sung by the heroine.However, it ends with a clear moral:

> The sheriff came out and got Frankie and led her off to the jail
> She's going to make her home there until her cheeks are worn and pale
> He was her man, but he done her wrong
> All of you girls who have sweethearts don't let them out of your sight
> And all of you guys who like living you better treat them right.

The ballad continues to represent indigenous American culture, but it is one that now offers little sense of the vitality and danger that originally drew audiences in the 1920s and early 1930s. In a 1949 dictionary of folklore, mythology, and legend, the editors note the ballad is sung widely by "both Negroes and whites and is popular among students."[67] Presumably the student performers and audiences (something separate from the racial categories of "Negroes and whites") represent the middle-class audience that Sandburg hoped would eventually come to celebrate the American vernacular alongside its European counterpart. However, its use in postwar films and elsewhere suggest a process of inoculation against the ballad's more lurid elements that would come to some sort of completion by the time of the folk song revival of the late 1950s and early 1960s.[68] The 1960s folksingers would reclaim an authenticity for the ballad that would help mitigate its nostalgic use by Hollywood in the late 1940s and early 1950s, but these late-twentieth-century troubadours and minstrels could not retrieve the sense of frisson the song carried for its audience in the late 1920s and early 1930s, so much of which depended on their proximity to a turn-of-the-century polyglot urban environment with its concomitant fears of miscegenation that the ballad so successfully exploited.

An example of just such a negotiation around the representation of modernity, race, and national identity is found in the opening of the 1934 Warner Bros. feature *Bordertown.* The film begins by portraying an urban polyglot ideal of the United States that is racially and ethnically inclusive.

The film starts in the "Mexican Quarter" of Los Angeles, with tracking shots along city streets ending at a shop window with a display of Mexican jumping beans and a sign that reads "English spoken." Just a little further down the street is the Pacific Night Law School; a sign outside advertises courses in English, Spanish, French, and Chinese. The camera moves inside the building, revealing a notice on each step of the staircase that leads up to the school that reads "Climb these stairs to success." Before entering the classroom, "America (My Country 'Tis of Thee)" is heard, sung by a graduating class made up of blacks, whites, browns, and yellows. Different races are united in the commonality of American citizenship. But the class's representative, Johnny Ramirez, who is characterized as a "savage" by a white society dame, is unable to hold his own in the courts of law. He reappears south of the border helping run the Silver Slipper, a gambling joint. In a poor echo of the law school's racial inclusiveness, the Silver Slipper is the last club on a street that welcomes customers with its neon signs for the "American Bar," "Cabaret Mexicana," and "International Bar." The inclusive equality of the law school has been exchanged for the liminal, anarchic, and miscegenated space of the border town. From out of the clubs pours a raw, jarring jazz music, a hybrid form that contrasts with the "pure" folk music Johnny's family had played at his graduation party. The progressive disavowal of the initial promise of inclusion that shifts into a logic of exclusion is finally validated at the end of the movie through the cautionary tale of the fate that awaited the two white women who had vied for Johnny's sexual attention: one is dead, and the other has gone insane and been imprisoned for murder. Compared to the women in his life, Johnny gets off lightly, and ends up back where, he tells us, he belongs, "with my people."

By ending *Bordertown* with Johnny Ramirez's professed desire to abandon integration and return to "where I belong," the filmmakers were attempting to erase the images of hybridity promoted earlier in the film and return to an idea of a segregated America. The cautionary example of what happens when miscegenistic desire is put into play (provided by the fate that befell the two white women) further confirms the film's reactionary racial politics. The great integrationist experiment is shown to fail; the film's closure suggests that whites, blacks, browns, and yellows are better off separate. But the resolution is not as clear-cut as the filmmakers may have wished, for not all evidence of hybridity has been erased. The character of Johnny may be Mexican, but he is played, in dark makeup, by Paul Muni—a white actor. At the very least, this conflicts with the idea of race as genetically defined, positing instead the suggestion that race is performative.

The image of race as performative is particularly apt in Hollywood's deployment of songs such as "Frankie and Johnny" or of jazz and blues more generally, which are used to condense meanings of class, gender, and race. Two further examples of this practice are *The Age of Consent* (RKO, 1932) and *Ten Cents a Dance* (Columbia, 1931). The latter film stars Barbara Stanwyck, an actor who appears regularly in the films of the early and middle part of this book, and is based on the Rogers and Hart song from which it borrowed its title. The song relays the torrid tale of a taxi dancer, and it is a good instance of how Hollywood exploited a preexisting pop song: "Come on, big boy, ten cents a dance."

Directed by Lionel Barrymore, *Ten Cents a Dance* begins with a shot of silhouetted dancers seen through the windows of the run-down Palais de Danse. It is intensely crowded inside the hall, where a cigar chewing bandleader throws spastic shapes as he encourages both the musicians and the dancers to let loose. In contrast to the revelry, bored hostesses lean against a barrier waiting to dance with some tobacco-chewing ape of a sailor with big feet and a pocket full of dimes. Of these poor unfortunates, the film makes no moral judgment—they do whatever they have to do to pay their rent. Barbara O'Neill (Stanwyck) has hit lucky with a punter, a slumming businessman. Bradley Carlton (Ricardo Cortez) has taken a shine to her and becomes her protector and friend; he respects her earthy honesty and she does nothing to compromise his social standing. As a way of saying yes to his proposal to eat dinner together, Barbara makes some vitriolic comment on the music and the band that has just kicked in with a particularly manic version of "St. Louis Blues." Rogers and Hart's "Ten Cents a Dance" had set the tone of female resilience in the face of economic depression and sexual exploitation. "St. Louis Blues," however, is used to anchor the story in a more sordid reality that counters false sentimentality and misplaced romanticism. Even if Barbara is about to go on a swell date with a rich and good-looking man, in this job she is about as low on the social ladder as you can get. The narrative twists and turns, throwing all sorts of obstacles in the path of the protagonists, but Barbara's innate goodness is never tarnished, and as the final reel winds to a close, she has shown herself, despite her occupation, to be worthy of her wealthy suitor, just as he has shown himself worthy of her.

Class lines are crossed in *Ten Cents a Dance* without anything untoward happening to the lovers because their love is based on mutual respect and trust. But in *The Age of Consent,* the crossing of class lines ends in disaster. College students Betty Cameron (Dorothy Wilson) and Michael Harvey (Richard Cromwell) have been dating for some time, but not all is well between them. Betty wants more laughs and thrills, but Michael wants to concentrate on his studies and demands commitment from her. Both aspire to marriage, but the whirl of college life appears as an insurmountable barrier towards achieving matrimony. Betty finds the sensations she craves in the company of playboy Duke Galloway (Eric Linden), who drives a sporty coupe. Michael becomes distraught when he fears he has lost her and finds himself falling into the open arms of a young waitress, Dora Swale. Dora takes Michael home and they become intoxicated on her father's bootleg liquor and each other. This sorry and squalid affair is accompanied by a rousing version of "St. Louis Blues" playing on her radio. Drunk, they sleep in each other arms. In the morning they are discovered together by her father, just returned from working the night shift. Arrangements for a shotgun wedding quickly follow. When Betty hears about the proposed marriage she turns to Duke and his fast car for comfort, but too much speed, wet roads, and a sharp bend means that they end up in hospital beds. Duke dies, Michael cries over Betty, and Dora, despite her father's threats and the certain knowledge that she is a ruined woman, withdraws from the marriage when she witnesses Michael's great love for Betty. The crossing of class lines—Michael descending into Dora's domain and Betty ascending into Duke's world—ends in disaster, at least for Duke and Dora. With the antagonists out of the way, the natural class order is reestablished.

This is not to contend that the two films are ideologically opposed, that *The Age of Consent* suggests that cross-class interaction is impossible while *Ten Cents a Dance* suggests it is possible *and* desirable. Rather, the two films operate on ground that is complicated by race, class, gender relations, and sexual ethics. Crossing the lines between classes is laudable and achievable when both partners show mutual love and respect, as with Barbara and Bradley, but when a relationship is not virtuous and aboveboard, as with Michael and Dora and Duke and Betty, it is ruinous. Before falling in love with Bradley, Barbara had been married to an educated upper-middle-class man. The Depression had deprived him of his livelihood, or so he said, but with Barbara's help he finds his feet again. However, he soon reveals his true self: he is a wastrel and gambler who once more becomes financially destitute. To both his colleagues and his gambling cronies, he had kept his marriage to Barbara a secret. In contrast, Bradley, who has been twice married and divorced, prominently displays in his home photographs of his ex-wives—so as not to forget what money-grubbing gold diggers they were. Honesty and integrity are of paramount importance in matters of romance, much more so than questions of class compatibility.

The romantic notion of true love that unites the two films is dependent on a shared understanding of what kind of obstacles lay in the path of love's wanderings. If class distinctions are a poor barrier to the formation of the couple, then the possibility of love's corruption must be located elsewhere. Part of the common currency shared by these two films is the idea that class relationships are always colored by the question of race. The use of low, bawdy, coarse, and vulgar jazz or blues music symbolizes not only a working- or under-class identity but also a racial identity. The use of "St. Louis Blues" in the two films signifies a compact of class and race that must be disavowed, if not obliterated, by the lovers if their true love is to be tendered and nourished. In the dance hall, Barbara rejects the music that accompanies her trade, implying a distinction between her and the other girls that makes her a suitable marriage partner. On the other hand, Betty, the young waitress, is defined by the blues music she plays in her home while making love to Michael. She is not a suitable marriage partner. The distinction may seem minor—one woman rejects the blues, the other embraces the music, and true love is either achieved or squelched—but the repetition of this distinction across the many films discussed in this book suggests that race music such as blues and jazz is absolutely central in American films' production of romantic intrigue.

Formulaic romances such as *The Age of Consent* and *Ten Cents a Dance* show a remarkable consistency in their articulation of what I identify as an American vernacular culture. And though neither of these films made any particular claim to an American provenance, they are, nonetheless, received as examples of an American culture, an idea absolutely confirmed by the films' use of vernacular black music. Though "Frankie and Johnny" can rightfully lay claim to being America's gutter anthem, its profile in Hollywood's productions was relatively limited compared with the use of W. C. Handy's "St. Louis Blues": no other song in the history of Hollywood has been used so repeatedly and with such symbolic resonance.

3

An Excursion into the Lower Depths: W. C. Handy's "St. Louis Blues"

Ashes to ashes and dust to dust, I said ashes to ashes
  and dust to dust,
If my blues don't get you my jazzing must.
—W. C. Handy, "St. Louis Blues"

Recalled for the line of dialogue spoken by Bette Davis—"I'd like to kiss you, but I've just washed my hair"—*The Cabin in the Cotton* (First National, 1932) should also be remembered for its eclectic and effective use of vernacular American music as part of its strategy for representing racial, gender, and class identity. Black spirituals, white hymns, blackface minstrel tunes, hillbilly string band music, rural blues, big band pop, and urban jazz play a major role in establishing and blurring identity in the film. The story is centered on the conflict between planters and tenant farmers on a cotton plantation in the Deep South. Caught between the rich and the poor, workers and bosses, is Marvin Blake (Richard Barthelmess)—the son of a tenant farmer and white-collar employee of a plantation owner. The use of music as a way of emphasizing and reinforcing an impression of location is established from the opening credit sequence when Stephen Foster's sentimental minstrel tune "Old Folks at Home" ("Swanee River") plays over the credits. It will be used again later in the film, plucked on a banjo; the credit sequence is a fully orchestrated version. Foster's tune fades as the last credit rolls, a spiritual is introduced over an image of black cotton pickers, and the music carries over the edit to the adjacent shot of a family of white tenant farmers also picking cotton. The shared location, activity, and music unite black and white even as they remain within separately framed compositions and shots. The black spiritual is later rhymed with a white hymn sung at a funeral for a tenant farmer. Separated by race, black and white cotton pickers nevertheless belong to the same economic class and are joined by music.

Marvin's family is ambitious and hopes an education will save him from a life of backbreaking labor. After his father's death, he works in the store owned by planter Lane Norwood (Berton Churchill), where Marvin mediates between him and his tenants. Marvin's untenable position is reinforced by the attraction he feels for both Norwood's daughter Madge (Davis) and his childhood friend and sweetheart Betty (Dorothy Jordan). He dances with Betty on her eighteenth birthday to the music produced by a string band ("Buffalo Gals," "Turkey in the Straw," "The Girl I Left Behind") while Madge is shown with one of her boyfriends outside the dance, laughing and looking in through a window. The scenario is later reversed when Madge throws a party and cotton pickers look in at her dancing with Marvin. For her party, Madge books a black jazz band to provide the entertainment. Mirror opposites of the string band, the Memphis Jazz Band, as their name implies, are from the city, and are professional musicians for hire (a very expensive $400). After playing a spirited "Willie the Weeper," Madge instructs them to play a tune to accompany the "Peckerwood Wiggle," a dance that parodies the cotton picker's frolic at Betty's party. As tenant farmers on the outside look in through the mansion windows, the band plays a jazzed-up version of "She'll Be Comin' Round the Mountain." "They're making fun of us," claims one of the farmers, which is true, but the filmmakers were also keen to reveal the similarities between the planters and the tenants, so a shot from Betty's party is cut into the planters' dance, making the tenants appear to be dancing to the music provided by the jazz band. By using music to first separate and then bring together (symbolically) the planters and tenants, the film is able to develop the idea that through cooperation and fair play the two sides can amicably work out their differences.

The use of black music produces a leveling effect. The tenants' abject poverty is confirmed by aligning them with those who are self-evidently at the lowest economic level in the Deep South. The hiring of a black jazz band further suggests that the planters might be economically powerful but are, nonetheless, the cultural equivalents of the powerless. As Marvin points out, the jazz band was paid for by the money "sweated out of my people," an image that suggests how thoroughly entwined the various parties are on economic and cultural terms. But the image of hybridity that best confirms this entwining is displayed outside of the Norwood mansion on the night of Madge's party. She has seduced Marvin, and while she is lying in his arms she sings a song played earlier by the Memphis Jazz Band:

> Did you ever hear the story 'bout Willie the Weeper?
> Made his living as a chimney sweeper
> He had the dope habit and he had it bad
> Listen, while I tell you about the dream he had.

Though the song's narcotics references comment upon Madge and Marvin's momentary feeling of delirium as they hold each other close, this is, to say the least, a strange number for her to sing to her lover. When Madge seduces Marvin a second time, she will again sing about Willie the Weeper and his cocaine addiction.

"Willie the Weeper" belongs to the family of black urban folk songs—"Frankie and Johnny," "St. James Infirmary," "Stack O'Lee," "Cocaine Lil"—that found considerable popularity as jazz standards in the late 1920s and early 1930s.[1] In 1931, the year before the film's release, the character of Willie the Weeper had been reintroduced to the American public in Cab Calloway's smash hit "Minnie the Moocher." Beyond its implication of sexual narcosis, the use of the song in *The Cabin in the Cotton* was timely. But a more pertinent argument for why the song was used would be due to its documenting of an illicit lifestyle and its reflection on Madge's wanton character. When she finishes singing to Marvin, an itinerant blind blues singer wanders past the mansion, he picks up on the music being made by the jazz band and adds his own musical turn for the lovers listening in the garden. The doubling of black musical forms, the modern and the primitive, surrounds the white couple, furthering the link between black music and illicit sexual behavior.

Madge is a sexual predator whose unruly desires can be implied but never fully stated. Jazz and blues songs like "Willie the Weeper," which are clearly suggestive of an urban, primitive, sexualized, feminized, non-white and low-class culture, a world placed precisely at the margin of legitimate American identity, enabled filmmakers to imply desires and actions that were otherwise unrepresentable in films intended for heterogeneous audiences. Filmmakers relied on an understanding of intertextual signifiers such as popular songs to allow "sophisticated" cinemagoers to arrive at a particular understanding of the nature of relationships while leaving the film sufficiently ambiguous on sexual matters so as not to offend the less sophisticated in the audience. To do so, filmmakers often drew upon commonly held ideas that equated moral values with racial characteristics. The more abject an individual, the more closely he or she is aligned with images of blackness. Because of its references to an illicit life lived in America's gutters, "Willie the Weeper" was an easy, and culturally vital, means for *The Cabin in the Cotton* to signify what it could not show. The end result of this process, however, is to produce an image of sexually assertive women as somehow blackened—figurative, if not literal octoroons.

Like "Frankie and Johnny," "Willie the Weeper" too overtly signified its illicit and racial provenance to be used with any regularity in Hollywood productions. The summoning of a more tacit and therefore less controversial signification of these songs' miscegenistic implications was more readily carried out through the use of "St. Louis Blues"—a less overt mediation on illicit black urban lifestyles. When Joseph Breen wrote to MGM in 1944 to advise them that the "Frankie and Johnny" vignette in *Ziegfeld Follies* was "unacceptable" on account of its "flavor of prostitution and excessive sex suggestiveness," his counsel was based on knowledge and experience gained during the 1930s.[2] If "Frankie and Johnny" was proscribed, there were, nevertheless, other songs, less controversial, that offered a similar means of expressing lewd and vulgar desires. For the Fred Astaire number in *Ziegfeld Follies,* Arthur Freed substituted "Limehouse Blues," a 1924 hit written by Douglas Furber and Philip Braham and introduced to America in the André Charlot Revue. As the historian of popular song Sigmund Spaeth pointed out in 1948, "Limehouse Blues" was "not at all 'Blues' in the American sense" but rather a "fascinating combination of words, melody and harmony, in the pseudo-Chinese mood of London's Limehouse district."[3] In the interceding twenty-odd years, however, it had become something of a jazz standard. The loss of "Frankie and Johnny" clearly posed few problems for the producers, who simply substituted a less contentious number but one that carried equivalent connotations of a racially mixed urban underworld. Hollywood understood "Frankie and Johnny" to be a particularly resonate signifier of urban black female sexuality, but it was clearly not the only song available to convey this message.

The producers of *The Public Enemy* (Warner Bros., 1931) dropped a proposal to use "Frankie and Johnny" in the film, replacing it with "Hesitation Blues." "Frankie and Johnny" was to be sung by Putty Nose to the boys at the Red Oaks Club, and was to be performed with "many sly winks and grimaces to bring out the suggestive part."[4] This, and subsequent scenes, were little affected by its replacement with the less-well-known (and therefore less controversial) "Hesitation Blues," a version of which W. C. Handy copyrighted as "The Hesitating Blues" in 1915.[5] In *Banjo on My Knee* (Twentieth Century Fox, 1936), the producers' original choice for a song that would be sung at strategic points during the film had not been "St. Louis Blues"—what appeared in the release prints—but "Frankie and Johnny." The PCA had advised them against including the latter as it was certain to be cut by local censor boards.

Of the choices available to producers, "St. Louis Blues" was the preferred alternative to "Frankie and Johnny." Neither "Limehouse Blues" nor "Hesitation Blues" had the same cultural cachet as the much more widely recognizable W. C. Handy composition. "St. Louis Blues" avoided the more overtly bawdy lyrical material of "Frankie and Johnny," thus remaining immune from censors' inquisitions, but was able to do the same dramatic work. The close relationship between the two songs was demonstrated in *Red Headed Woman,* an unambiguous celebration of a working-class gold digger. After failing to get her man, Lillian (Jean Harlow) wallows in her sorrows by playing "Frankie and Johnny" on her phonograph. In the scene that follows, she has won her man, and, now leading him around by her apron strings, she plays "St. Louis Blues."[6] But "St. Louis Blues" was not simply a substitute for "Frankie and Johnny": it was also used because of its own unique attributes, and it was featured by a variety of Hollywood studios between 1929 and 1937 with more consistency and in more complex ways than any other comparable popular song.

First popularized in vaudeville and in the emerging nightclub scene of the 1910s and early 1920s, by the end of the 1930s "St. Louis Blues" had become the most recorded of all blues songs.[7] Copyrighted by its author W. C. Handy in 1914, "St. Louis Blues" was first featured in black vaudeville circa 1916 by Charles Anderson, whom blues singer Ethel Waters described as "a very good female impersonator." It was from Anderson that Waters first learnt the song: at seventeen she performed it in her vaudeville debut, becoming the first female African American to feature "St. Louis Blues" in her act.[8] The first phonograph recording of the song took place in London, performed by Ciro's Coon Club Orchestra in 1916. Recorded by coon shouter Sophie Tucker in 1917, it became one of the year's biggest selling phonograph records.[9] The song's first commercial release by black musicians was in 1919 by Lt. Jim Europe's 369th ("Hell Fighters") Infantry Band—a seminal group in the development of jazz. In 1921 the white Original Dixieland Jazz Band (ODJB)—an act held responsible for helping turn the verb "jazz" into a noun—recorded their version. On this occasion, the white blackface singer Al Bernard, who had already recorded a version of the song two years earlier, augmented their lineup.[10] "St. Louis Blues" would become a staple of blackface performances, spawning a subgenre of minstrel parodies and pastiches, notably Emmett Miller's "The Ghost of St. Louis Blues" (1929) and the Cotton Picker's "St. Louis Gal" (1929).[11] From these low and vulgar beginnings, the song entered into the public imagination.

"St. Louis Blues" was recorded in almost every conceivable pre–World War II style—rural and vaudeville blues, jazz, hillbilly, Hawaiian, croon, swing, ragtime, symphonic—and by artists as diverse as Bing Crosby with Duke Ellington (1932), the Quintet of the Hot Club of France (1935), the Dorsey Brothers Orchestra (1934), the Lew Stone Dance Orchestra (1935), Louis Armstrong (1929, 1933, 1934), Cab Calloway (1930), the Callahan Brothers (1931), Bessie Smith (1925), Weaver and Beasley (1927), Jim and Bob, the Genial Hawaiians (1933), Jim Jackson (1930), Paul Robeson (1936), Paul Whiteman and His Orchestra (1926), the Sons of the Pioneers (1934), LeRoy Smith and His Orchestra (1928), Benny Goodman (1936), Bob Wills and His Texas Playboys (1935, 1937, 1954), and scores more. Even the Nazi swing band Charlie and His Orchestra got in on the act, producing the propaganda parody "Blackout Blues."[12] Jazz critic Brian Peerless believes that "St. Louis Blues" is the "jazzman's Hamlet," while musicologist David Schiff argues that "St. Louis Blues" "changed the landscape of American music."[13] A notable number of jazz and blues scholars consider the version by Bessie Smith accompanied by Louis Armstrong as exemplifying the pinnacle of these musical genres as well as Armstrong's and Smith's artistic achievements.[14] For my purposes, the plenitude of instrumental and vocal recordings of "St. Louis Blues" gives weight to the argument that the song would be instantly recognizable to a wide cross-section of cinema patrons during the period from 1929 to 1937.

The song begins with a woman's lament for the end of the day: "I hate to see de evenin' sun go down."[15] Her man has left her for another woman, whose powder, paint, and "store bought hair" proved a temptation too great for him to ignore. The song plays upon the listener's recognition of two female archetypes—the abandoned lovelorn woman and the sexual temptress—who compete with each other for the attention of a feckless male. Hollywood's use of the song recognized this scenario: in some cases it suggested ambivalence about whether a character was sexually exploitative or exploited (*Rain,* produced for United Artists in 1932, for example) while on other occasions it would help to underpin a character's duplicitous use of sex (as in *Red Headed Woman*) or a woman's destitute and loveless status (as in *Banjo on My Knee*). However, a contemporary audience would have responded to the song not only because it recorded the plight of these female archetypes but also because of its play with representations of a black urban underclass.

On the basis of the song's popularity, Handy has been called "The Father of the Blues" and rather less generously, by Ian Whitcomb, the "stenographer of the blues."[16] Jelly Roll Morton simply wished Handy branded the most "dastardly impostor in the history of music."[17] The truth lies somewhere in between these claims. In a manner analogous with the artists of the Harlem Renaissance, Handy reworked his folk material.[18] By retaining ties to older forms, for example, folk blues and spirituals, Handy's modern (but not modernist) articulation and commercial exploitation of these musical styles suggested an evolving continuity between the old world of the southern plantation and the new world of the northern city. This is certainly implicit in his own account of the composing of "St. Louis Blues." Above all else, however, Handy considered himself to be an *American* composer, which is to say that he worked with indigenous black musical forms.[19] With "St. Louis Blues" his aim, he explains, was to

> combine ragtime syncopation with a real melody in the spiritual tradition. There was something from the tango I wanted too. . . . This would figure in my introduction, as well as in the middle strain.
>
> In the lyric I decided to use Negro phraseology and dialect. I felt then, as I feel now, that this often implies more than well-chosen English can briefly express. My plot centered around the wail of a lovesick woman for her lost man, but in the telling of it I resorted to the humorous spirit of the bygone coon songs. I used the folk blues' three line stanza that created the twelve-measure strain.[20]

The central theme to emerge from this characterization of the song is its rootedness within traditions of representing blackness—hence its appeal for blackface minstrels—but this is not a song contained by the legacy of plantation minstrelsy. Rather, the song addresses the experience of modernity in the milieu of the black habitués of the urban *demi-monde*. Remembering the incidents in his life that influenced the composition of "St. Louis Blues," Handy writes in his autobiography:

> I have tried to forget that first sojourn in St. Louis, but I wouldn't want to forget Targee Street as it was then, I don't think I'd want to forget the high-roller Stetson hats of the men or the diamonds the girls wore in their ears. Then there were those who sat for company in little plush parlors under gaslights. The prettiest woman I've ever seen I saw while I was down and out in St. Louis. But mostly my trip was an excursion into the lower depths.
>
> Still I have always felt that the misery of those days bore fruit in song. I have always imagined that a good bit of that hardship went into the making of the "St. Louis Blues" when, much later, the whole song seemed to spring so easily out of nowhere, the work of a single evening at the piano. I like to think the song reflects a life filled with hard times as well as good times.[21]

The more immediate inspiration for the lovelorn protagonist of the song derived from an impression Handy gained on Beale Street in Memphis, which offered a similar urban experience to St. Louis's Targee Street: "Scores of powerfully built roustabouts from the river boats sauntered along the pavement, elbowing fashionable browns in beautiful gowns. Pimps in boxback coats and undented Stetsons came out to get a breath of early evening air and to welcome the night."[22] A drunken woman passes by him on the street muttering, "Ma man's got a heart like a rock cast in the sea." He asks another passing woman what the lush meant, and she replied, "Lawd, man, it's hard and gone so far from her she can't reach it." "Her language," he explains, "was the same down-home medium that conveyed the laughable woe of lamp-blacked lovers in hundreds of frothy songs, but her plight was much too real; to provoke laughter. My song was taking shape. I had now settled upon the mood."[23]

The song's "mood" drew upon the ambience of black urban nightlife, but not as its unmediated document. Rather, the portrayal was to be filtered through earlier song types that dealt with a similar subject matter, in particular ragtime numbers such as "Frankie and Johnny" and less specifically religious spirituals and the profoundly secular coon song tradition. Finally, giving the whole a contemporary edge, elements from the latest dance fad—the tango—were incorporated. This hybrid of styles and traditions, which left "spaces for vocal or instrumental improvised breaks," partly explains the song's popularity with such a wide range of performers. Its roots in the past (coon songs) along with its embracing of the contemporary (the tango) made the song both comfortably familiar and excitingly new. Recalling the ODJB's recording of "St. Louis Blues," trombonist Eddie Edwards remembers the modernist expression of clarinetist Larry Shield's performance:

> A ribald gross denial. Larry hated New York City. . . . This annoyance is carried on to the fourth measure, is followed by a wavering of indecision and inertia, helpless in its efforts to rise above it. On into the blue notes, characteristic of the . . . moods, lights, colors, and shadows of his urban dislikes and indecision. Noises at times, exuberant and pathetic, and lonely. Chaos is all about. It is dismal and gruesome. This is the first strain of twelve measures. The second chorus of [the] strain follows with screaming hate.[24]

Though Eddie Edwards made this observation in the 1950s (as part of a wider project on behalf of the surviving band members to assign historical importance to their role in the development of a jazz idiom), it is remarkably faithful to the band's iconoclastic intent. In a 1920 interview, ODJB leader Nick LaRocca stated, "Jazz is the assassination, the murdering, the slaying of syncopation. In fact, it is a revolution in this kind of music . . . I even go so far as to confess we are musical anarchists . . . our prodigious outbursts are seldom consistent, every number played by us eclipsing in originality and effect our previous performance."[25] The anarchic aspects of jazz were no doubt part of its attraction, particularly for high-modernists like Carl Van Vechten, author of *Nigger Heaven* (1926) and tour guide to "primitive" Harlem nightlife for slumming whites. The preeminent role of "St. Louis Blues" as a sound track for the 1920s can be gauged by Van Vechten's snobbish rebuke of William Faulkner for not being hip to the modern sounds of New York. Accompanying him on a tour around Harlem, Van Vechten recalled a mild embarrassment at "Faulkner's persistent request of the musicians to play the 'St. Louis Blues' when that song was out of fashion."[26] This was an act of cultural betterment on Van Vechten's part, a dig at Faulkner; the song was still very much in vogue with musicians until the 1940s. The song's form meant that it could be readily rearranged and hence reinvigorated by introducing an element of novelty to wrap around a series of easily identifiable refrains, an idea brilliantly demonstrated in the versions recorded by Louis Armstrong. English poet, librarian, and jazz fan Philip Larkin wrote: "Louis Armstrong's

1929 'St. Louis Blues' is the hottest record ever made. Starting *in medias res,* with eight bars of the lolloping tangana release, it soon resolves into a genial uptempo polyphony. . . . Louis leads the ensemble in four blistering choruses of solid riffing. By the third chorus the whole building seems to be moving."[27] Armstrong made an equally house-rocking version for RCA-Victor in April 1934, but with two further versions recorded six months later with a pick-up band in Paris, he not only rocked the house, he brought it down. Maybe Larkin never heard these, but by October 1934 Armstrong had stripped away any attempt at melodic sophistication and simply let rip—everything gives way beneath the insistent riffing upon which Armstrong blows fast, high, and hard. It was a model that the plethora of boogie-woogie versions produced in the late 1930s—the early 1940s could only hope to emulate, never surpass.[28]

Despite its claim upon modernity, the song was also locked into a rural premodern past. The ODJB's 1921 recording of "St. Louis Blues" (among others) featured the atavistic blackface vocals of Al Bernard. Produced five years before *Billboard* first alluded to the "'jazzing up' and modernization of minstrelsy," this relatively archaic performance of blackface in the context of a jazz recording, while not wholly vitiating a modernist interpretation, suggests that not all is chaos and uncertainty as alluded to by Eddie Edwards.[29] Early in his career, Al Bernard specialized in recording Handy's blues and also published a number of songs with Handy's company. Handy notes that at the time, "Negro musicians simply played the hits of the day" while white performers "were on the alert for novelties. They were therefore the ones most ready to introduce our numbers." On the other hand, "Negro vaudeville" artists wanted songs that would not conflict with "the white acts on the bill. The result was these performers [such as Ethel Waters and Charles Anderson] became our most effective pluggers."[30] No doubt this was how Bernard first heard "St. Louis Blues." In any case, he recorded the song five times between 1919 and 1928, including one version as a blackface monologue.[31] Bernard's 1927 version produced under the pseudonym John Bennett would have a lasting impact on the western swing band leader Bob Wills, whose three commercially released versions and two-sided radio transcription disc all drew upon the blackface minstrel's recording.

But what does it mean for a white man in blackface, or a Texan in a cowboy hat, to sing a song written to give a black woman's point of view? Bernard and the other blackface minstrels who performed "St. Louis Blues" were the heirs to a nearly century-old tradition of white men not only crossing the line between races but also between genders. On phonograph recordings such as those by Al Bernard and the ODJB, neither the mask nor the performance can be seen: connotations of racial and gender transgression, then, must be carried by sound. But as Dale Cockrell argues, the *"noise—the ear—*that which always accompanies ritual representations of blackness, is a much richer indicator of the presence of inversion rituals than mere blackface."[32] In this context, it becomes possible to argue further that the ODJB's cacophonous recording of "St. Louis Blues" is less "modernistic"—an elitist artistic response to modernity—than "urban primitive": its sense of "chaos" and "anarchy," both in the music and in the blackface play with persona, function as a lowbrow populist rebuke to the dehumanizing subjugation of modernity. The particular narrative and musical strategies described by Handy in his composing of "St. Louis Blues" suggests that the song could operate as a signifier of both the traditional and the modern symbolized in the play with blackness implied in the vocal characteristics of Al Bernard and his usurpation of a female subjectivity. In the context of a jazz recording, Bernard's appropriation of a black female subjectivity suggests a world outside modernity: the southern plantation evoked through minstrelsy and his invocation of female sexuality. But it also connotes a confinement within modernity: the technologically disembodied voice of the phonograph recording that addressed an urban audience and the brutal swing and attack of the jazz band that accompanies his vocal.

Bing Crosby, who appeared in blackface in at least two feature films— *Holiday Inn* (Paramount, 1942) and *Dixie* (Paramount, 1943)—and who flirted with blackface personae in songs such as "Mississippi Mud" (1928), later featured in the Paul Whiteman film *King of Jazz* (Universal, 1930), and "Black Moonlight" (1933) featured in *Too Much Harmony* (Paramount, 1933), forsook both the female point of view, as implied in Handy's original lyrics, and blackface ventriloquism for his version of "St. Louis Blues." Despite this apparent refusal to cross racial and gender lines, Crosby retains an authenticity for the recorded performance by singing with Duke Ellington and His Orchestra.[33] Crosby's association with Ellington—who, as jazz and film historian Krin Gabbard suggests, strove to present an "uptown" "sophisticated" image—works to mitigate the vulgarity that is central to Handy's copyrighted version and Al Bernard's performance. Nevertheless, because of Ellington's association with the Cotton Club, his collaboration with Crosby maintains a sense of the song's roots in a black urban vernacular.[34] The recording has a three-part structure. Ellington's orchestra introduces the musical themes of the song with an arrangement that suggests the slow, powerful, rhythmic pull of a locomotive train. The tone then changes in order to incorporate Crosby's trademark crooning, which scans across, rather than emphasizes, the blue notes. The final section attempts to harmonize the distinct styles of Ellington and Crosby by returning to the opening arrangement with Crosby scat-crooning to the recording's end. In the middle section, Crosby shuns an alignment with the song's female point of view by changing the lyrics so that it is a man who has been abandoned by a woman rather than the other way around. This inversion severely deforms the song's logic because the woman, who has "done lef dis town," and left the singer feeling so blue, has done so for another woman—the temptress in "powder" and "store bought hair."[35] A strange affair, but not quite as befuddled as the King of Western Swing became on his several versions of the song.

In the first of the commercially released Bob Wills versions, Wills plays a minstrel endman interpolating commentary between the lines delivered by singer and de facto interlocutor Tommy Duncan (the band's singer). Duncan begins by taking the song from the point of view of an objective observer. A woman is singing about how she hates to see the evening sun go down, but then he switches from her to tell about a man from St. Louis with a diamond ring who takes a girl around by her apron strings. In feigned disbelief, Wills' endman wants confirmation that a man who wears diamond rings exists. Shifting into the character, a high-pitched minstrel dialect, Duncan takes the point of view of the bejeweled lover man, confirming his existence and his hold over women. However, when he gets to the lyric where his heart is described as hard, the masculine point of view breaks down and Duncan assumes the role of the lovesick woman. Following a steel guitar solo, Duncan reassumes the point of view of a male, which he stays with to the end of the song. Two years later in 1937, Wills and his band recorded another version under the title "New St. Louis Blues." Despite shifting Leon McAuliffe's steel guitar solo to the song's introduction, not much was new about this recording, and it retained the confused and confusing points of view. Wills' 1954 recording, however, takes the muddled narration to new levels of absurdity. Beginning with a warning to "rounders" (card players and drinkers) to stay away from his gal (an image straight out of Jimmie Rodgers' songbook), Wills through the technique of overdubbing is now able to sing and speak to himself; his first interpolation is to mention that he can hear a "little Negro" in the singer's (his own) voice. Following a version laid down by his old musical sparring partner Milton Brown on a 1935 recording, he emphasizes the song's black heritage and his knowledge of the idiom by ditching the more familiar stanzas in exchange for blues clichés—"woke up this morning," "come here and tell me whose muddy shoes are these?" He returns to Handy's verses towards the end of the song in order to discuss the vital issue of store-bought hair—he naturally prefers black to bottle blonde.[36]

The song was recorded by a large number of male vocalists, many of whom refrained from following Bob Wills and undermining the song's female point of view, or all points of view for that matter. Though it does not appear to have been the case with "St. Louis Blues," leaving the gendered structure of address intact in popular songs was often dictated by music publishers. But it was also, as is the case with Wills, consistent with acts of vocal transvestism that were legitimized by the long tradition of blackface cross-dressing. Bob Wills' play with gender and race is a particularly resonant and anarchic example of Cockrell's idea that minstrelsy "conceals and promises reordering": gender and racial boundaries are simultaneously collapsed and reinforced. The pleasure is in the dissembling of identity, not in the reinforcement of any particular gender and racial alignment.[37]

In any case, few versions of "St. Louis Blues," regardless of the singer's gender, are sung beyond the first three verses in Handy's original and therefore do not attempt the passages that are particularly marked by female desire: "Blacker than midnight, teeth like flags of truce / Blackest man in de whole St. Louis / Blacker de berry, sweeter am de juice."[38] When Ethel Waters used the song in her vaudeville routine, it began with her slumped in a chair as her lover, acting disgusted, tells her, "I'm going off to see my other chick." "Don't leave me, sugar," she pleaded. "Please don't leave me." After her lover departs, she sits on the stage "rocking sadly and slowly . . . 'When I see how my man treats me,' I'd moan, 'I get the St. Louis Blues.' Then I would sing 'St. Louis Blues,' but very softly."[39] This image of a lovesick protagonist was carried over to the scenario for the Bessie Smith short *St. Louis Blues* (1929) that W. C. Handy helped produce and that was also, Gabbard suggests, partly scripted by Carl Van Vechten.[40]

The short film opens in the hallway of a run-down rooming house where a group of black men in shirtsleeves are playing craps. Things liven up when Jimmy, Bessie's lover, appears with a young woman on his arm. Discovering Jimmy and the girl in her rooms, Bessie first fights the girl and then alternately threatens and pleads with Jimmy. He walks out. Later in a crowded bar, a dejected and downbeat Bessie sings "St. Louis Blues."

Publicity poster for Bessie Smith in *St. Louis Blues* (author's collection)

Jimmy enters and her mood lightens, they dance together, and Jimmy surreptitiously takes her roll of money. Leaving race and class aside for the moment, the performances of Waters and Smith make clear that the song addresses a female sexuality habituated to exploitation by men. Bessie Smith's performance resonates from the explicit display and invocation of active female sexual desire. But it is a form of desire that is reduced to an "irresistible, destructive sensuality."[41]

On Smith's role in the film, Gabbard has argued that Bessie Smith the blues singer "does not 'play' a blues singer. Rather she is entirely contained within a narrative of unrequited love and its spontaneous, unmediated expression in song."[42] The idea that the film denies artistic agency is further developed by Angela Y. Davis. In discussing the blues of Ma Rainey and Bessie Smith, she notes, "They are far more than complaint, for they begin to articulate a consciousness that takes into account social conditions of class exploitation, racism, and male dominance as seen through the lenses of the complex emotional responses of black female subjects."[43] Davis also notes:

> St. Louis Blues [the 1929 film] deserves criticism not only for its exploitation of racist stereotypes but for its violation of the spirit of the blues. Its direct translation of blues images into a visual and linear narrative violates blues discourse, which is always complicated, contextualized, and informed by that which is unspoken as well as by that which is named. St. Louis Blues, the film, flagrantly disregards the spirit of women's blues by leaving the victimized woman with no recourse. In the film the response is amputated from the call. . . . It is precisely the presence of an imagined community of supportive women that rescues them from the existential agony that Smith portrays at the end of St. Louis Blues.[44]

Rather than present the consciousness-raising that Davis believes is present in female blues performances, Hollywood used blues songs in stereotypical fashion as a sound track to displays of urban primitivism. Hollywood's use of the blues often reduced the form's potential for meaning to an existential play with surfaces—a smearing of blackness on a world otherwise imagined as white.

Like the Bessie Smith short, Hallelujah! (dir. King Vidor, MGM, 1929) used the song without regard to its full potential for representing black female subjectivity. Vidor's Hollywood sound film was made with a cast composed entirely of African American actors. The story is set in the Deep South and concerns the trials and tribulations of a cotton sharecropper,

Zeke (Daniel L. Haynes), and his amorous relationship with a streetwise hussy, Chick (Nina Mae McKinney), whose pimp, Hot Shot (William Fountaine), gets her to help con the naive hero of his money and dignity in a barroom craps game. In the violent argument that follows, Zeke's younger brother is killed. Zeke returns home a chastened and hopefully wiser man, and commits himself to the Lord. He becomes a successful preacher, but his missionary work brings him back into contact with Chick and Hot Shot. Zeke once again cannot resist her temptations and leaves his calling, marrying Chick and finding work in a lumber mill. Hot Shot finally tracks them down and seduces Chick. As they make their plans to leave, Zeke returns from work; Hot Shot makes a hasty retreat out the back door. To cover his exit and her nervousness, Chick begins to sing "St. Louis Blues"; the song underscores her sexual enchantment of Zeke, but it also comments upon her duplicity.[45]

Zeke's geographical move from plantation to town is paralleled by a shift in musical idiom from rural to urban—from folk to jazz. Until the point Zeke first comes to town to sell his cotton crop, the musical sound track had been a mix of spirituals and ersatz "Negro" folk tunes. Zeke's seduction, however, is accompanied by the roughhouse music of a jazz band. In her high-heeled shoes, short satin dress (which is emblazoned on the right of her chest with two patches representing dice), hoop earrings and sassy sexual deportment, Chick appears as a natural habitué of urban hostelries. Like "St. Louis Blues," she symbolizes a world caught between the primitive and the modern.

As James Naremore and Adam Knee argue in their essays on *Cabin in the Sky* (MGM, 1943), the binary opposition between the city and the country that structures *Hallelujah!* is also present in the other all-black-cast films produced in Hollywood between 1927 and 1954: *Hearts in Dixie* (Fox, 1929), *Green Pastures* (Warner Bros., 1936), *Stormy Weather* (Twentieth Century Fox, 1943), and *Carmen Jones* (Twentieth Century Fox, 1954).[46] Naremore writes:

> The social tensions and ideological contradictions expressed by this opposition were always crucial to any art or entertainment that involved blackness; notice, for example, how the country-city polarity functioned in early uses of 'jazz.' . . . Was jazz a primitive music, a people's music, or an entertainment music? All three possibilities were suggested by critics, and the term seemed to oscillate between diametrically opposed meanings. On the one hand, jazz was associated with flappers, skyscrapers, and the entire panoply of twentieth-century modernity; on the other

Daniel L. Haynes and Nina Mae McKinney in *Hallelujah* (courtesy of the British Film Institute)

hand, because it originated with African Americans who migrated to the northern cities, it connoted agrarian or precapitalist social relations, and could be linked to a pastoral myth.[47]

Discussing the space of the urban saloon in *Cabin in the Sky,* Knee argues that, although it represents the film's "freest African American self-expression, a realm that allows sexually allusive dialogue, open physical movement and dancing combined with sweeping camera dollies, and spontaneous performance in the relatively free, unrestrained idioms of jazz," it is "ultimately condemn[ed] and destroy[ed]."[48] In a similar manner, the playing or performing of "St. Louis Blues" in Hollywood's productions of the 1930s sanctions, but finally condemns, a transgressive female sexuality.

Jazz, then, appears simultaneously as a product of an overcultivated metropolitan sensibility and the natural primitive instinctual urge of a rural premodern sensibility. This cultural instability, I want to argue, is precisely what is available to Hollywood for representing the sexually transgressive woman. More particularly, the locus of the conflation of sexual desire, gender, race, and urban primitivism is found in the figure of the symbolic octoroon whose discursive hybridity, as Jennifer DeVere Brody has argued, replays an "anxiety about the destruction of one's whiteness" as a legacy "expressed through references to the figure of the blackened woman."[49] Lorraine O'Grady suggests a similar paradigm when she argues that "The female body in the West is not a unitary sign. Rather, like a coin, it has an obverse and a reverse: on one side, it is white; on the other, not-white or, prototypically, black. The two bodies cannot be separated, nor can one body be understood in isolation from the other in the West's metaphoric construction of 'woman.' White is what woman is; not-white (and the stereotypes not-white gathers in) is what she had better not be."[50]

"St. Louis Blues" helped to organize discourses of sexuality, race, and gender imagined as transhistorical, but which are in fact historically specific: formed by the economic and social transformations of modernization. Race and gender became "identical *as constructs*," according to Jazz Age historian Chip Rhodes, "transhistorical signs for the embodiment of a potency that the capitalist production process vitiates. In this sense, blacks in general, and black women in particular, serve the same end." Excluded from the mainstream of modern America, "they are clearly not excluded from the world of social desire." Rhodes argues that "blacks" proved useful in representations of "primitive" desires because (at least before the Great Migration) "they were largely excluded from the alienating production process that both modernism and consumerism promise to counteract."[51] White espousal of black blues, then, is underwritten by primitivistic desires, which are not performed in the *agrarian* past of the plantation, but in a more immediate and modern context of a black *urban* vernacular—but one constructed as unencumbered by the constraints of modernization and modernity: salaried labor, domestic responsibility, and bourgeois morality.

Beyond the pale of bourgeois mores, then, but absolutely defined by them, black women, as Stanley Aronowitz has written, are "labeled temptress, symbolically considered the embodiment of the dark side that links race with sexuality."[52] Conversely, sexualized white women in American films are "blackened"—that is, symbolically constructed as octoroons. In *Hallelujah!* and *St. Louis Blues,* the sexually aggressive women are played by actors with a light skin tone, and their moral, sexual, and gender "transgressiveness" is attributable to their coding as racially uncertain and therefore impure, sullied. The image of race mixing is present in "St. Louis Blues" in the figure of the temptress characterized through her use of the "whitening" devices of "powder and store bought hair," which suggest a face powder to lighten skin tone and a wig made of straight hair. The instability of racial "boundaries" becomes conflated with a woman's moral standing, which is thereby corrupted.

From these accumulated readings, it should be clear why Hollywood's use of the song "St. Louis Blues" was not a random choice. Barbara Stanwyck's portrayals in the early to mid-1930s of sexually transgressive women are ably assisted in a number of films by the musical signature of "St. Louis Blues," making the song something of an intertextual signifier of her star persona. In turn, the repetitive use of "St. Louis Blues" in Stanwyck's early to mid-1930s star vehicles confirms the song's claims to represent an "excursion into the lower depths" of female sexuality.[53] In *Baby Face* (Warner Bros., 1933), in which Stanwyck plays an archetypal gold digger, the song follows her on her sexual journey from the beer parlor of a midwestern steel town to the penthouse of a city skyscraper. Her amorality and rise out of an illegal drinking shop, where her father forced her to sleep with his customers, to eventual wealth and marriage is both qualified and commented on by the presence of her black friend/servant (Theresa Harris) who punctuates the narrative with her rendition of "St. Louis Blues." The song, which is both vocalized and used as a musical motif, acts as a constant reminder of Stanwyck's character's lowly status. "St. Louis Blues" functions like an aural birthmark, a sign of vulgar beginnings and flawed character that remains with her regardless of how much wealth she accrues. The film's resolution has Stanwyck's character return, penniless but happily married, to the city from where she started out. Although this ending is tacked on to provide a morality lesson and to placate the censors, it is also confirmation of who she is, where she has come from, and where she must stay.

In the majority of the films that use "St. Louis Blues," it is an instrumental version that is played, and recognition of the song's subject matter is thus dependent on the cinema patron's identification of the tune. In *Baby*

Theresa Harris and Barbara Stanwyck in *Baby Face* (courtesy of the British Film Institute)

Face, however, an African American woman sings the song, so its racial and sexual connotations are relatively unambiguous. "St. Louis Blues" comments overtly on Stanwyck's character:

> St. Louis woman, wid her diamond rings,
> pulls dat man roun' by her apron strings.
> 'Twant for powder an store-bought hair,
> De man ah love—would not gone no where.

Stanwyck's character has an equivalent role to the active protagonist in the song—she is the woman with "a heart like a rock cast in the sea," and the temptress who can make a "freight train jump the track" and a "preacher ball the jack."

Just how useful a song such as "St. Louis Blues" could be in expressing a transgressive female sexuality is perfectly summarized in the Joan Crawford vehicle *Rain*—the second Hollywood adaptation of W. Somerset Maugham's short story. Sadie (Crawford), a prostitute, has arrived in the South Sea Island of Pago Pago by way of Kansas, San Francisco, and Honolulu. A particularly raucous instrumental version of "St. Louis Blues" is used as a recurring motif throughout the film, played on Sadie's omnipresent phonograph. In Pago Pago, she comes into conflict with the missionary reformer Davidson (Walter Huston). Sadie's sexuality is as strident (and as "primitive") as the native islanders Davidson and his wife are hoping to convert to Christianity.

Holding true to its title, the film begins with images of overcast skies that pour rain relentlessly. The emphasis on the elemental is echoed in Sadie's physically unfettered deportment, yet it is the city and its "civilized" manners that have transformed Sadie from an innocent teenage orphan from rural Kansas into a San Francisco chippie and sexual primitive. Though *Rain* deals almost wholly with American characters, the South Seas context helps create a universal parable of corrupted innocence, thereby avoiding accusations that the film depicts an exclusively American prurience. Similar concerns dictated the geographical relocation of the story of Frankie and Johnny from the Barbary Coast to an unidentified island off the southern coast of the United States in *Her Man* (Pathé, 1930). The effect is to place the characters within an Oriental primitivism that paradoxically confirms their essential American characteristic. With its denotation of a black feminized American urban milieu, "St. Louis Blues" exemplifies an American primitiveness. The sexualized lower-class woman's distinctly American characteristic is fostered through connotations of "blackness" that accrue through her being identified with this prototypical blues song as well as through cultural stereotyping that conflates primitivism with African American identity.

The song's denotation of a black feminine urban America is supported by its use in the 1939 British gangster film *Murder in the Night* (U.S. title: *Murder in Soho*), wherein "St. Louis Blues" is used to help distinguish the Chicago mobster from the English representatives of the law and upper classes. The American (Jack LaRue) is coarse, vulgar, and brutish. He is identified as feminine through his obsessive concern with appearance and as black through his identification with jazz in general and "St. Louis

Sadie (Joan Crawford) with whiskey, men, and her phonograph (courtesy of the British Film Institute)

Blues" in particular. The linking of feminized gangsters with "St. Louis Blues" also occurs in Cornell Woolrich's short story *Hummingbird Comes Home* (1937), which features a homicidal protagonist who sings the song before and after assassinations. Less obscurely, it is used in nightclub sequences in the gangster films *Scarface: Shame of a Nation* (a Howard Hughes production, 1932) and *Quick Millions* (Fox, 1931). It is also used with rather more narrative complexity in the prison picture *Ladies They Talk About* (Warner Bros., 1933). Barbara Stanwyck plays the part of a gangster's moll who is sent to prison for her role in a bank job. While serving her sentence, she plays an instrumental version of "St. Louis Blues" on a phonograph to cover the sound of prisoners trying to dig their way out. The choice of the song fits neatly alongside the film's exploitation of the abject and vulgar femininity displayed by Stanwyck's character and her fellow inmates. However, "St. Louis Blues" is also used to underscore the essential loneliness of the emotionally abused heroine—the woman who has lost her man.

In *Banjo on My Knee*, Stanwyck again plays a lower-class character, but Pearl's heart is not hard, just broken. She is "love-sick" and, contrary to the sexually meretricious woman played by Stanwyck in *Baby Face*, she does not lead her man around by her apron strings. The core dramatic dilemma is that she and her husband, Ernie (Joel McCrea), are unable to consummate their marriage. The setting is a cluster of rafts tied to an island in the middle of the Mississippi. Pearl's father-in-law Newt (Walter Brennan) enjoys playing his banjo, and, as his riverboat neighbors had serenaded him and his bride as they consummated their wedding, he now wishes to do the same for his son and daughter-in-law. The tune he chooses to accompany their lovemaking is "St. Louis Blues"!

Banjo on My Knee was well received by the American press, which responded positively to "the novel characters and situation."[54] Yet the narrative conceit of an unconsummated marriage created difficulties between the production company and the PCA. A reader of the first complete script complained about the "excessive drinking" and "the suggestive running gag showing Newt's efforts to have Pearl and Ernie sleep together so that the marriage may be consummated." Darryl Zanuck, the film's producer, in a fit of (phony) outrage, responded with a three-page tightly typed letter that made the countercomplaint that "Your reader has injected smut and sex where none was ever intended. . . . We are telling a beautiful love story laid among a certain type of river people that exist on the Mississippi today. . . . It is a real human romantic drama, about real human beings. . . . They are not drunks, they are not whores."[55] Zanuck clearly felt that his film had been slighted, yet the PCA reader's view is not without considerable foundation. Even after a number of changes had been made in the script to bring it in line with the Code, the film remained sexually suggestive. This was because the characters' authenticity as "a certain type of river people" was based on traits that are by necessity vulgar—how else to characterize an underclass given Hollywood's world view? For Zanuck, the vulgar is ameliorated by playing on stereotyped ideas of an American vernacular and through the construction of the characters as childlike. As such, at least for Zanuck, any sexual innuendo simply does not exist.

Barbara Stanwyck and Lillian Roth behind bars in *Ladies They Talk About* (courtesy of the British Film Institute)

The ambiguity carried by the characters—sexual adults or innocent children—is similar to that found in *The Bowery*, which also used comedy to deflect criticisms of its suggestive play with sex.

The production was motivated in large part to cash in on the success of the Broadway play of Erskine Caldwell's *Tobacco Road*, adapted by Jack Kirkland (author of the Broadway version of *Frankie and Johnnie*). *Tobacco Road* featured similar character types to those on display in *Banjo on My Knee*, but in the latter's aligning of white characters and Hollywood stars so closely with images of blackness not distanced and displaced through the mask of blackface, or through a presentation that nostalgically evokes a theatrical tradition, the film raised the possibility that the key distinction between black and white is economic rather than racial. This clearly

Walter Brennan (*far left*) and his musical contraption, Barbara Stanwyck, and Buddy Ebsen in *Banjo on My Knee* (courtesy of the British Film Institute)

is an untenable idea for the period's dominant ideological construction of race, but it is mitigated by playing the film as a grand farce, an innocent celebration of a vernacular American culture, and by the exclusion of the riverboat community from the mainstream of American life.

The beginning of the film creates a view of a primitive yet vital community that draws heavily from combined stereotypes of poor Southern whites and blackface minstrels. One of the marginal characters, Buddy (Buddy Ebson), who performs accompanying dances to Newt's music making, belongs firmly within the minstrel tradition. Much is made of the excessive drinking, the frivolity of the singing and dancing, and the centrality of the sexual act in party making. The blackface tradition that this is being drawn from is also signaled in the film's title, taken from Stephen Foster's "Oh! Susanna." Following a series of incidents, Pearl and Newt end up performing in a New Orleans bar, Café Creole, where she wows a slumming sophisticated audience with sentimental ditties and he gets them dancing as he plays his bones and banjo, and bangs out a medley of nineteenth-century minstrel tunes on a weird musical contraption that harnesses all sorts of homemade instruments. Newt and Pearl, despite their success and acclaim, drift back to their river home. Ernie also returns to the riverboats and Newt finally plays "St. Louis Blues" for the couple as they consummate their marriage in the film's closing moments.

In *Banjo on my Knee,* the black origin of "St. Louis Blues" is visually confirmed during a scene in the last third of the film when Stanwyck's lovesick character, roaming the back streets of New Orleans at sunset, hears a black woman singing the song (performed, as in *Baby Face,* by Theresa Harris). Cut into the scene are vignettes of black laborers bent double by the weight of the cotton bales they carry on their backs. The scene both adds poignancy to the evocation of lost love and works to suggest how close the white riverboat community are to becoming "black." Indeed, the lighting of Stanwyck changes from the opening scenes where she gives off a white radiance to the scenes in the Café Creole (an appropriately named setting) where she becomes markedly darker. In *Baby Face,* Stanwyck's character is symbolically "shadowed" by Theresa Harris, who rarely leaves her side until her final atonement—when moral ambiguity (her "shadow") needs to be expelled from the narrative in order to confirm the correctness of her decision to give up material desire and return to her working-class roots as a married woman.

As with "Frankie and Johnny," Hollywood used "St. Louis Blues" as a means of articulating racial instability in its characterization of women who represent problems in terms of their sexuality, their morality, and their lower-class status. "St. Louis Blues," however, insured that this representation was never lacking in complexity and, significantly, ambiguity. The 1937 version of *Stella Dallas* provides an indication of the complex ideological work that was often performed by the song.[56] Working-class Stella (Barbara Stanwyck) has married Stephen Dallas, a man of upper-class bearing, whom she hopes will teach her about the better things in life. However, following the birth of their daughter, the marriage disintegrates and they drift apart. Stella devotes herself to the raising of Laurel, who grows up to embody all the social graces she cannot or will not adopt.

To fulfill her role as a "good" mother, Stella has to give up her hold over Laurel. To ensure that Laurel is able to make a guiltless shift into the domain of the patriarch, Stella must successfully cut the ties that bind her to her daughter. To achieve this, she must *appear* to transgress the role of the loving mother. Against the evidence mustered earlier in the film that suggests she is a paragon of the self-sacrificing mother, Stella, then, has to give the appearance of embodying that which ultimately threatens the maternal.

Stella's deportment, dress sense, and public behavior is coarse, improper, and utterly tasteless, but her heavily marked acts of sartorial and public vulgarity have previously signaled her lowly class status, not her sexual availability: "There isn't a man alive who could get me going anymore." However, to make the break with her daughter she will need to convince her that Stella does have sexual desire, and that Laurel stands between her and her sexual fulfillment. Stella tells Laurel that she will marry Ed Munn (a kindhearted man but an incorrigible gambler and lush). She further enacts the transition from mother to sexualized woman by indolently lying on a sofa smoking a cigarette, reading a trashy romantic magazine, and playing "St. Louis Blues" on her phonograph. Supported by the sound track of "St. Louis Blues," this masquerade finally rends asunder Laurel's resolve and she leaves.[57] Stella's *enactment* of a sexual persona has countered Laurel's image of her as a good mother, but it does not alienate the audience, who remain sympathetic to Stella's plight.

What evil did Laurel hear emanating from her mother's phonograph? Was it the same that bluesman Robert Johnson sang about on his 1937 recording "Phonograph Blues"?—"Beatrice, she got a phonograph, and it won't say a lonesome word. / What evil have I done, what evil has the poor girl heard?" Probably not. What Laurel heard was an incursion of black culture into a white domestic environment. Enabled by the new technology of the phonograph (and later in the 1950s via radio), the cultural advance of black culture into spaces previously foreclosed to it proceeded apace in the 1930s. Hollywood dramatized this incursion in terms of a nonwhite culture's assault on the sanctity of white middle-class femininity. The effects could be calamitous to the listener, and woman's control over the domestic sphere is revealed as precarious due to the threat posed by the easy access she grants to pernicious recorded musical forms.

From the late 1920s to the late 1930s, Hollywood represented women as exclusively in command of the technology of the phonograph, at least initially. The didactic drive of the narrative eventually wrests away her

Barbara Stanwyck in *Stella Dallas* (courtesy of the British Film Institute)

control in order to save her from her own self-destructive tendency. The
playing of phonograph records, particularly jazz and blues, is extraordi-
narily pervasive in studio-era Hollywood films. This was not done simply
to provide interior and aural decoration; the phonograph is rarely used
simply as a domestic appliance—an idle and harmless distraction for the
family—nor was it used simply as a filmic device for locating a musical
source. Rather, the diegetic use of a phonograph is always motivated by
something more than mere function because the *kinds* of music played
condition the meanings the phonograph can convey. As both vehicle
for the reproduction of signification (in its re-presentations of socially
meaningful music) and an autonomous signifier of wider social meanings
around modernity, domestic leisure, commodity ownership, mechanical
reproduction, and relations to mass culture, the phonograph is a historically composite technology—it is never just a neutral technology of reproduction.

As a mirror image of the patriarchal control of filmic institutions that
primarily address a female audience, the control of the phonograph in
Hollywood films is most often shown to be in the hands of women, just as
the music she plays is aimed at a male intimate. Siegfried Kracauer's ideas
on the consumption of popular phonograph records suggest they aid in
the diminishing of his representative consumers, the petit bourgeois shop
girl or typist "for whom it is characteristic that she cannot hear a piece of
music . . . without chirping along its text. But it is not as if she knows all
the hits; rather, the hits know her, they catch up with her, killing her softly."[58] American films, however, make use of the phonograph to empower
not belittle its consumers; in films the phonograph's importance lies in a
woman's ability to use it as a means to seduce the male. The phonograph
is used to invent fantasies of female control over reproductive technology
as a means of attaining authority in heterosexual relationships. More than
an ankle bracelet or overrouged lips might, the phonograph signifies a
provocative and insubordinate female sexuality that through the music
it reproduces (blues and jazz) is also coded as raced and classed.

Although the music played on phonographs—"Frankie and Johnny"
and "St. Louis Blues" in *Red Headed Woman,* for example—is self-evidently
sexual, the phonograph machine itself can carry this kind of connotation. In Louis Armstrong's "(I'll be Glad When You're Dead) You Rascal
You," he sings: "You gave my girl a Coca-Cola, so you could play on her
Victrola," the period's most popular make of phonograph standing in
for Armstrong's girl's body. In "Come Up and See Me Sometime," her

1934 parody of Mae West, Ethel Waters sings, "You'll be at ease, you can relax and stay as long as you please / Just bring a needle for my talking machine—get what I mean?—and we can dance in between / Come up and see me sometime."[59] Blues yodeler Cliff Carlisle used a similar metaphor in his 1936 recording "Nasty Swing": "Wind my motor honey, / I've got a double-spring / Put the needle in the groove and do that nasty swing."[60] Rhythm and blues star Moose Jackson's 1952 recording "Big Ten Inch Record" linked his sexual prowess to a phonograph record: "I really get her going when I take out my big ten inch [pause] record of her favorite blues."[61] On his 1937 recording "Phonograph Blues," bluesman Robert Johnson found bragging about his sexual prowess came less easily. To his girlfriend Beatrice he sings, "I love my phonograph, but you have broke my windin' chain / And you have taken my lovin', and give it to your other man." Impotent and cuckolded, poor Robert can only ruminate on what once was: "We played it on the sofa, now, we played it 'side the wall." Though he soon returns to his present pitiful condition: "My needles have got rusty, baby, they will not play at all."[62]

The absence of a potent male is what drives the narrative forward in *Female* (Warner Bros., 1933). Where once men ran industries, in the new world order effected by the Depression, women find themselves in control. The woman at the head of a car production company uses her position of power, as men have done before her, to buy the sexual affections of the opposite sex. Along with liberal amounts of vodka, the phonograph, which plays a lush instrumental version of "Shanghai Lil," is a key tool in her seduction of young men. In *I'm No Angel* (Paramount, 1933), Mae West makes comic capital out of this idea when Tira (West) seduces her suitor, who is from Dallas, Texas, by playing a phonograph recording of "No One Loves Me Like That Dallas Man"—other discs in her collection include "No One Loves Me Like That Memphis Man" and "No One Loves Me Like That Frisco Man." The use of phonograph recordings by characters like Tira suggest the woman is the active agent in the dance of seduction, an idea that would be less persuasive if the music was played by either a live band or over the radio. Broadcast music or its live performance is outside of a woman's control, but the domestic domain that the phonograph occupies is registered as female and under her management.

But female control over reproductive machinery does not come without a cost to the operator. In his essay on art and mechanical reproduction, Walter Benjamin notes how "process reproduction," of which phonograph records are an example, no longer guarantees the authority and

authenticity of the original and this is primarily because "technical reproduction can put the copy of the original into situations which would
be out of reach for the original itself. Above all, it enables the original to
meet the beholder halfway . . . the choral production, performed in an
auditorium or in the open air, resounds in the drawing room." One of
the effects of this process is to reactivate the object that is reproduced,
and for Benjamin this leads to a "tremendous shattering of tradition."[63]
Hollywood's use of phonograph recordings produces a less culturally
catastrophic impact, but on an individual level the effect is often literally devastating.

The phonograph's ability to reactivate the original, to bring the dead
back to life, is an idea toyed with in Twentieth Century Fox's adaptation of
Vera Caspary's 1942 novel *Laura*. Investigating the murder of Laura Hunt,
Detective Mark McPherson becomes obsessed with her painted image.
His attempt to give better shape to his fantasy draws him towards Laura's
phonograph; over and over again he plays her favorite recording:

> Waldo Lydecker: What do you know and how do you know so much?
> . . . You act as though you've been Laura's friend for years.
> McPherson: I looked at her records . . . I even played some of them.[64]

But rather than fill the lack at the center of his dream, the phonograph
only brings her absence more fully into focus ("Had he known and lost a
living love, he would never have been so marked as by this short excursion
into necrophilia").[65] McPherson's experience is similar to that discussed
by Greil Marcus, who has noted, "the oddity of the fraternity that comes
together when one is listening to and feeling at one with the dead, who
on records are more physically present than in any other medium: on
the page, on the screen, even in a personal memory of a night when you
were there to see the singer, alive."[66] The structuring absence of the original that phonograph recordings implicitly evoke leads in *The Hard Way*
(Warner Bros., 1942) to the suicide of Albert (Jack Carson), a vaudeville
trouper. Albert is separated from his wife, who is enjoying critical and
popular success as a singer on Broadway. In his dressing room, depressed
and forlorn, he plays a phonograph record she has made, but the recording does not ease his sense of separation. Rather he more keenly feels his
wife's absence, and, as the record plays, he shoots himself. Listening to
the music outside his door, a fellow trouper comments that if he were in
Albert's shoes he would go to New York rather than sit and listen to her

records, but at this point in his life the only relationship Albert has with his wife is with her disembodied voice.

In his classic essay on popular music and standardization, Theodor Adorno argues that there are two basic responses to popular music, rhythmic and emotional. One says "come and dance," the other says "come and weep." As with his colleague Kracauer, Adorno proffers the figure of the shop girl as the weeper and principal consumer of emotional music. "Hollywood and Tin Pan Alley may be dream factories," writes Adorno, "but they do not merely supply categorical wish fulfillment for the girl behind the counter." Rather than identify herself with a character in a film or the female protagonist in a pop song, as is commonly assumed, she confesses to herself what "the whole order of contemporary life ordinarily forbids [her] to admit, namely, that [she] actually [has] no part in happiness."

> What is supposed to be wish fulfillment is only the scant liberation that occurs with the realization that at last one need not deny oneself the happiness of knowing that one is unhappy and that one could be happy. The experience of the shop girl is related to that of the old woman who weeps at the wedding services of others, blissfully becoming aware of the wretchedness of her own life. Not even the most gullible individuals believe that eventually everyone will win the sweepstakes. The actual function of sentimental music lies rather in the temporary release given to the awareness that one has missed fulfillment.[67]

Leaving the question of gender aside, Adorno's thesis strikes me as an indisputable truth, and Hollywood, to a degree, also concurred, using the phonograph to posit a partial critique of modernity that was otherwise absent from the fabric of its films.

In *In This Our Life* (Warner Bros., 1942), the phonograph has a much more serious dramatic function than the comic role it is given in Mae West's film. It is again controlled by a woman, and, as it does so often in film, it indicates a significant lack at the heart of the central character's life. The story concerns the love lives of the bizarrely named sisters Stanley (Bette Davis) and Roy (Olivia de Havilland) Timberlake. Stanley is engaged to Craig Fleming (George Brent) but is having an affair with her sister's husband Peter (Denis Morgan), a doctor. Stanley is headstrong, self-centered, and a thrill seeker. When she and Peter run away to Baltimore, they leave behind a string of broken hearts, but living in the moment they could not care less. The passing of time and the need to earn money to support themselves means that Peter and Stanley are separated for long periods, and to ease her sense of loneliness Stanley buys an expensive Victrola; playing rumba records, she daydreams about nightclubs and dancing. When things go from bad to worse between her and Peter, she stops playing dance records and plays a blues tune performed by a big band. Peter demands that she "shut that thing off," but she only plays her Victrola louder. After he is killed, she still plays the blues on her Victrola. Following his funeral she returns to her family, and her life of drudgery continues. Even after she throws out her mourning clothes, she cannot find anyone to dance with and so dances the days away in an alcoholic haze accompanied only by her phonograph. The phonograph records do not fill the lack in her life; instead they work to make her feel the absence of excitement even more keenly. In a letter to his friend Paul Eluard, surrealist Andre Breton, feeling a little lovesick himself, wrote: "Less and less exchange of ideas or conversations worth having. Endless games. The phonograph. What's the use of it all?"[68] The phonograph is not an alternative to life and love; the music can feed desire but it cannot satisfy. "The so-called releasing element of music is simply the opportunity to feel something," Adorno argued. "But the actual content of this emotion can only be frustration." In seemingly numberless films produced during the 1930s and 1940s that had scenes of women weeping along with phonograph records, Hollywood seconded Adorno's argument. But unlike the German Marxist, it did not resist popular music's blandishments: "Music that permits its listeners the confession of their unhappiness reconciles them, by means of this 'release,' to their social dependence."[69] Hollywood movies offered little relief, and certainly no release, from emotional (or social) dependency.

The blues tune that Stanley plays is "Blues in the Night," written by Johnny Mercer and Harold Arlen and published in 1941. Warner Bros. controlled the screen rights for the song's use and exploited it in a number of their films in the early 1940s. It was used as a passing musical motif in *Lady Gangster,* the studio's remake of *Ladies They Talk About* (1933), replacing "St. Louis Blues" that was used so notably in the earlier version. "Blues in the Night" covers similar terrain to Handy's blues, but the gender of the duplicitous protagonist could be more easily reversed, pigtails for knee pants, a worrisome man for a sweet-talkin' woman.

> My momma done tol' me,
> When I was in knee pants.

My momma done tol' me,
"Son, a woman will sweet-talk
And give you the big eye.
But when that sweet-talkin's done,
A woman is two-faced, a worrisome thing
That leaves you to sing
The blues in the night."

But for all the points of comparison that could be made between the two songs, it is the differences that are most remarkable, and though "Blues in the Night" was successful in the marketplace and would become a standard performed by most of the period's major artists, its strict meter and Mercer's clever rhymes allow little space for instrumental or vocal exploration of the song's form and meaning. "Blues in the Night" belongs more firmly to the school of Broadway blues exemplified by "Ol' Man River" than to a black musical vernacular.

Whatever its pedigree, "Blues in the Night" still signified blackness, as its use in the Warner Bros. picture *The Gay Sisters* (1942) testified. Fiona Gaylord (Barbara Stanwyck) is the oldest of three sisters, and when their father is killed in the Great War she takes responsibility for the household. Because other parties are contesting her father's will, the sisters' inheritance is held in suspension. On reaching the age of twenty-one, Fiona can claim $100,000 from her aunt but only if she is married. Desperately in need of money, she resolves to find a man, marry him, and then pay him off with $25,000. Eventually she discloses to her sisters the consequences of acting on this plan, portrayed as a flashback with Fiona providing the narration. Fiona assumes the role of the sweet-talkin' duplicitous woman, who appears in "Blues in the Night." Her courtship and seduction of the unsuspecting Charles Barclay (George Brent) is reported in a dispassionate voice seeped in irony. Fiona deconstructs the rituals of mating for her audience—the rugged feel of his leather jacket as he carries her across a stream, the blossom on an apple tree under which they make love, the chirruping of two caged canaries, moons in June, and so on. Until her wedding day, the whole scenario is presented as an absurd joke. After the wedding ceremony, Fiona fakes an illness and Charles leaves her to get some medicine from a drugstore; however, before she can make her escape he returns. Upon reading the letter that accompanies the $25,000 Fiona had left on a table, George tells her she can leave but not until the morning. George's assertion of his conjugal rights changes the whole atmosphere of the sequence. Gone is the jokey ironical tone, replaced by an ambience ripe with sexual threat: the lighting darkens, "Blues in the Night" rises up on the sound track, and George forcibly takes Fiona in his arms. That this relatively new composition is able to carry such melodramatic weight has little to do with its uniqueness and everything to do with its links to earlier blues, not in the least "St. Louis Blues." "Blues in the Night" "convincingly suggested the mood and style," wrote Sigmund Spaeth, "if not the actual form, of true Negro-folk-music."[70] For Hollywood, mood and style was everything—it certainly wasn't, at least in the early to mid-1930s, interested in "true Negro-folk-music." Because the performance suggested the need for a much more complex understanding of the position of black Americans within modernity, the concerns that fired the performance of blues songs by black female singers such as Bessie Smith would be excluded from Hollywood's use of the blues.

"St. Louis Blues" and it progeny ("Blues in the Night") symbolically supported Hollywood's characterization of female sexuality as simultaneously transhistorical and as the product of modernity, aiding the conflation of race with sexual transgression—and thereby creating a uniquely American discursive circuit for signifying female desire. As such, in the films discussed here, "transgressive" female sexuality is rooted in both an apparently eternal concept of the female temptress and the historical causality of consumer desire defined as modern American. Upon arriving in the big city, Stanwyck and Harris's characters in *Baby Face* watch a rich young woman in a fur coat climb into an expensive automobile: the fur coat and the automobile standing as two eminent symbols of American glamour, wealth, and modernity. Harris's character simply gawks, but Stanwyck's response is more telling: "What I want to know is how did she get it?" The unspoken answer is "sex"—male sexual desire feeding female material desire—caught in an urban American web of class, race, and gender.

By 1937, repeated use by filmmakers of "St. Louis Blues" (and other songs of equivalent black urban origin) for representing "transgressive" female sexuality meant that it had accreted connotations for contemporary audiences of racial and sexual imperfection.[71] In *Stella Dallas,* these meanings are evoked to enable the filmmakers to suggest credibly to Stella's daughter—against the evidence of her experience—that her mother is unworthy of her continued familial loyalty. However, because "St. Louis Blues" is double-coded in its address to both an exploitative and exploited female sexuality, it helps maintain the audience's sympathy for Stella as the abandoned wife who has lost out to another woman. Social and cultural convention demanded that Stella's masquerade as a sexually active woman coded her as "black." This racial marking overdetermines the representation of the morally suspect, lower-class, sexualized women as literal or figurative octoroons, a process of representation that is, in large part, guaranteed through the use of songs such as "St. Louis Blues."[72]

4

Voices of Smoke and Tears:
Torch Singers and Sin-Songs

She came to the city where nobody cares.
And thousands have wondered before
And it's there she will stay till they lay her away,
In the city where nobody cares.
—Charles K. Harris, "In the City Where Nobody Cares"

In her combination of perfume and jazz with alcohol and unfaithful
men, the 1920s figure of the torch singer offered a compelling *white*
female counterpoint to black female blues and jazz performers. Simultaneously, the torch singer was differentiated from other contemporaneous
white performers such as Sophie Tucker and Mae West who espoused
personae of unruly concert-saloon women. In contrast, the torch singer's
identity is grounded in the sophisticated modernity of metropolitan life
and defined by its heightened experience of emotional vicissitudes. The
performers responsible for establishing the abiding image of the torch
singer as an authentic voice of a woman who has experienced the best and
worst of men were Helen Morgan, Ruth Etting, Lillian Roth, and Libby
Holman. All except Holman appeared with some regularity in early Hollywood sound movies. At one point in 1932, RKO, Universal, and Paramount had each attempted to register the title "Torch Singer." To clarify
matters, Paramount studio executive Maurice McKenzie wrote to Jason
S. Joy at the MPAA. Joy replied that the

story contemplated by Universal was one that was published recently as a serial in some magazine. The story was about a girl of the Libby Holman type and contained incidents which are said to have occurred during her career. This studio also had two or three of its writers trying to develop an original story using the Libby Holman incidents and character, but finally gave up the whole thing. RKO has purchased an original story written by Stella Block. I am advised by them that it has nothing in it that would suggest Libby Holman but it is, rather, about a nightclub singer of the Lillian Roth type, and they intend to use it to feature Arline Judd. However, they have no immediate plans.[1]

The distance between the life the torch singer sang about and the life she lived was often hardly noticeable, or so it was made to seem. Helen Morgan's film career, in particular, confirmed this image. "Helen Morgan was a white chanteuse who specialized in torch songs sung perched on, or against, pianos," Linda Williams writes; she "could convey infinite pathos, and even at a young age her face and voice suggested deep dissipation and ruin."[2] In both her private life and in her personal, theatrical, and film appearances, as well as with her phonograph recordings, Helen Morgan epitomized the popular image of the torch singer. Helen Morgan's unique talent was her ability to give expression to a body and soul tortured by unrequited love for a good-for-nothing man.

Morgan rose to fame as a featured singer in the *George White Scandals* and the *Ziegfeld Follies* (restaged in the 1929 film *Glorifying the American Girl*), and, of course, through her performances on stage and in film in *Show Boat.* But it was her very public arrests for running speakeasies, her relationship with known felons and hoods, and addiction to alcohol that fueled the gossip columns.[3] This image of her was both supported and exploited by her theater and film roles. In a scene in the 1927 stage production of *Show Boat,* her character Julie is described in a manner already familiar to fans of her *Follies* and *Scandals* appearances, as standing by, sitting, or leaning on a piano as she sings. But it is her drinking that gives the scene its dramatic resonance: "From time to time, she furtively takes a drink from a pint flask she keeps in her handbag. At Jim's urging, she reluctantly agrees to try out a new song. Julie goes to the piano and, sitting atop it, sings 'Bill.' When she exits, Jim observes how quickly she fell apart when her husband deserted her."[4] That final point about her ill luck in love was more fully exploited in the film version of *Frankie and Johnnie,* while her relationship with gangsters is used in her role in Al Jolson's *Go into Your Dance* (Warner Bros., 1935) and in the only adaptation to date of Dashiell Hammett's novel *Red Harvest,* which was released under the title *Roadhouse Nights* (Paramount, 1930). In *Marie Galante* (Fox, 1934) she plays a café singer entertaining a motley bunch of ex-patriots, deadbeats, and spies washed up alongside the Panama Canal. In one of her few lines of dialogue, she explains to the film's ingénue the economic benefits of getting the customers to buy drinks. In *Applause* (Paramount, 1929), she galvanized all these elements of her personal and public life. Helen Morgan died in 1941 in Chicago of liver failure brought on by alcoholism.

Libby Holman had the misfortune, or fortune, to marry but then become implicated in the death of playboy and tobacco heir Smith Reynolds. A court eventually decided it was suicide, but the stories circulating around the trial added to the torch singer's image of glamour and star-crossed love.[5] Before Ruth Etting was famous, she married Martin Snyder, otherwise known as "Moe the Gimp," who used his underworld connections to get her radio and nightclub bookings. By 1927 she was appearing in the *Ziegfeld Follies,* which featured her singing the Irving Berlin number "Shakin' the Blues Away"; she also recorded the torch song standards "Body and Soul," "What Wouldn't I Do For That Man," and "Mean to Me," but it was with "Love Me or Leave Me," showcased in the Eddie Cantor revue *Whoopee* (1928), and the Rogers and Hart classic "Ten Cents a Dance" that she found particular renown. Like Helen Morgan, Lillian Roth suffered from alcoholism, but unlike Morgan she survived the disease, a story she told in her autobiography *I'll Cry Tomorrow,* which was filmed by MGM in 1955. In the same year, MGM also made the story of Ruth Etting and Moe the Gimp, played by Doris Day and James Cagney, as *Love Me or Leave Me* (MGM, 1955). Helen Morgan was given the biopic treatment in *The Helen Morgan Story* (Warner Bros., 1957) starring Ann Blyth, while Libby Holman's story had been used as the basis for *Written on the Wind* (Universal, 1957).

Discussing her new one-woman show *Blues, Ballads, and Sin-Songs* (1954), Libby Holman told a French reporter: "I've been working backwards from where I began as a singer of torch songs." "The torch song is a song of unrequited love. It's a modern thing. Nobody carries a torch in the early American songs. If the one they love doesn't love them, then, the hell with it, they can get themselves another girl or man. People in early American ballads just don't feel sorry for themselves."[6] This in part defines the difference between the blues singer and the torch singer, as Angela Davis argues: "what gives the blues such fascinating possibilities of sustaining emergent feminist consciousness is the way they often construct seemingly antagonistic relationships as noncontradictory oppositions. A

female narrator in a women's blues song who represents herself as entirely
subservient to male desire might simultaneously express autonomous
desire and a refusal to allow her mistreating lover to drive her to psychic
despair."[7] Being in a state of "psychic despair" is precisely the emotional
space occupied by the torch singer.

The distinctive differences in the address of blues and torch singers
can be heard in the versions of "Frankie and Johnny" recorded by Ethel
Waters (1939) and Helen Morgan (1934). In the latter, the ballad is given
a mournful and melancholic introduction by a string section. There is
no lift in the emotional pitch of the song when Morgan begins singing,
and the sense of a woman defeated by a no-account man continues to the
denouement. Sung in the first person, Morgan's identification with the
character of Frankie is total. Waters, on the other hand, sings the song
in the third person and produces a more upbeat rendition. She appears
to revel in the particulars of the story—the collecting of the .44 from the
pawn shop, telling the "madam and her floozies" to stand well back or
she'd blow them all straight to hell, even the regret she reports that Frankie
expressed as she stood upon the gallows high for killing her man. Waters
struts through the ballad's narrative vicariously enjoying its pleasures,
while Morgan wallows in its apparent verities unable to find any possibility of transcendence.

In a celebratory note, the columnist and broadcaster Walter Winchell
wrote of Libby Holman that "she is the torch singer par excellence—the
best of those female troubadours with voices of smoke and tears, who
moan and keen love's labors lost to the rhythm and boom of the Roaring Twenties." Holman had achieved popular recognition following her
appearance in the Broadway production of Howard Dietz and Arthur
Schwartz's *The Little Show* (1929) due, in particular, to her rendition of
"Moanin' Low." This was an original song written for her by Dietz and
Ralph Rainger, which, according to one of her biographers, "had its origins in Harlem. Clifton Webb, one of the most stylish dancers of his day,
had long wanted to do a scene in which he could dance and play the part
of a pimp—a sweetback, as the breed was known in Harlem—'a young
man who allows a lady friend to keep him in change.' Libby, Webb, and
Dietz worked on the idea together, attempting to devise a scene and an
appropriate song for Libby's husky voice. For inspiration, they went up to
Harlem—to slumming parties, to black-and-tan cafés, to the Easter Parade
on Lenox Avenue."[8] Whether they actually bothered to visit Harlem or
just played a few phonograph records for inspiration, is less important

than noting that this is another moment of whites authenticating their art through an apparently direct association with black culture. The biographer's description of the scene in which the song was eventually featured is worth quoting at length, due to the similarities between the story and the ballad of "Frankie and Johnny" as well as its almost perfect match with the scenario, produced in the same year, used for the Bessie Smith film *St. Louis Blues*. None of this, however, should detract from the image of Clifton Webb making "snake-hip movements" in a "frenzied" dance. For those who only know of his work through such exaggeratedly fey film performances in, for example, *Laura* (1944), *The Razor's Edge* (1946), *Dark Corner* (1947), all Twentieth Century Fox, the description that follows is truly remarkable, if not wholly unbelievable:

> Ultimately the staged scene of "Moanin' Low" would show Webb, the drunken sweetback, asleep in his gaudy suit, tan makeup and exaggerated sideburns. Libby his high-yaller whore, creeps into their dingy Harlem bedroom and, while crooning her love for him, hides part of her earnings in her stocking. Webb wakes up, takes his money and performs a frenzied dance, utilizing the "snake-hip" movements he had learned from Buddy Bradley, the famous black dancing instructor. He then makes love to Libby, practically raping her, and discovers the concealed cash in her stocking. Outraged, Webb chokes her to death, he believes, and exits terror stricken. Libby recovers, crawls to the door, beating futilely against it, while singing a throaty obbligato, a scatting improvised growl, that no white woman had ever attempted on Broadway before.[9]

Whether it is Holman performing as a "high-yaller whore," Morgan in the role of Julie in *Show Boat,* or Lillian Roth posing in blackface in imitation of Al Jolson in a publicity photograph with the caption "Black and Blues. A little of the first on the face and plenty of the second in the tones—and you have Al Jolson as Lillian Roth sees him,"[10] the torch singer walks in the shadow of the blues, appropriating an emotionalism intrinsic to white constructions (minstrelsy) of black culture, but maintaining an aura of sophistication and urbanity absent from 1920s and 1930s constructions of blues singers. In contemporary reports, Helen Morgan, for example, was sometimes called both a ballad or blues singer, two forms apparently interchangeable, but more usually adjectives associated with the blues—"torrid voiced," "husky-toned," "tragic-faced"—were attached to the description of her as a torch singer, which kept the image of blackness associated with the blues only a little apart from the singer.[11]

A little of the first on the face and plenty of the second in the tones—and you have Al Jolson as Lillian Roth sees him. Add to this a *Sonny Boyish* bob and the imitation is better than Harry Richman's

Black and Blues

Al Jolson as Lillian Roth sees him, *Motion Picture* magazine, 1930 (author's collection)

Sigmund Spaeth thought *The Little Show* "the most important event of the year [1929] in popular music."[12] But the success of that show and its two featured songs "Why Can't We Be Friends?" and "Moanin' Low" was overtaken the following year by the production *Three's a Crowd,* which reunited the three leads from *Little Show,* Webb, Holman, and comedian Fred Allen. *Three's a Crowd* featured Holman in a similar scenario to that which gave a context for "Moanin' Low" but was now given a "social protest" angle by "bemoaning the plight of the mulatto, unloved by the white world."[13] The featured song was "Yaller," which has not entered the public's consciousness; however, two numbers did survive the show to become classics of American popular song. "Something to Remember You By" was also sung by Holman and would become a much-recorded standard, but it was Johnny Green's "Body and Soul" which was truly outstanding, becoming *the* anthem for torch singers. In popular culture of the 1920s and early 1930s, the kind of sexual yearning explicit in a song like "Body and Soul" was unique to the torch singer, which is why Hollywood featured them in films and drew upon their image for story material. Moreover, the torch singer exemplified an image of urban dissipation.

Forgetting "at a minimum, several dozen" other essential works concerned with the city of New York, critic Luc Sante, nevertheless, finds space for *Applause* (Paramount, 1929), the Helen Morgan vehicle directed by Rouben Mamoulian. Among those New York stories Sante has remembered are Stephen Crane's *Maggie,* Walt Whitman's *Specimen Days,* F. Scott Fitzgerald's "My Lost City," Herbert Asbury's *Gangs of New York,* Weegee's *Naked City,* Jules Dassin's *Naked City,* the photographs of William Klein and Louis Faurer, Chester Himes's *Blind Man with a Pistol,* Martin Scorsese's *Mean Streets,* and Joseph Mitchell's *Up in the Old Hotel.*[14] This is heady and vital company for a film all but forgotten except by historians of early sound cinema.[15] *Applause* had something of a reputation in the late 1960s and early 1970s as young auteurists sought to place Mamoulian in the pantheon of Hollywood greats, but now it has fallen into an abyss of forgetting.[16] Yet the film is a tour de force, a brilliant examination of American modernity. Helen Morgan, the greatest of the 1920s torch singers, takes the two-dimensional archetype Beth Brown's source novel had essayed, and creates a character rich in pathos—a lonely aging soul, aching for companionship and sexual fulfillment in a world otherwise characterized by the false laughter, phony bonhomie, and sleazy lifestyle of a run-down, beat-up burlesque company. "Shake 'em up!" Hitch would command. "This ain't a church social! Now let me tell you what the men want when they come to see a burlesque show. Let me give you the low-down." And he did, concluding with, "Just forget you were ever in a convent school. See? More wiggle, more shake! Get those hips in action! Don't be an iceberg. Come on! Start thawing!"[17] Paramount studios produced the lowdown on hips in action and thawing icebergs in their adaptation of *Applause* that formed part of a cycle of backstage dramas released in the late 1920s and early 1930s. *Applause,* however, has more in common with the pessimism of Vidor's *The Crowd* than with the gaiety of *Broadway Melody* (1929). It is less a tale of show folk and more a tale of the city with show folk as its representative citizens. Like *Show Boat,* it begins in the 1890s and ends in the present, but unlike the former, cultural refinement and the lights of Broadway and the legitimate stage are not part of the film's conclusion. Kitty Darling's (Helen Morgan) career and life end backstage of a run-down burlesque house: she has poisoned herself so as not to burden her daughter (in an echo of *Stella Dallas*) who is leaving show business to marry a sailor.

The basic story is trite and begins with "The Queen of Hearts" Kitty Darling, the leading lady of the Gaiety Girls Burlesque Company, riding in a barouche at the head of a parade. Kitty receives notice that her husband, who is in Sing Sing, has not been granted a stay of execution, and, pregnant with his child, the news causes her to collapse—she gives birth backstage to a girl, April. Because "burlesque is no racket for a child," April is sent to a convent. When she is seventeen, she rejoins her mother who is hooked up with another ne'er-do-well, Hitch Nelson (Fuller Mellish Jr.). Kitty's career is all but finished. She is with the Parisian Flirts, a shoddy burlesque company, and Hitch, a man much younger than her, is fleecing her for all she is worth while carrying on an affair with a showgirl. Hitch forces April (Joan Peers) onto the stage and attempts her seduction. When Hitch acts improperly towards her, April walks the city streets and meets a young sailor called Tony (Henry Wadsworth); they fall in love and plan to marry. But April becomes torn between her love for Tony and the need to support and provide for her mother. As for Jolson's character towards the end of *The Jazz Singer,* her situation seems impossible: should she do the dutiful thing and look after her mother or should she go with the man she loves? She chooses her mother, and Tony leaves her to rejoin the navy rather than go home to his family farm in Wisconsin (as they had planned to do after they had married). A life in burlesque is April's future, although unknown to her, Kitty, thinking April is now safe and secure with a man she loves and who will love her, takes poison so she will not be a burden. April seems to have lost everything—but wait, Tony reappears;, hurrah, he did not rejoin the navy. Wisconsin beckons for the couple.

This is maudlin, sanctimonious, sentimental, and clichéd, but Mamoulian's direction and the central performance by Helen Morgan turn this hackneyed story into raw modernist art and make it one of the great American films. The film's narrative is anchored on the binaries of a Manichean world view—good and evil, purity and impurity, spiritual and secular, rural and urban, productive and nonproductive labor—which Mamoulian reworks to give a more thrilling, vital, and modernist spin. The attractions of the city are intoxicating in their complexity and deny any easy recourse to telling a morality story, a cautionary tale of the big bad city. *Applause* has two musical sound tracks, one formed from old and newly fashioned Tin Pan Alley tunes, the other from the sounds of the streets, the subway, and the air space of Manhattan. Together they form a modernist jazz imbroglio.

The first indication of the film's modernist principle of making art from modernity follows April's arrival at Penn Station in New York. The scene is set by having previously shown her life at the convent as heavenly in its serenity: a picture book, fairy-tale world summoned earlier in the film by a tableau of April with the Mother Superior in the grounds of the convent in a reflective, iconic pose. In his monograph on Mamoulian's films, Tom Milne describes the "beautiful chiaroscuro sequence" as April prepares to leave the Mother Superior to rejoin her natural mother: "with the camera tracking slowly down corridors where nuns glide past or kneel in prayer, and out to the gardens where children play on the lawn, nuns stroll by the lake and swans float gracefully on the water. Largely silent, except for an 'Ava Maria' sung on the soundtrack, the scene enshrines a sense of pure tranquility, almost as incorporeal as the nuns who flit like black and white shadows through it."[18] April is escorted out of the convent; a man in worker's clothing awaits her on the other side. In close-up, we see her pensive face and the man's hand pulling open the convent's wrought-iron gate. There follows a match dissolve to April staring out of a window in the door of a train; a man's hand enters the frame and pushes the door open. The movement is accompanied by a loud clang, followed immediately by an explosion of ambient sound: a great cacophony of grinding noises produced by the collision of machines and people on the move, all amplified beneath the great steel and glass roof of the train terminal. The camera tilts back to reveal the vast architectural space above the travelers' heads, the monumental steel and glass roof contrasting markedly with the stained glass windows and iron gate in the convent. This is April's rude arrival in New York—the shock of the new where all that is solid melts into air. The camera tilts back down to eye level to record the crowd moving along the platform and up the stairs to exit into the even greater noise of the street outside. The almost polite sound of train bells fall asunder beneath the mighty blaring of klaxons and honking horns of taxicabs vying for passengers; all human sounds are obliterated. In the rhythmic rush of the crowd, April is lost to the viewer, but not to the camera, which catches her entering a cab; following dissolves from the cab's meter to its lights, the scene moves forward to the Star Hotel where April is greeted by yet another man opening doors for her. Kitty is not at home.[19]

Escorted by a young man from the hotel, April is taken to see her mother's stage show. Following a cootch dancer, the chorus line troops on to the stage led by Kitty. The number is "Yacka Hula Hickey Dula," a faux Hawaiian tune first popularized by Al Jolson in his show *Robinson Crusoe Jr.* (1916). The dancers are overweight, middle-aged, and amateurish, and so is the song's execution. On gartered spindly legs, supporting an overweight torso sheathed in a tutu and with a mess of bleached blonde hair, Kitty looks well past her prime; a point echoed by an audience member who shouts in April's hearing that "they ought to pension off that old blonde." April has not seen her mother perform for twelve years, and her distress at seeing how much she has aged and how far she has fallen down the burlesque ladder is made apparent in the montage of close-ups on performers and audiences' faces as the number draws to a close. The edits bounce between the audience and dancers, their matched gaping mouths full of rotten teeth, before dissolving to Kitty's face and then on to a horrified April. This catalog of those on both sides of the stage's footlights is a display of grotesquerie without equal in American film.

Later that night, April relives the day's events in a dream in which the Mother Superior's face is replaced by Kitty's, the steel and glass of the train station obliterates the convent, the monstrous faces of the dancers and their audience obscure those of the nuns, and "Ava Maria" is drowned out by "Yacka Hula Hickey Dula." Towards the end of the dream, she returns to the pastoral image of swans swimming languidly around the convent's pond and "Ava Maria" is restored. But modernity wins the day, if not the night, when she is woken by the sound of the telephone ringing.

Hitch starts teaching April to dance, but she is an unwilling student. During one lesson held in their hotel rooms, he tries to seduce her and is only stopped by the timely intervention of Kitty, who brings news that she must attend an after-show "stag smoker" at a men's club. This is the lowest rung on the burlesque ladder; she is to give a private performance that is only a sex act away from being prostitution. Rather than return to the hotel with only Hitch for company after the evening's performance, April walks out of the burlesque house on her own. Filmed from below the waist in a long tracking shoot, April is met by a line of stage-door Johnnies and mash-men—"Hello kid," "Hey, give us a kiss," "Where you going, baby?" "Wait a minute sweetheart," "Come on baby, give me a break"—before she is rescued by a handsome young sailor from Wisconsin (not uncoincidentally where her convent was located). The sequence is accompanied on the sound track not only by the men's solicitations and whistles, but also by a yapping dog and by a less raucous, but no less insistent, chorus of bells, klaxons, and horns than that heard earlier outside Penn Station. The scene visualizes Jelly Roll Morton's 1926 recording "Sidewalk Blues" that W. T. Lhamon Jr. used as means to extemporize on Jolson's two-handed whistle in the middle of "Toot Toot Tootsie" in *The Jazz Singer*. Morton's recording begins, writes Lhamon, with a "minstrel whistle, wolf-whistle subfamily":

> Morton interrupts it by overlaying the whistle with a klaxon horn, then with dialogue between an interlocutor, playing streetcar conductor, and a pedestrian endman:
>
>> Hey, get on outta the way. Whadya tryin' to do, knock the streetcar off the track? You so DUMB you should be president of the Deaf and Dumb society.
>> I'm sorry, boss, but I got the sidewalk blues.
>
> This strutter dusts off his pride, tentatively, at first. But soon his stride is swinging a rejoinder to the conductor's abuse. His music is eloquent answer to the conductor's klaxon, the very opposite of "dumb." Every time the streetcar's rude noise intercedes, the strutter whistles his own little undertune. He picks up his swing, extending the dialogue which began the recording, but he makes the terms his own. He reclaims his right of way, building his own momentum.
>
> At the song's end, the conductor's voice is still trying to break through, still stalled, but not silenced either. He is shouting out ambiguously and perhaps converted to the strutter's swing, "Let 'em roll." The music of the margin, of the sidewalk, has talked back to his klaxon command.[20]

This is how April first finds herself in the city: she is trying to build her own momentum against the very men who once opened doors for her and who have now closed them against her. Cornered, she is unable to pick herself up and answer the sounds of the street. The sailor's intervention gives her the opportunity to return to the state of grace she enjoyed at the convent, but with heterosexual romance replacing divine love.

In a cafeteria, the couple chat and drink coffee into the small hours before watching the dawn from the Brooklyn Bridge; the long lonesome sound of ships' sirens punctuates their courting. With morning breaking, they return to the Star Hotel, where their enchanted evening ends abruptly. As they part, the sounds of the city reappear followed by the arrival of a very drunk Kitty, home at the end of the stag smoker and mimicking the blaring city soundscape by blowing into a party horn. Tony has four days left before he has to return to his ship or give up the navy, and in this time the couple fall very much in love. On the fourth day, Tony proposes to April on the roof of a skyscraper. Alone above New York, they wonder at the sights before them: the Battery, the Woolworth building, and the Statue of Liberty. The future seems to be theirs. After they have married, he says, they will live on a farm in Wisconsin and "raise swedes, have a Ford, a radio, and. . . ." Unsure of what other worldly goods he can claim, Tony finishes his little speech with "oh, several things!" Their view of the future, then, is not outside of modernity—a retreat to a rural idyll—but within it: the sights of New York, the Ford automobile, the radio and, oh, several things. Their lovemaking is interrupted by the noise of an airplane circling the skyscraper, but it is not a fearful intrusion. She says yes to his proposal, and they return to the hotel to tell Kitty.

Kitty is delighted and they plan a celebration at a chop suey house. After Tony's departure, Hitch returns and is infuriated to hear that April will be leaving. He announces that Kitty is washed up and that without the youthful April in the act, they will not secure new bookings. He storms out leaving her distraught. April is faced with the cruel dilemma of whether to stay with the act and her mother or leave and find happiness with Tony. Kitty begs off going to the restaurant, and, in the following scenes that cut between the chop suey house and her hotel rooms, she takes a dose of poison.

The restaurant sequence opens with a rush of excitement: a jazz band is pumping out a fast, peppy arrangement of Dolly Morse and Joe Burkes's "Give Your Little Baby Lots of Lovin'," and dancing couples fill the floor. Over by a wall sit a very happy Tony and a melancholy April. As he becomes more aware of her emotional state, the music changes. First the tempo drops as the band plays "Flying High," but the optimism of the song sounds false as April tells Tony she cannot marry him. The tempo drops again as the band plays "What Wouldn't I Do For That Man," which Kitty had sung to herself earlier in the film as she rummaged around old showbiz mementos and photographs of April and Hitch.²¹ The music of the jazz band is so prominent it almost drowns out April and Tony's conversation. But whether the listener can hear all of the talk or not, it is clear that even if April has decided she must follow her mother on to the burlesque stage in order to provide for her, she will not become her, she will not sacrifice herself to a man.

Very reluctantly, Tony accedes to April's wishes and the two leave the restaurant. He declares that he will rejoin his ship, and they walk together to the subway. She accompanies him to the platform where they wait with a crowd of travelers for his train. Disconsolately idling, Tony pumps coins into a vending machine and passes the sticks of gum to April, a hopelessly inadequate token of his love. When the train pulls out, April is all but alone; only a fat old drunk is left on the platform—"Missed your train? There'll be another along in a minute." *Applause* begins on an empty street, the camera recording the flight of a torn and tattered poster of Kitty Darling, star attraction of the Gaiety Girls Burlesque Company. As the poster recedes down the street, the ominous boom of a bass drum on the sound track becomes part of a marching band's recital of the coon song "Hot Time in the Old Town Tonight," whereupon the street becomes filled with people rushing to watch and join the parade led by Kitty in her barouche. "Apart from its sheer brilliance as film-making," writes Milne, "the sequence is cleverly contrived as a foundation for the whole film. It plants the idea that Kitty's fame will be short lived, undercutting the slightly hackneyed 'fickleness of fortune' theme by getting in first, as it were; and more importantly, it establishes in terms of harsh, grimy lasciviousness the weary reality that lies behind that fame."²² The scene of April, first alone in the crowd with Tony by her side and then her long walk up the empty subway stairs that only moments earlier had been filled with travelers, is the mirror image of the film's opening.

As April had finished drinking a glass of water in the chop suey house, the scene had cut back to Kitty finishing the last of the poison. The sound of the jazz band in the restaurant is replaced by the honking horns of automobiles and shouted greetings of citizens outside Kitty's open window. Inside her hotel room, the clock on the mantelpiece ticks methodically in counterpoint to the random ambient sounds. As April reaches the top of the subway stairs, another edit returns the viewer to Kitty. The poison has begun to take effect, and the ambient sounds have now turned into a murderous wail of noise. As her last conscious act, Kitty drags herself to the burlesque house where April prepares to go on in her place. She dies as April steps onto the stage singing "Give Your Little Baby Lots of Lovin'" and kicking out a jazz dance in a sequined bathing suit. The phony gaiety of the dance and the interaction between performers and audience contrast with the song's earlier recital by the jazz band in the chop suey house—a peppy number that had everyone (except April and Tony) dancing. On seeing her mother's body, April is totally distraught, but as she leaves the theater, there waits Tony in front of a huge poster of Kitty Darling. They kiss. The end.

Notes on the film produced for, and collected by, the SRC are very positive, particularly in regard to direction and technical effects. The National Board of Review thought it "Very excellently directed . . . The photography is remarkable and at times exquisitely beautiful." Jason Joy writing to Will Hays noted that "the direction and photography are quite unusual, and, in our opinion, the picture will cause considerable commendable discussion."[23] In a letter to one of the film's producers, Walter Wanger, Joy wrote: "The direction, photography and general production value seem to us to be examples of a new forward step in picture building which, I am sure, will greatly please the regular motion picture patrons and which should attract to the theatre new and more critical patrons who are not in the habit of patronizing the usual motion picture."[24] Reported *Film Daily,* "Outstanding features of the picture include careful and refreshingly new direction from Rouben Mamoulian . . . a high grade of sound recording and a brand of photography which is as excellent as anything we've seen to date."[25]

But while the film's direction and photography did create some discussion, it was neither considerable, nor generally commendable. The regular reviewer for the *New York Times,* Mordaunt Hall, thought Mamoulian "rather lets his penchant for camera feats run away with suspense . . . he delights in swinging his camera back and forth and in many instances he does so with a certain effect. . . . In most cases, however, Mr. Mamoulian commits the unpardonable sin of being far too extravagant. He becomes tedious in his scenes of the convent and there is nothing but viciousness in his stage passages."[26] The film seems to have excited and bored reviewers in equal measure: despite approving of the film's technical aspects, *Film Daily* thought the picture as a whole was a "drab drama of backstage burlesque life, with only a sprinkling of comedy. A melancholy undercurrent runs through the picture and makes it heavy stuff."[27] In one of the few reviews published in fan magazines, *Photoplay* thought "when this is good it's very, very good and when it's bad it's—you know."[28] Paramount obviously concurred because it seems to have given the film little promotional push following its New York premiere in October 1929, preferring instead to give advertising space in both trade journals and fan magazines to the first feature film starring the blackface duo Mack and Moran, to the *The Virginian* with Gary Cooper, and to *The Dance of Life,* another backstage burlesque drama but with a more traditional romantic story and a happier ending. Perhaps the company concurred with *Film Daily*'s appraisal that "It's highly probable that the picture will appeal to class houses but it's speculative product for the average audience."[29]

The *New York Times* reviewer noted that Mamoulian was a Theatre Guild director, which would have signaled to eagle-eyed readers his cultural capital and helped explain the more "extravagant" aspects of the film's production. *Variety* found it almost inconceivable that a theater director could have been responsible for such a daring production: "No doubt Mr. Mamoulian did direct the stage work of the burlesque show and the attendant scenes back-stage, but to ask one to believe that a stage director on his first try could turn out this film as it has been turned out is asking one to believe as big a lot as a studio occupies."[30] Mamoulian had been working for the Theatre Guild company since 1926 and had enjoyed considerable success with the 1927 production of *Porgy.* Previously employed by the American Opera Company (1923–25), he had also worked as a director in London's West End. Born in Tiflis, Georgia, in 1898, he studied at the Moscow Art Theater under the tutelage of Yevgeny Bragrationovich Vakhtangov before leaving Russia in 1922. This range of experience explains Paramount's willingness to engage the services of Mamoulian and helps to locate the film's modernist principles, particularly his background in revolutionary Soviet theater. The images of the burlesque agents and bookers in *Applause,* shot from low angles to exaggerate their corpulent bodies, are reminiscent of Eisenstein's representations of capitalists in his early films; similarly Mamoulian's use of montage while Kitty sings "Yacka Hula Hickey Dula" are clearly drawing upon the Soviet master's theory and films.

But the sound track, to my ears, has no precedent in either European avant-garde cinema or in highbrow theater. The mobility of the camera and the sound track's novel qualities were deemed at the time to be worth exploiting in studio publicity material: "Bringing to his first screen directorial effort a wealth of originality, imagination and technical dramatic knowledge which is his, he developed a motion picture technique of his own which differs radically from the accepted forms of film story telling. . . . Mamoulian tells the story of *Applause* by constant movement of the photographic recording instrument. Approximately 85% of the scenes in the picture are photographed in motion and the director has achieved a smoothness of action and an accentuation of dramatic values by this method never attained before."[31] Writing in 1929, cultural critic Gilbert Seldes considered the "essential problem" of sound cinema is to "find the proper relation between the camera and the microphone":

> A satisfactory relationship can be maintained and that will be found when the nature of the mechanics of each has been understood. The camera is a recording instrument, but the record it makes is an illusion; the microphone is a recording instrument and the record it makes is a duplication (within quite narrow limits) of the actual. Thus, at the beginning we have the juxtaposition of two instruments with different and frequently incompatible capacities. The next point about the two is that the camera is, in practice, mobile almost without limitation whereas the microphone is practically stationary. The problem of reconciling these two instruments is complicated by a non-technical and non-esthetic fact: the moving picture has accustomed us to quick movement and the microphone, attached to the movie, is an interesting novelty; so that either habit or curiosity must be given first gratification until a compromise is effected.[32]

Of the early sound films, *Applause* comes closest to effecting the compromise Seldes calls for. It does this through allowing ambient sound sourced from the location in which the camera moves to dominate the sound track. Years after the fact, Mamoulian would discuss how he had experimented with "syncopated rhythms" and a "Symphony of Noises" in his production of *Porgy,* but this was to provide an authenticating rhythmic sound track to accompany his portrayal of "Negro life": in this sense the soundscape is simply a play on racial stereotypes.[33] *Applause* does something else. The sound of the city is the music of the city *(musique concrete).* It is not abstract or metaphorical, but emanates from tangible sources: automobiles, locomotives, airplanes, telephones, phonographs, human voices. Mamoulian has edited and orchestrated these sounds, but they nevertheless remain true to their source: sounds produced by the clatter and whirl of technological urban life. The recital of popular music is similarly precisely located, such as that produced by the jazz band whose music continually threatens to overwhelm April and Tony's conversation—the music is never subordinate to the dialogue. The ragtime and coon song tunes "Hot Time in the Old Town Tonight" played by the marching band or "Waiting for the Robert E. Lee" punched out by the pit orchestra in the film's first burlesque sequence are also orchestrated expressions of an urban dissonance. The only harmonious musical moment is when Kitty sings softly "What Wouldn't I Do For That Man" to herself. But this moment of repose is soon shattered by the untimely arrival of Hitch, and later the tune is appropriated and given a syncopated reprisal by the jazz band that virtually mutes the tune's melody. If you throw away the story of *Applause,* you are left with a film that presents itself as an extraordinary carnival of urban music, dissidence, and noise.

Yet the story is worth keeping. The film's modernist superstructure rests upon the time-honored tale of a mother's love, and sacrifice, for her child. Using the figure of the torch singer, it was a story Hollywood returned to again and again throughout the 1930s. In Paramount's *Torch Singer* (1933), starring Claudette Colbert, the story's theme is transcendent maternal love. Separated from her lover after he leaves for China, Sally Trent is broke, heavily pregnant, and unmarried when the film begins. Following the birth of her daughter, Sally teams up with another single mother, but they soon find they are unable to hold down steady employment and look after their children. When her friend marries, the situation becomes even more desperate for Sally, and she gives her daughter up for adoption. Without the difficulty of having to look after a child, she soon finds work singing in a saloon where she is discovered by Tony Cummins (Ricardo Cortez) who manages her rise to stardom as a torch singer, graduating from saloons and cafés to nightclubs and Broadway revues. With fair-weather, good-time friends to distract her, Sally seems not to miss her child. By a happy accident, she becomes the hostess of a children's show on which she is known as Aunt Jenny. The fan letters she receives unlock her maternal instincts, and she begins a search for her daughter that will end with her reunited not only with her child but also the child's father.

The fan magazine *Motion Picture,* in its review of the Sophie Tucker star feature *Honky Tonk*—"The story of the mother who became a vulgar café singer in order to give her daughter 'advantages' only to have the daughter ashamed of her"—noted that this kind of film was "Made according to the tried and true movie recipe, so much mother love, so many tears, one café set, a few laughs, and a song about a broken heart." But in defense of these clichés, or "old stuff," the review claimed a universal appeal for "mother love and heartache."[34] Even the most hard-boiled of the 1930s torch singers Mona (Jean Harlow), in *Reckless* (MGM, 1935), finds her maternal feelings overwhelm all other considerations. This formula was given particular social relevance in the *Torch Singer* by the filmmakers who posit an unmistakable link between the dissolution of families and the economic effects of the Depression.

Marlene Dietrich's character in *Blonde Venus* (Paramount, 1932), Helen Faraday, similarly sacrifices everything in her attempt to hold onto her child. In Germany she had been a cabaret singer, but when she meets and marries an American she gives up the stage and returns with him to New York. He is a chemist who through his work contracts radium poisoning. There is a possibility that a cure can be found in Europe, but they are without funds. She persuades him to let her return to the stage to try to earn some money. For her first engagement, she wears a gorilla costume which she strips away before singing "Hot Voodoo"—the exotic European vamp who appeared in *Der Blaue Engel* (UFA, 1930) and *Morocco* (Paramount, 1930) is transformed, via a white-sponsored fantasy of Africa, into an American jazz singer. After the show she meets a wealthy playboy (Cary Grant) who is smitten by her. He gives her the money to pay for her husband's trip to Europe, and in his absence they begin an affair that lasts until he returns. When her husband discovers how she has raised the money for his hospital treatment, he demands that she leave him and give up their child. Rather than accede to his demands, she leaves New York with their son. Unable to find work as a singer, Helen and child are soon living rough and trying to keep one step ahead of the detectives her husband has hired. For reasons that are never explained, their time on the road and living in cheap hotels takes them ever deeper into the rural American south. Even as their direction of travel counters contemporary migrations, it draws comparison between their plight and the Depression's economic migrants. Helen only relinquishes responsibility for the child when it is clear she can no longer provide what he needs. But in his way, her husband proves to be an equally inadequate single parent—they live almost in squalor, he fails to wash the boy properly, and he makes rotten puddings. Only a complete restoration of the family can provide all that the child needs and should have.

Susan Hayward played Lillian Roth in the screen version of the singer's autobiography, *I'll Cry Tomorrow* (MGM, 1955). It was a part she was eminently suited for, having previously taken the roles of an alcoholic singer in the Walter Wanger production *Smash-Up: The Story of a Woman* (Uni-

Body and Soul

versal, 1947) and of real-life singer Jane Froman in *With a Song in My Heart* (Twentieth Century Fox, 1952). Industry gossip suggested that *Smash-Up* was based on Bing Crosby's marriage to Dixie Lee, and there are more than a few points of comparison, but Wanger was right to vehemently deny any intentional similarities—the story of a mother struggling with personal demons had already been told in previous Hollywood dramas of torch singers.[35] In *Smash-Up,* Angie Evans' career as a singer is ascendant when she marries the out-of-work big band singer Ken Conway (Lee Bowman), but their fortunes are reversed following the birth of their daughter. After a long period of unemployment, Ken finds work as radio's Melancholy Cowboy. Clearly bored by the whole cowboy shtick, he and his accompanist take the opportunity provided by the news of his daughter's birth to air an original number. The (cloying) sentimentality of the song, combined with Ken's (oh-so-sincere) baritone voice is an instant hit, and his rise to fame is recorded in a montage of theater marquees carrying his name in lights.

As Ken's career takes off, Angie slumps into the bottle. Before long, even the simplest of domestic chores are beyond her, and Ken has no choice but to take their baby and leave her to embrace John Barleycorn with even greater ardor. The separation from her husband and child eventually stirs Angie to attempt a recovery and get back to singing. She secures an engagement at an uptown nightclub: "We have a special kind of clientele here you know," the manager tells her, "it's not one of those bang bang places." She does not appear on her opening night, and instead hits the bars, joints, and clubs of New York's famed 52nd Street—bang bang places—Leon and Eddie, the Bayou Club, Onyx Club, Swing, Club Downbeat, and the Three Deuces. Angie passes out in the street and wakes up the following day in a stranger's bed. The sound of children playing outside the tenement building in which she finds herself remind her of her own child, and, after one more setback, she gets back on the road to recovery.

The collective image of 52nd Street's neon signs is the film's third and last montage sequence. The montage of Ken's rise to fame and fortune had earlier been rhymed with a montage of Angie's rise from anonymity. That montage recalled Claudette Colbert's character's rise to stardom in *Torch Singer:* a sequence of ever more luxurious and refined nightclub scenes that are linked together by the performance of a single song. The basic theme of *Torch Singer* and *Smash-Up* is the same; whatever wealth, fame, and independence a woman gains, it is no substitute for maternal feelings and the equally necessary love of a good man. As *Motion Picture*

132

magazine pointed out, the story was old when Sophie Tucker played the singing mother in 1929 in *Honky Tonk*; by 1947 it was ancient.

Other than the maternal concerns displayed in these films, the torch singer was also used to portray women in the autumn of their lives. Marlene Dietrich's most intriguing portrayal of a saloon or cabaret singer was in Fritz Lang's *Rancho Notorious* (RKO, 1952). Dietrich's role was conceived as a reflection on her past characterizations, particularly Frenchy in *Destry Rides Again* (1939) and Lola Lola in *The Blue Angel.* Lang does not simply repeat these parts but instead ruminates on the effects of aging. Dietrich's dialogue is laden with allusions to growing old ("Every year's a threat to a woman." "He's young and handsome, and it's easy to take a fancy to him. He makes you remember yourself a long time back." "I wish you'd go away and come back ten years ago."), and her given name, Altar, is a play on *alter,* a German word for an old man.[36] In "Get Away, Young Man," one of three songs commissioned for the film, Altar offers the advice of an experienced woman to a novice lover:

> A young man is full of adventure
> and eager to do what he can!
> He may be a boy
> But don't send a boy
> To do the work of a man.

But most significantly, Altar is a woman with a history.

The film begins with a close-up of Vern (Arthur Kennedy) kissing his fiancée—"There's nothing better than that to make a man feel agreeable," he says when they have ended their embrace. But his agreeable demeanor is shattered when his fiancée is raped and murdered. Setting out on the vengeance trail in pursuit of the murderer, Vern collects clues that suggest the man he is looking for is somehow connected to a singer called Altar Keane and a gambling game called Chuck-a-Luck. The first story he hears about Altar has her as a saloon girl: the storyteller recalls being the mount to her jockey in a race with other girls riding on the backs of cowboys. It is an image of high jinks and merry hell that recalls similar barroom scenes in *Destry.* The next character that Vern discovers with a memory of Altar is the aged and drink-sodden Dolly. She recalls how Altar had the world at her feet, riding in a barouche accompanied by a black maid and with men of wealth and good standing at her beck and call. "She was a glory girl in those days," Dolly remembers, but "she'd shut the door on a cattle baron if she had a fancy for a cowboy." In the next vignette, Altar appears in more straitened circumstances: in an echo of Lola Lola she is shown with a cigarette dangling from her lips while singing a mournful ballad. After she kicks a customer who has been pawing at her, the bar owner, who calls her Angel, gives her the sack: "you don't smile enough," he says. "I'm sick of smiling," she says in reply. Escorted out of the bar by Frenchy (Mel Ferrer), a gentleman outlaw from the Old South, he reminds her of three men that fought a duel over her—all died—and of the time she rode a white horse into a grand hotel. But now she lives in a hovel on a street lined with lousy brothels. Frenchy rescues her from this sewer and helps her to set up a hideout for outlaws called Chuck-a-Luck.

Other than Lang and Deitrich's reputations, what makes the film stand out from the hundreds of Westerns produced in the 1950s is its use of a nondiegetic singing narrator. William Lee sings the "Legend of Chuck-a-Luck," with its refrain of "hate, murder, and revenge," that was intended to provide narrative information not shown on the screen, but, in fact, it only reinforces what the viewer already knows. Nevertheless, beyond its novelty value, it does help confirm the idea that the film is concerned with myth and not history—that Vern, Altar, and Frenchy are archetypes drawn from folk ballads, rather than psychologically complex characters that belong to realist fictions.

The idea of the characters as archetypes is reinforced by the use of the ballad "Gypsy Davey" that Altar sings while smoking a cigarette. "Gypsy Davey" is credited to Ken Darby, but he is no more the author of this ballad than Frank Crumit was of "Frankie and Johnny." "Gypsy Davey," or as it is better known in the United States, "Black Jack David," was a sixteenth-century English ballad that was one of many examples of British folk song that survived in America and was anthologized by Francis Child, the father of American folk song collectors. The ballad was subsequently recorded by a number of pre–World War II hillbilly, old-time, and folk musicians.[37] The story told in "Gypsy Davey" has direct parallels with events in Altar Keane's life. Given the choice of a cosseted life of luxury or a game of chance with a cowboy, Altar has always chosen the latter, which is why she falls for Vern's "pretty talk." When she is introduced singing "Gypsy Davey," she is already well into the verses, but the essential meaning of the ballad is contained in the few lines we hear:

How could she leave her high-born Lord?
How could she leave her baby?
How could she leave her bed and board

> And elope with Gypsy Davey?
> Last night she slept in a goose-feather bed
> Along with her Lord and baby
> Tonight she sleeps . . .

She cuts the song off, but it would have continued: "tonight she sleeps on the cold, cold floor / Beside Gypsy Davey."

What spell has Gypsy Davey cast that could hold the girl in such thrall? What enchantment could make her leave her feather bed, her child, and her master? The belief that the supernatural explains her actions denies, of course, any agency on the girl's part and any recognition of her desires and lusts. The impression is, time and again, that as a woman the chanteuse is incomplete, that she needs a child and a man. In the stories that are told about her, Altar Keane always says "no" when what is expected of her is to say "yes." This gives an entirely different perspective on the lines in "Get Away, Young Man," which are reinforced by Dietrich's dialogue:

> A young man will come when you call him,
> And leave when you tell him to go.
> But someday he'll guess a woman means yes,
> Whenever a woman says no.

However masochistic her character, it does not diminish the rare image in Hollywood films of the period of a middle-aged woman with sexual desire and refusing to conform.

Though "punished" for her wrongdoing at the end of the film, Dietrich's character maintains her dignity while expressing her desires; self-esteem and respect were not traits allowed Claire Trevor's character in *Key Largo* (Warner Bros., 1948). Her portrayal of an aging, alcoholic gangster's moll suggested that the masochistic, emotionally damaged torch singer was a figure of the past. She was once a great singer, but time and drink have taken their toll. Sadistically toying with her, Johnny Rocco (Edward G. Robinson) promises her a drink, but she has to sing for it. She introduces herself: "My gowns were gorgeous, always low-cut—very *décolleté*. I wore hardly any make-up, just some lipstick, that's all . . . They'd play the intro in the dark, and the spot would come on and there I'd be." Unaccompanied, she gives a rendering of Libby Holman's signature song "Moanin' Low" that is both wretchedly grotesque and unbearably beautiful. The song signals her age: it is anachronistic, locating her personal history and performance style firmly in the past. Since the late 1930s, the persona adopted by white female singers had undergone something of a revolution. The new singers—Lee Wiley, Peggy Lee and Anita O'Day, for example—did not identify with the masochistic psychic suffering of the torch singer and instead projected an image of worldly independence and professionalism. Moreover, styled as "one of the boys" along with the band produced an image of femininity that was not readily susceptible to victimhood and that moved decisively away from the raw, unpolished mode of personal testimony that characterized the torch singer's emotional instabilities.[38] The Hollywood actor who best portrayed this character was Ida Lupino, whose box office appeal, according to *Variety,* depended upon her ability to exhibit a "portrait gallery of hard, warped women with a psychological edge . . . feverish, cunning, sexy."[39] Lupino played this type with notable aplomb in *The Man I Love* (Warner Bros., 1946) and *Road House* (Twentieth Century Fox, 1948).

Based on Maritta Wolff's 1942 novel *Night Shift, The Man I Love* was pitched as a platform for some of the best-known torch songs—the opening titles list Gershwin's "The Man I Love" and "Liza," Kern and Hammerstein's "Why Was I Born" and "Bill," Johnny Green's "Body and Soul," and Henry Creamer and Johnny Johnson's "If I Could Be with You"—but things are not like they used to be.[40] It is not the nightclub singer Petey Brown (Ida Lupino) who is suffering from psychic despair, but the man she loves, San Thomas (Bruce Bennett). After cutting some hot piano sides, San had been a big noise among the musicians and club-goers of New York's 52nd Street but, following his marriage to a rich society dame and subsequent divorce, had dropped out of the scene.

The film opens with a lush orchestral version of the title song played over the credit sequence and across a nighttime panoramic view of New York City. The orchestral version is faded down in the mix and replaced by a variation on the theme performed by a small jazz ensemble during an after-hours jam session at Club 39 on 52nd Street. Before an off-screen vocal is heard introducing Petey Brown, the band is seen in a series of close-ups of the soloists. The setup is informal but serious. After several solos, Petey cuts in—she is leaning on the piano, smoking and drinking while she sings. The song is about a woman's longing for the perfect partner who will provide her with a home for two, from which she'd never roam—"who would, would you?" Jazz critic Otis Ferguson described the tune as having a "strange running sadness," which is precisely how it is sung here.[41] Petey sings "The Man I Love" as if she has lived it, but afterwards when asked what has happened to her boyfriend George she shows

Ida Lupino and Robert Alda in *The Man I Love* (author's collection)

a different side: "what a pill he turned out to be—stole my only watch." You mustn't worry about him, she is told. Her response is hard-bitten, but without cynicism or false sentiment: "I've never worried about a guy in my life."[42]

Petey's family lives on the West Coast: two sisters and a brother who share an apartment. The eldest of the two sisters, Sally, is married to a serviceman hospitalized with shell shock with whom she has a young son. Brother Joey lacks parental guidance and is working as a gopher for club owner Nick Toresca. Their kid sister is shy Virginia who has a harmless crush on her neighbor Johnny who is married to Gloria, a gadabout with baby twins. Toresca is a notorious womanizer and is attempting to woo Sally, who shows no interest in him. When she returns home for Christmas, Petey takes things in hand and turns Toresca's attention away from Sally and onto herself. She gets a spot singing at Toresca's club, and he and she appear to be something of an item. Following two chance encounters with a tall handsome man on New Year's Eve, it is clear that neither Petey nor Toresca feel much for each other. The stranger turns out to be San Thomas, who still carries a torch for his ex-wife and has given up music to become a sailor in the merchant marine. On the verge of making love to each other, he tells Petey that, if she falls for him, she'll end up singing the blues. Ten days of loving bliss follow, but it seems the memory of San's ex-wife still won't go. "Stick with me in my gutter," Petey tells him, but he decides he is better off looking up at the stars and standing in mud of his own making. He, not Petey, sings the blues, signing on for another tour as a sailor.

At the film's close, Petey sees San embark; maybe they will get together when he returns, but it is not certain. She turns away from his ship and walks towards the camera. Raising her head, she wipes away a tear, puts a smile on her face and a kick in her stride, and walks purposefully out of the frame. Earlier she had knocked a pistol out of Johnny's hand and slapped him hard when he was gunning for Toresca, who had seduced his wife and was indirectly responsible for her death. Petey took charge of the situation, just as she had taken care of her sisters' and brother's problems. Partly thanks to Petey, Sally's husband has left the veteran's hospital and is back home. His return marks a restoration of patriarchal order at the apartment, but Petey had never moved into the domestic confines of "home." Living and working elsewhere on terms she determined, neither Nick Toresca, San Thomas, nor the return of Sally's husband seriously challenge her self-imposed autonomy.

Though Petey is introduced as the torch singer, it is not her renditions of the title song or "Why Was I Born" that registers a soul in torment with the audience. Rather, it is San's emotive piano workouts on "The Man I Love" and "Body and Soul" that suggest psychic disorder. The hard-boiled torch singer and the damaged, vulnerable male was a theme used again in *I Walk Alone* (Paramount, 1947).[43] Nightclub singer Kay (Lizabeth Scott) tells Frankie (Burt Lancaster), "we've had fun, let's let it go at that. I've been singing around this town for six years. In that time I've learned more than just how to put a song over. I've learned to play every kind of angle there is, except, maybe, the right one." Because of the final note she attaches to the end of her little speech, he accuses her of being sentimental. "Perhaps I've sung too many torch songs," she replies. Later she sings "Don't Call It Love," and when a customer requests "I Lost My Man," she tells her she doesn't know the words. "You should learn them," the customer replies. Kay never does. What makes her interesting and attractive to the men in the film and as a character is that, like Petey, she is no man's plaything. She will not be hurt or conform to a masculine ideal of masochistic femininity.

Kay thinks she is in love with Noll Turner (Kirk Douglas), who owns the club she sings in, but he is also seeing divorcée Mrs. Richardson, whom he intends to marry in order to ensure that she continues to bring high-class patronage to his club. Queried about Kay, Mrs. Richardson tells her companion that "every man has a girl who sings someplace in his life." Kay won't play that role, which is why she drops Turner and is in turn attracted to Frankie—"I've been waiting just once to meet a man who will tell me the truth." Frankie and Kay share an understanding that all new songs sound alike. Frankie tells her, "for a song to stick you've got to be with a girl while the music's playing. Yeah, the old songs really stick." The "old songs" are Richard Rodgers and Lorenz Hart's "Isn't It Romantic" and Frank Loesser and Hoagy Carmichael's "Heart and Soul," sentimental titles that suggest purity in the devotion shared by the songs' lovers. Kay sings neither of these tunes in her show.

A year after she appeared in *The Man I Love,* Lupino reprised the role of a singer in *Road House.* Hired as the in-house entertainment at the ultra-modern bowling alley and night club Jefty's Road House, Lily Stevens (Lupino) is a hit with the customers, turning in nicotine and whisky-soaked renderings of Johnny Mercer and Harold Arlen's "One For My Baby (And One More for the Road)," "Again," written for the movie by Dorcas Cochran and Lionel Newman, and "The Right Kind" by Don George, Charles Henderson, and Lionel Newman. Other than her husky-voiced singing and her barrelhouse piano accompaniment, what makes her particularly appealing to club customers and management alike is her insouciant attitude to both her performance and her life. A female customer asks her boyfriend what the singer has apart from the gravel in her voice. He tells her, "she reminds me of the first woman that ever slapped my face." For Jefty (Richard Widmark), the club's indolent owner, she is the best thing he has ever seen—"she does more without a voice than anyone I ever heard"—for the club's manager Pete Morgan (Cornel Wilde), she's just the "new equipment" that Jefty has brought with him from Chicago.

All men are boys to Lily, until, perversely, Pete's indifference and coldness toward her makes him increasingly attractive. Lily's desire for Pete is also abetted by the competition provided by Sally, the club's cashier, for his attentions. By the time Lily has broken through Pete's emotional armor, Jefty has completely fallen for Lily. But like Sally's love for Pete, Jefty's desire for Lily is unrequited, and when Jefty discovers that Lily and Pete are lovers he becomes psychotically disturbed. Significantly, neither of Lupino's characters nor Lizabeth Scott's singer in *I Walk Alone* have children, nor do they show any maternal instincts. The absence of any familial distraction in these films seems to ensure that the tortured body and soul belongs not to the torch singer but to the male who holds her flame. The autonomous self-defining singer, as played by Lupino and Scott, did not simply replace the figure of the emotionally damaged torch singer, but she did suggest that Hollywood fictions could allow for a broader spectrum in their representation of (white) femininity.

While rejecting the image of victim, the hard-boiled nightclub singer maintained the low cultural caste that stigmatized female performers, a social status underpinned by the racial inflections produced by singing the blues. As cultural historian Linda Mizejewski has shown in her study of the Ziegfeld girl, racialized productions were central to twentieth-century theatrical female performance styles: "The circulated images of white women were dependent for their value on the presence and performance of other racial and ethnic identities. Beginning in the 1890s, the desirable African American female body 'on show' in a parallel theatrical venue heightened the stakes of the upscale chorus girl's whiteness and in one sense necessitated the rhetoric of the Glorified American Girl."[44] The invoking of blackness in others guaranteed an idealized whiteness displayed by the Ziegfeld girls. The performance of cross-racial dressing, shows that featured the girls as "dusky belles," or African American choruses featuring light-skinned dancers "offered to white audiences the thrill of a forbidden sexuality; the display of their light skin exposed miscegenation, cross-racial desire."[45] Yet as the discourse of racial hybridity was heightened in these performances, it was mitigated by the effect of fully "demarcating an authentic [white] body from its more threatening others."[46] In the same manner that the torch singer offered a more acceptable image of femininity against the excessively vulgar performances of the coon shouter, the nightclub singer as personified by Lupino in her roles in *The Man I Love* and *Road House* found her counterpart in the black jazz singers of the period.

The Murder Men (MGM, 1962) was originally aired as an episode of the television crime series *Cain's Hundred* (1961–62) called "Blues for a Junkman," which with additional material was given a theatrical release. Dorothy Dandridge plays Norma Sherman, a jazz singer addicted to heroin. The film version opens with Norma giving a particularly heartfelt performance of "The Man I Love." As she brings the song to a tremulous halt, a voice-over explains that this is "Norma Sherman, famous American jazz singer—like too many jazz artists addicted to narcotics and by current American law, a criminal." After spending two years in prison, she is released into the protection of Nick Cain (Mark Richman), who is presently involved in organizing a major narcotics investigation. She has her freedom, but things are far from easy. Her trumpet-playing husband has left her for another singer, and she is not able to return to her old gig at Club Troy because, as a former junky with a close relationship with Nick Cain, she would bring unnecessary police attention to the activities of club owner Arthur Troy (James Coburn), a mob stooge involved in prostitution, the jukebox racket, and a drug-running ring.

Norma Sherman's character is slightly drawn; her relationship with her husband hardly exists outside of the time they spend together on stage. Her drug addiction is explained by the irregular hours led by musicians and the easy graduation from smoking marijuana to the intravenous use of heroin. Yet, because the character corresponds so closely to earlier Hollywood portrayals of emotionally damaged singers, Norma evokes an aura of authenticity by drawing upon the tragic figure of Billie Holiday, who died a drug addict in 1959. The "authenticity" of the characterization is further enhanced by the fact that she is played by the light-skinned black actor Dorothy Dandridge (star of Twentieth Century Fox's 1954 production of *Carmen Jones*) who would also die in 1964 from drug addiction.[47] Norma's particularly abject lifestyle and lack of control over the vicissitudes of love place her in the same category of torch singers played by Helen Morgan. Yet what differentiates Norma from Morgan's characters is that she has never risen above the downbeat and lowlife; her world has always been only one step away from the gutter.

The film's end credits roll over an illustration that evokes the paperback cover of a contemporary pulp novel. In the middle-ground, the singer is shown lying on a bed; with an iron bedstead in the foreground and a vanity chest mirror in the background reflecting an image of a generic American urban skyline, the result is that Norma is held between the long vertical bars of the bedstead and the reflected city. This image is not drawn from the iconography of the torch singer, but from the directory of B-girls, burlesque dancers, and strippers who populated the abandoned city of the late 1940s and 1950s and who, like Norma Sherman, suggest a tragic compact of hurt and degradation that pulp wisdom would describe as a world of "hot dames on cold slabs."

5

The City Stripped Bare: Burlesque and the Postwar Urban Underworld

I went down to the St. James Infirmary
Saw my baby there
Stretched out on a long white table
So sweet . . . so cold . . . so fair
—"St. James Infirmary"

The backdrop of the Depression that underpinned so many of the narratives about torch singers brought with it a politicization of certain genres of popular music, most notably folk and jazz.[1] Young, politically conscious performers and fans sought to establish an overt link between musical forms and social groups economically and racially ostracized from the American mainstream. The communion between fans and performers of what became known as hot jazz was part of a process of politicizing popular music that functioned as a rebuke to official culture and a recognition, however slight, of black music's true provenance. Some Hollywood films—*Blues in the Night* (Warner Bros., 1941), *Crossfire* (RKO, 1947), and *Body and Soul* (Enterprise Productions, 1947), for example—helped encourage the shifting perspective on what black music signified to white audiences. Not coincidentally, these films had significant input from filmmakers who identified with the politics of the Popular Front.

Though a spent force in the postwar years, the Popular Front, neverthe-less, kept a hold on the imaginations of many artists and creative workers who came to a political maturity during the 1930s. Their critical vision of contemporary society, allied to postwar demographic shifts—black migra-tion to urban centers and white, middle-class flight to the suburbs—en-gendered a bleak and pessimistic view of America's cities. Urban spaces in the years following World War II were overwhelmingly represented as inhospitable, populated by life's misfits and the riffraff of America's underclass. With a sound track of sleazy jazz as an aural backdrop, the nocturnal streets of the cities were ideally represented in these films by the figure of the burlesque dancer who symbolized a dead or decaying culture. America's gutter music found fertile ground in this milieu to continue its play with race, gender, and class.

Blues in the Night was based on Edwin Gilbert's play *Hot Nocturne,* which was retitled *New Orleans Blues* and then changed to *Blues in the Night* to capitalize on the popular success of Johnny Mercer and Harold Arlen's tune. Following a fracas in the St. Louis Café, a joint that promises in neon "Hot Jazz, Hot Food, Hot Drinks," hot jazz piano player Jigger Pine (Richard Whorf) and his friends are jailed. Looking through the bars at the city outside, Jigger nonchalantly comments, "St. Louis from a jail window." "Yeah," replies his tubercular sidekick Peppi, played by former Dead End Kid Billy Holga, "we've seen a lot of towns in this country from jail windows, ain't we, Jigger?" The claim to having had more than just a passing acquaintance with three walls of stone and a fourth of steel bars is a bid for authenticity by these white musicians, an assertion of being "in the world" with "the people," a testimony to having had "real" experi-ence of hard times and hard luck. It is also a declaration of intent: with an evangelist preacher's passion, Jigger describes the kind of music he has dreamed of playing and the type of band he wants:

> It's got to be *our* kind of music, *our* kind of band. The song's we've heard
> that have been knocking around this country, real blues, the kind that
> comes out of real people. Their hopes and their dreams, what they've
> got and what they want. The whole USA in one chorus. And that band
> ain't just guys blowin' and poundin' and scrapin'. It's five guys—no
> more—who feel, play, live, and even think the same way. That ain't a
> band it's a unit. It's one guy multiplied five times. It's a unit that breathes
> in the same beat. It's got a kick all its own and a style that's their own
> and nobody else's. It's like a hand in a glove, five fingers, each that fits
> slick and quick.

Written by Communist Party member Robert Rossen, Jigger's speech rehearses Popular Front rhetoric of the period. The linking of music and music making with class struggle, and its potential to function as cultural cement between the disparate citizens of the United States is the film's underlying theme. Yet the film falls far short of achieving this admirable aim.[2]

Following Jigger's speech, an overexcited Peppi tells him, "Maybe right here in this jail the dream you've got is born." A coughing fit causes Peppi to collapse; a doctor is called for, which attracts the attention of a black prisoner in a nearby jail cell. The prisoner's inquiry about Peppi's health and whether he has got the "miseries" stirs a fellow black inmate into song. The scenario reinforces the, apparently, mandatory need in American films to have at least one black prisoner in jailhouse sequences and, if at all possible, have him provide a momentary musical distraction. The cliché becomes noteworthy in the Warner Bros. 1936 program filler *Road Gang* when a white prisoner comments on the black prisoners heard singing "Swanee" and "Swing Low Sweet Chariot": "Those darkies always find something to sing about."[3] (One-time Communist and Popular Front sympathizer Dalton Trumbo wrote *Road Gang*.) The St. Louis jailhouse inmates have nothing more specific to sing about than, as Jigger defines it, "The real miseries." "You could beat that out, couldn't you, Jigger?" says a recovering Peppi about the jailhouse blues they have just heard. "We all could," says another member of Jigger's putative band. "We all will," says Jigger. "Boys, that's the blues, the real New Orleans blues." The imagery in the song "Blues in the Night," which the jailhouse minstrel has been singing, shifts from warnings a mother gives her young son about the dangers of sweet-talking, two-faced women to images of escape and the clickety clack of train wheels humming from Memphis to Mobile. The song continues over a montage (one of three produced for the film by Don Siegel) of stock footage of black cotton-pickers and laborers carrying cotton bales, levee workers eating and toting watermelons, and paddle steamers navigating the Mississippi, intercut with maps suggesting a journey south towards New Orleans. The image that heralds the end of the montage and that confirms the music's roots as having come from New Orleans is a close-up of the bell end of a trumpet out of which pours high blue notes. But despite the image of the anonymous black jailhouse singer and the montage of black laborers, the source of the music is not black but issues instead from the embouchure of white New Orleans horn player Leo Powell (Jack Carson). As film and jazz scholar Krin Gabbard has noted, this is just one among many examples of Hollywood's jazz-centered entertainments that acknowledged the black origin of jazz only to disavow black control over the music through white musicians ability to transform "folk" material into art.[4]

By the movie's end, Jigger has translated and refined the jailhouse monody he heard—"Blues in the Night"—into a quasi-classical piano piece. The racial crossings and sleights of hand that are needed in order to achieve this image are myriad. White songwriters Mercer and Arlen's "Blues in the Night" was definitely not born in a jailhouse, and its kindred relation to a black vernacular cleaves closer to blackface minstrelsy than to the ballads of Huddie Ledbetter, but it nevertheless signifies blackness. Similarly, Jigger's name—one consonant away from "nigger"—signifies blackness, and special attention must be paid to Leo Powell's trumpet solos. These can best anything a black musician has to offer, so we are shown (Leo playing up against Jimmie Lunceford's band) and told ("We ran them clear out of the hall. Leo's hot licks had them [Harlem jazz musicians] turning in fire alarms"). This assertion is made even though the solos were ghosted by the black horn player Snooky Young, confirming Gabbard's observation that Hollywood's representation of jazz musicians will always disavow the music's black provenance. When jazz and film critic for *The New Republic* Otis Ferguson wrote about the "native true spirit" of American music, its proponents could be either black or white, but when he discussed music as belonging to a people, it was inevitably black music and black people: "There is a gay abandon and all that, up the one and only Lenox Avenue [Harlem]; there are lights and people carrying on and whatnot. To be sure. And that is about half of it. It is out of the lives of the people here that the music comes, and so if you will stand here you may suddenly feel it, the whole of it with undertones and overtones, its abandon and bitter sorrow."[5] Only in the context of a jailhouse is recognition of this facet of black American life and culture given in *Blues in the Night*. The musical art of "the people" celebrated in the film is simple, uncomplicated, and direct, but in reality the white expropriation of black culture is never lacking in ambivalence—the shared cultural pool is never fed by pure naturally filtered spring water but is always polluted and muddy.

Jigger's jailhouse sojourn is a holiday compared to his experience after he quits the band and has given his heart to sweet-talking, two-faced Kay Grant (Betty Field). His punishment is to end up as the monkey to the organ grinder Guy Heiser, who fronts a big band in white tuxedos, playing pop pap and featuring teeth grindingly awful novelty acts. Heiser's band represents a hollow, shallow, commodified, white, and feminized American culture. As a featured pianist in a band that shares similarities with the sugary pop confections produced by the likes of Rudy Vallee and His Connecticut Yankees, Paul Specht and His Orchestra, and particularly Kay Kyser and His Orchestra (who Guy Heiser's band so obviously parodies), Jigger's defection is musically akin to class betrayal.[6] At the beginning of the film, he hit a customer who requested "I'm Forever Blowing Bubbles." The joint's manager told Jigger, the "customer is always right, even if he spits in your face," so Jigger hit the manager as well. The customer is not always right, as the artist knows. But Jigger has now given up the fight and sold out to the customer and commerce. As a traitor to his art and to the people, Jigger must atone for his sins by wandering from bar to bar in an alcoholic haze. When he rejoins the band, he has a nervous breakdown. His dreams mirror his life: they begin with him creating a people's music, which he abandons for the love of a wanton woman, who then nightmarishly assumes the role of every musician in Heiser's band. Jigger, however, soon recovers and is back among the people playing his "Blues in the Night" concerto at the Jungle, a New Jersey roadhouse and gambling joint.

The Jungle's audience of "kids" rhapsodically listens to Jigger's masterpiece and then dances with exhilaration when the band accompanies him in a boogie-woogie arrangement. The easy shift the audience makes between aesthetic appreciation and the physicality of dancing suggest that Jigger and his band have found a means of uniting high and low culture, premodern and modern, folk with commercial music, and black with white without sacrificing authenticity or their vision of a people's music. The film ends, à la Woody Guthrie, with the band riding the rails, traveling in a boxcar, taking their music to the people: "Their music beats against the clatter of the wheels as they set forth again, playing the blues."[7]

It is a shame that Otis Ferguson never published his opinion on the film, but it is safe to assume that he would have ridiculed its racial confidence tricks, laughed at its political naiveté, and considered its exploitation of the vogue for hot jazz among the left-leaning youth of the period as equally comical.[8] The ardent male jazz fan is represented in the film by fast-talking, mother-loving, ethnically distinct Nickie Haroyan, played by Elia Kazan in his most ingratiating manner: "I'm a student of jazz." He announces at one point, "I know the anatomy of swing, not only musically but theoretically. I've read everything from *Le Jazz Hot* [Frenchman

Hugues Panassié's groundbreaking study published in 1934] and *Down Beat* [the period's preeminent jazz journal]." He is such a parody of an impassioned young fan that real aficionados of hot jazz who viewed this film must have wanted to bust him in the jaw.

Blues in the Night is easy to dismiss as just another film exploitation of the latest musical craze, which, courtesy of Rossen and Kazan, has a hint of radical politics hanging off its shirttails. Less easily dismissed is the postwar, socially conscious movie *Crossfire,* which used hot jazz in a much more subtle and politically radical manner. One of the most closely analyzed of Hollywood's immediate postwar productions, *Crossfire* has a "test case" status in debates on film genre—is it a male melodrama, film noir, murder mystery, or social problem film?[9] Because the story concerns the murder of a Jew (in the source novel the victim was a homosexual), the film also has a notable place in debates over Hollywood's representation of religious, sexual, and racial prejudice.[10] Its status as an example of radical filmmaking in the conservative environment of Hollywood, and the filmmakers' subsequent blacklisting during the Communist witch hunts, have all assured a continued interest in the film.[11] What interests me, though, is one of the ways in which it signaled its political radicalism to a sympathetic contemporary audience.

As film scholar James Naremore notes at the beginning of his superb analysis of the film, generic hybridity and the story's potential for political consciousness raising were part of the appeal of Richard Brooks's novel *The Brick Foxhole* (1945) for the film's producer Adrian Scott, its director Edward Dmytryk, and screen writer John Paxton. All, as Naremore notes, were "strongly identified with *tendenz* films (*Tender Comrade* and *Till the End of Time*), and they had recently achieved major box-office success with a pair of antifascist, hard-boiled thrillers starring Dick Powell (*Murder, My Sweet* and *Cornered*). *The Brick Foxhole* presented an opportunity to combine the two styles."[12] The adaptation of Brooks's novel is centered on a police investigation into the murder of Joseph Samuels (Sam Levene), a Jew. Samuels was murdered by the bigot Monty Montgomery (Robert Ryan); the chief suspect, however, is a fellow soldier, Mitchell (George Cooper). Mitchell does not have an alibi, or at least one that can be confirmed. He met Samuels in a bar and accepted an invitation to continue their conversation back at his apartment. After leaving Samuels, Mitchell had wandered around the city streets and bars before meeting B-girl Ginny (Gloria Grahame), who he befriends, and he spends the rest of the night at her apartment. Discovering that he is suspected of Samuels' murder, he contacts his buddy Keely (Robert Mitchum), who leads the police away from Mitchell and towards Montgomery.

In Brooks's novel, the murder victim was Mr. Edwards, an interior decorator and homosexual. Changing the character to a war veteran and a Jew was imposed by the Production Code Administration, but the specifics of what particular burden of representation the victim was made to carry were apparently not important. Film historian Saverio Giovacchini writes:

> According to the inclusive, but not assertive, notion of "people" shared by Cultural Fronters Scott and Dmytryk, gender, ethnic, and racial differences were "interchangeable." "In the book [the soldier] murders a fairy," Scott wrote to RKO producers William Dozier and Charles Kormer. "He could have murdered a Negro, a foreigner, or a Jew. It would have been the same thing." Remaining substantially faithful to their 1930s notion of the "people," Scott, Dmytryk, and Paxton focused on a definition that was inclusive, rather than one that articulated gender, sexual, or ethnic difference.[13]

The interchangeability of the subject of Montgomery's prejudice was certainly shared by Brooks. In the novel Montgomery is described as "strongly American. Frenchmen were Frogs, Negroes, niggers; Poles, Polacks; Italians, wops; Chinese, Chinks; Jews, Christ-killers."[14]

To avoid potential objections from censors, Naremore notes that the producer and scriptwriter removed all "references to homosexuality."[15] But, as he also writes:

> even when *Crossfire* does exactly what the Breen Office and the studio wanted, it enables us to "see" (in Christian Metz's sense) many of the things that censorship was trying to repress. Notice, for example, how it conveys something of the forbidden homosexual content of Richard Brooks's novel even when it works hard to assure us that Samuels, the murder victim, is heterosexual . . . though Samuels appears motivated by nothing more than decency and concern for a veteran, and even though we are told that he and Mitchell talk mostly about baseball, the scene has sexual ambiguity. The effect is heightened because of the Socratic intensity of the conversation, because the actor playing Mitchell is boyishly handsome, and because the bizarre setting creates psychological tension. The city streets, bars, and hotel lobbies are surreally crowded with uniformed men, and Dmytryk's *misé-en-scéne* occasionally resembles an expressionist, militarized locker room. In this

place, as one character remarks, "the snakes are loose," and nobody seems purely innocent.[16]

The impression of sexual ambiguity that circulates around the figure of Samuels is also aided by the playing of big band records in his apartment for his and Mitchell's mutual pleasure. Men do not play phonograph records for other men in Hollywood films of this period, not unless the filmmakers implicitly want their audience to question the characters' sexuality. In the equivalent sequence in the novel, Mitchell is also in the company of two other soldiers, all equally inebriated, when Mr. Edwards, frustrated by the constant interruption of commercials, turns off the radio and begins to play his favorite phonograph records: "for the last two hours the phonograph had been grinding. The complete score from the stage hit 'Oklahoma,' had been played. Eddie had also brought forward a favorite of his, Hildegarde singing 'Leave Us Face It.' Floyd couldn't see what was good about Hildegarde's singing. He thought her English was bad. The first trouble started when Eddie played a recording by a well-known Negro singer."[17] Big band music may not be such an overt signifier of homosexuality as phonograph records of show tunes and a popular soprano jockeyed by an interior decorator, but regardless of the musical genre, the phonograph's primary role in scenes of feminine seduction adds immeasurably to *Crossfire*'s sexual charge.

Within the context of *Crossfire* or *Blues in the Night,* big band pop is conceived as feminine. After he deserts his hot jazz band and joins Guy Heiser's orchestra, Jigger, it is suggested, is symbolically emasculated in both his private and professional being. During his nervous breakdown, the feminized vision he has of the orchestra with Kay assuming all the roles is matched later by the image of him playing the piano with Kay on his left and Character (Priscilla Lane), the band's vocalist and mother figure, on his right. As the two women vie for his very soul, Jigger's piano keys turn into glutinous elasticated slime. Only the homosocial bonds of the band can assure the return of stiff piano keys and a firm right hand. In *Blues in the Night*, hot jazz is defined against the inauthenticity and femininity of big band pop. Similarly, in *The Fabulous Dorseys* (United Artists, 1947) brothers and band leaders Jimmy and Tommy Dorsey, after playing a gig with their big band, relax by going to hear, and jam with, a "real musician," the black pianist Art Tatum who is playing in a small club. This is the background against which it is possible to better recognize the aura of homosexuality, domesticity, and femininity suggested by Samuels' phonograph records in *Crossfire*. It is an aura confirmed by its opposite—hot jazz, an authentic, heterosexual, public, and masculine music that pours out of the city's bars and clubs, and out into the streets.

Roy Webb produced the musical score for *Crossfire,* but Kid Ory's band performed the hot jazz tunes "Muskrat Ramble" and "Shine." Like Jelly Roll Morton, Louis Armstrong, and King Oliver, Ory was a New Orleans original, a pioneer disseminator of jazz, but for much of the 1930s he had given up professional music making, due in part to changes in musical fashion and the effects of the Depression, and had taken to raising chickens in California. By the mid-1940s, he had returned to playing professionally and was making regular appearances on radio shows with Orson Welles as compère. His change of musical fortune was the result of a West Coast revival of Dixieland-style jazz, led by white musicians Lu Watters and Turk Murphy and supported by the growing membership of the United Hot Clubs of America.[18]

The United Hot Clubs of America were an idea initiated by New Yorker Milt Gabler, jazz fan and record collector, who ran his own music shop and later label, Commodore Records (founded in 1938). The idea was that groups of like-minded fans would organize places and people to promote and listen to hot jazz. He had borrowed the idea from Europe where Hot Clubs in Germany and France catered to fans of American jazz, and, in particular, he was responding to the enthusiasm of Hugues Panassié, who, on his first visit to America in 1938, sought out an older generation of American jazz musicians to make phonograph records for the fan market in Europe. The now instantly recognizable figure of the dedicated young male record collector whose interest is served and fed by equally dedicated independent phonograph record producers is rooted in the Hot Clubs of Europe and America. These young fans, some of whom would go on to positions of incredible influence in the American music industry—John Hammond at Columbia, Milt Gabler, first with Commodore, later at Decca, Alfred Lion with Blue Note, and Ahmet Ertegun with Atlantic Records—played an equally important role in the regendering of record consumption.[19] By emphasizing connoisseurship of arcane discographical information alongside the acquisition of historical and biographical data concerned with the production of the music and its major exponents, and the promotion of select phonograph records as artistically valid documentation of a particular musical style (rather than a distracting three minutes of recorded music for dancing to, or making love to), members of the hot jazz clubs produced a nonfeminine space for the consumption of phonograph records. New York journalist Joseph Mitchell suggested just such a gendering when in 1938 he linked boxing with his collecting of Bessie Smith phonograph recordings: "I had a bet on Joe Louis to win in the first round. I bet $1.50, and won $16 but it will not do me any good, because when Arthur Donovan counted ten I jumped up and knocked a table-lamp to the floor in my home and kicked over a cabinet in which I had a collection of Bessie Smith records, any one of which was worth $16, now that Bessie is dead and gone."[20] When *Crossfire*'s filmmakers chose to feature the music of Ory, they were consciously drawing upon the image of authenticity this music had gained through its promotion by young white male jazz fans. The assertion that Ory's jazz was a true representation of an urban American folk music, unsullied by cheap, superficial, and feminized commercial imperatives, also supported the left-leaning ideological concerns of the Hot Club membership. In his monumental study of the Popular Front, Michael Denning notes that the most influential writers on jazz were associated with left-wing politics, "including Ralph Ellison, John Hammond, Otis Ferguson, Charles Edward Smith [who in 1936 published an article in *Esquire* magazine called 'Collecting Hot'],[21] Fredric Ramsey, and R. D. Darrell, not to mention such key European leftists as André Hodeir, Joachim Berendt (who debated with Adorno), and Eric Hobsbawm. Indeed, the most important early study of jazz, *Jazz: A People's Music* (1948), was written by a Popular Front critic, Sidney Finkelstein."[22] Denning is at pains to point out that the subtitle of Finkelstein's book did not imply it was just another "work of folk sentimentality or romantic authenticity"; instead it was a work that criticized earlier primitivist and nostalgic views of jazz, which is the whole cloth that Jigger and Nickie Haroyan in *Blues in the Night* are cut from.[23] It should also be noted that the founder of the West Coast's premier revivalist label Good Time Jazz was blacklisted filmmaker Lester Koenig, who had worked with William Wyler and was for a time employed by Paramount.[24] For *Crossfire*'s filmmakers, Ory's revivalist music (he recorded more sides for Good Time Jazz than for any other label) signified both a people's music and an aural confirmation of their progressive political beliefs.

The expression of progressive political beliefs was also an explicit theme with the cycles of boxing movies—*Champion* (United Artists, 1949), *Set-Up* (RKO, 1949), *Iron Man* (Universal, 1951), *The Ring* (King Brothers, 1952), *Flesh and Fury* (Universal, 1952), *Glory Alley* (MGM, 1952), *Square Jungle* (Universal, 1955), *Somebody Up There Likes Me* (MGM, 1956), and *The Harder They Fall* (Columbia, 1956)—that followed the box office and critical success of *Body and Soul*. A critic for the *National Board of Review* wrote: "Here are the gin and tinsel, squalor and sables of the depression era, less daring than when first revealed in *Dead End* or *Golden Boy* but more valid and mature because shown without sentiment or blur." Paul Buhle and Dave Wagner, historians of Hollywood's blacklist, argue that even though *Body and Soul* first appeared in 1947, it "could be described as the last film of the 1930s," the "culmination of the Depression generation's struggle to emancipate American dramatic art from the film corporation's control."[25] Indeed, the film does not make a single reference to the war, but neither is it wholly tied to a prewar sensibility. On its initial release, reviewers tended not to emphasize its links to the Depression era but instead highlighted its opportune subject matter.

The Hollywood Reporter headlined its review of *Body and Soul* "Fight Yarn Gets Rugged Treatment" and followed up with "Enterprise steps out, with a walloping fight film, exposing the vicious rackets still being worked behind the scenes of the boxing game by unscrupulous promoters and greedy managers who allow their boys to fight themselves to death. With newspapers splashing these stories all over their pages, the subject is plenty timely and also box office."[26] *Variety* (Weekly) concurred, with the *Reporter* calling the film as "Timely as today's headlines."[27] The daily edition of *Variety* filled in some of the detail concerning its timeliness: "Topical yarn obviously designed to take advantage of the recent New York inquiry into 'sports fixing,' with an emphasis on some of the crookedness manifested in professional boxing, *Body and Soul* has a somewhat familiar title and a likewise familiar narrative. It's the telling, however, that's different and that's what will sell the film."[28] The trade press reviews that link the film's temporal location to a contemporary concern with corruption in the fight game are not in contradiction with the other reviews and later critiques that stress a continuity with the concerns of the 1930s. The subject of boxing allows for both versions, facilitating an allegorical reception of the film as an individual's and a community's struggle with the vicissitudes of capitalism and more simply as a melodramatic realization of the world of pugilism. Whichever version of the theme is accepted, the shadow cast by the Depression was not easily banished in the postwar years. As the artist and film critic Manny Farber said, "I'm not someone who ever survived the Depression. It's not the sort of experience you ever really get over."[29]

Enterprise's *Body and Soul* (1947) provided a more structurally resonant image of "the people" than the cartoonish *Blues in the Night* or the "realism" of *Crossfire*. It achieved this by wedding the generic story of "ghetto boy makes good" with the musical refrain of Johnny Green's torch song "Body and Soul." The film is the story of a poor Jewish New York boxer who throws aside friends, family, and lovers in his obsessive drive to succeed; it was John Garfield's first post–Warner Bros. production. With his producer Bob Roberts, Garfield assembled a number of Hollywood's preeminent left-wing filmmakers, notably director Robert Rossen and scriptwriter Abraham Polonsky. Paul Buhle and Dave Wagner, Polonsky's biographers, describe *Body and Soul,* and the writer's directorial debut *Force of Evil,* as embodying "the highest achievement of the American Left in cinema before the onset of repression," echoing the historian of the blacklist Thom Andersen's comment that these were the first (only?) American films to "implicate the entire system of capitalism in their criticisms."[30]

Much critical debate on *Body and Soul* has centered on the film's ending: Charley Davis (Garfield) has been told by the racketeers, who think they own him body and soul, that he must throw his defense of the title. Charley and the mob's money is bet, against the odds, on him losing, but the little people, as Charley's old neighborhood grocer Shimen explains to the boxer, are backing him. As Charley leaves the ring after winning the fight, he tells the racketeer: "What are you going to do, kill me? Everybody dies." It is a moment of redemption that affirms an abiding union between Charley, his friends, family, and neighbors that extends beyond the working class to include a socially committed intelligentsia (represented by Charley's girlfriend, Peg, a bohemian and commercial artist). The director's original choice had been to show Davis at the end of the film with his head in a garbage can, shot and killed for betraying the racketeers, but as Polonsky successfully argued, it would be "crazy" to kill the proletariat.[31] The film ends with Davis and Peg, arm in arm, back in the old neighborhood, which, as a prerelease synopsis for the film confirms, finds him "at peace with himself" and among "his people, his friends."[32] As the end credits roll over the image of Peg and Charley, the film's theme tune wells up on the sound track—ownership of Charley's body and soul has been passed back to the people, where, in Polonsky's terms, "the moral authority is."[33]

Decades later Polonsky described the film as a "fairy tale, a myth of the streets of New York," even "a parable." But it was the idea that the film owed something to "musical structures," and in particular "the structure of a fugue" that is his most illuminating comment on the film's conformity to generic types. A fugue is a polyphonic composition in which a

153

repeated melodic subject is first established and then developed so that the many parts form a whole. This is not only true of the film's structuring theme of the struggle for ownership over the boxer's body and soul, but is also the case with the film's sound track, which returns to a musical theme provided by the popular song "Body and Soul" as a way of underpinning Charley's family's, friends', and Peg's claim on him that counterpoints the racketeers' corrosive influence.

Composer Johnny Green wrote the song for torch singer Libby Holman, who performed it first in a 1930 Broadway revue. Three lyricists made contributions to the song's theme of unrequited love—"Your heart must be like stone / to leave me all alone / When you could make my life worth living / By simply taking what I'm giving"—though they really brought nothing special to Green's achingly beautiful melody beyond the then taboo in popular song of stressing physical love as equal in importance to spiritual love—body *and* soul. The physical is amplified in the sense of longing and desperation that torch singers of the caliber of Holman, Helen Morgan, and Ruth Etting could deliver through the song. But the lyrical suggestion of giving one's self freely to another is clearly key to Charley's mother's and Peg's relationship with him:

> My heart is sad and lonely,
> For you I sigh, for you dear, only.
> Why haven't you seen it?
> I'm all for you, body and soul.
> I spend my days in longing
> And wond'ring why it's me you're wronging
> I tell you I mean it,
> I'm all for you, body and soul.

This is why the song is only played during the course of the narrative when Peg is on screen.

Nobody sings the song—it only ever appears as an extra-diegetic instrumental motif on the sound track—but as with "Frankie and Johnny" or "St. Louis Blues," the film's producers could rely on audience recognition to put the intended meaning across. Apart from Hoagy Carmichael's "Stardust," no song was more alive in the popular consciousness of the 1930s than "Body and Soul." New York journalist Joseph Mitchell implied as much when he described a trip he made as a member of the merchant marine to Russia in the early 1930s: "After dinner the family sang. The girl knew some English and she asked me to sing an American song. I favored them with the only one I could think of, 'Body and Soul,' which was popular in New York City when I left. It seemed to puzzle them."[34] The song may have perplexed Mitchell's Russian hosts, but contemporary reviews of the film all highlighted the use of Green's song (conducted by Emil Newman with musical direction by Rudolph Polk) and applauded the work of the film's musical composer Hugo Friedhofer.[35]

Though consistently part of swing bands' and torch singers' repertoires at the end of the 1930s, "Body and Soul" took on a new lease of life and became part of the foundation for a musical revolution after jazz saxophonist Coleman Hawkins produced his landmark 1939 phonograph recording. His version of "Body and Soul" became a model for bebop improvisation. Arnold Shaw describes its evolution and effect:

> Coleman Hawkins said, "after a couple of quarts of scotch, very late, I'd sit down and kill time and play about ten choruses on 'Body and Soul.' And then the boys would come in and play harmony notes in the background until I finished up. That's all there was to it. But then Leonard Joy came in the club and asked me to record it." . . . The Hawkins disc made ["Body and Soul"] a jazz classic . . . [he] captured on wax [a] languorous late-hour mood. . . . For this matter it did not matter that he did not play melody or what chords he evoked. So long as he caught the early-morning feeling of longing, loneliness and lust. . . . It was the erotic chemistry of the deserted-street scene on 52d.[36]

As much as the torch song versions (and Lee Wiley's 1946 version is exceptionally brilliant), *Body and Soul* played upon the images of night and the city in Shaw's description of Hawkins' rendition.

The musical theme is introduced as the opening credits roll. It drops away as the film's first image, a swinging punching bag, appears on the screen. The theme returns when on the eve of his title fight Charley visits his mother and learns from her that Peg has been staying there. As he gently touches Peg's silk night dress and then holds an engraved silver-backed hair brush he had given to her, "Body and Soul" swells up on the sound track, anticipating Peg's entrance. After Charley flashes back to the beginning of his career as a fighter, the song appears in a waltz-time arrangement that accompanies his first meeting and dance with Peg. In the scene that follows, it appears twice more, first following Charley's claim that it is "every man for himself" and then as Peg gently ushers him out of her apartment, telling him he is an innocent and quoting William Blake. The song, then, acts as a commentary on Charley's blind and selfish ambition—"money, money, money"—and on Peg's freely given and unconditional love for him.

Charley's Faustian bargain with the racketeer Roberts (Lloyd Goff) puts an almost insurmountable barrier between him and Peg. From this point on, when Peg and Charley are together, the destructive effect that his contract with Roberts has on Peg's love is commented upon by the musical director's refusal to conclude the refrain of "Body and Soul." The opening phrase of the song is introduced, but the movement towards its completion is frustrated—that is, until Charley makes a commitment to Peg and promises to quit the fight game. The eventual resolution of the song's refrain is climatic—audience and characters surrender themselves to the moment—producing a sense of relief akin to walking out of a room filled with dead air into the bright, clean morning of the street outside. And this is what Charley has done: following a party at his apartment, he has left behind the nightclub singer Alice ("Am I Blue") and drunken fly-by-night friends and appears at Peg's door clutching her milk and morning newspaper.

The idea of starting over, of leaving the corruption of boxing behind, of pulling himself out of the gutter, is short lived. Charley wants money to retire on and that means betting against himself and throwing the fight, despite betraying his neighborhood friends and hurting (yet again) his mother and Peg. As the fight reaches the final rounds, Charley realizes he has been betrayed by his manager and Roberts. He will not be allowed to lose with dignity on points; his opponent intends to knock him out. Charley turns on his owners and wins—he tears up his contract with the devil and, for the first time, gives freely, to his people and Peg, his body and soul. Until production began in January 1947, the film's pretentious working title was *The Burning Journey*. The decision to change it to the more meaningful *Body and Soul* suggests a desire on the part of the filmmakers to have a title that, through their love affair with Johnny Green's melody, already belonged to the American people.

As an exemplary example of Cultural Front politics, *Body and Soul* inadvertently posed a question about the validity of the Front's influence in the postwar age.[37] In his 1947 essay "The Legacy of the 1930s," liberal critic Robert Warshow asked how was it possible to break free of the grip on intellectual inquiry that was dominated by the verities of Popular Front ideology? How could Communist dogma, which built barricades between the individual and his experience of the world, be overturned? "The half-truth was elevated to the position of principle," wrote Warshow, "and in the end the half-truth, in itself, became more desirable than the whole truth." The issue was pressing because of the limitations imposed on critical thinking: the "terms of discussion are still fixed by the tradition of middle-class 'popular front' culture . . . and we are still without a vocabulary to break through the constriction it imposes on us." The vocabulary he was searching for would enable him and others to "regain the use of our experience in the world of mass culture."[38]

But in postwar "mass culture," the legacy of the 1930s was not posed as an intellectual conflict; rather it was dramatized as a permanent economic struggle symbolized by the image of the city abandoned by the middle classes and occupied by the dregs of society: a criminal fraternity of syndicate operatives, grifters, gamblers, strippers, B-girls, and guttersnipes. This image of the "abandoned city" is examined by David Reid and Jayne Walker in an essay that is ostensibly about Cornell Woolrich's stories and subsequent film adaptations but which is in fact a highly persuasive revisionist attack on the dominant conception of film noir as located within, and produced by, a "post-war depression and the reorganization of the American economy" that situates the feelings of "loss and alienation" felt by noir characters. According to the authors, there was no postwar depression: "At no time did the economy seriously threaten to contract to the dimensions of the 1930s, nor did the specter of mass unemployment at Depression levels ever come close to materializing, despite widespread fears that both of these things were virtually inevitable. If the conditions of 1938 (one in five out of work), let alone of 1933, had ever returned, there would have been more dramatic results to reckon with than a vogue for moody pictures."[39] The postwar "depression," then, was a fear not a reality.

Similarly, the postwar threat to the phallic order posed by working women and symbolized in the figure of the femme fatale was not a product of a wartime economy, but a prejudice produced during the Depression when women had an increasing profile (as men's decreased) in the employment market. In a review of *Female* (1933) produced for the PCA, it was noted, as justification for the lead's more nefarious acts of sexual assertiveness, that the film constituted a "discussion of the current problem of the business woman displacing men in high official positions."[40] If it registers social anxiety, film noir does so on terms of a widespread and generalized fear that following the war the economy would return to its prewar condition.

This anxiety is expressed in figures such as Frankie Madison (Burt Lancaster) in *I Walk Alone* (Paramount, 1947), who, after being jailed for fourteen years, returns to ask for his share in the wealth and good times his old buddy, Noll Turner (Kirk Douglas), has enjoyed. Told that 1933 was a good year for champagne, Frankie barks back that it wasn't a good year for him. In the postwar context, Frankie is a literal and symbolic return of the repressed. This is also a theme in more socially conscious movies such as *Sound of Fury* aka *Try and Get Me* (United Artists, 1950) directed by Cy Enfield (later blacklisted during Hollywood's Communist witch hunt). Frank Lovejoy's role is less symbolic than Lancaster's in *I Walk Alone,* but in his hapless and frustrating pursuit of employment that leads to his eventual collusion in a kidnapping, he is very much a symptom of the late 1940s and 1950s fear that the Depression will return.

This helps explain, I think, Hollywood's willingness to adapt Depression-era novels—*The Postman Always Rings Twice, Mildred Pierce, Detour, Thieves Like Us* (filmed as *They Live By Night*), *Thieves' Market* (filmed as *Thieves' Highway*), and the Woolrich adaptations examined by Reid and Walker—with their emphasis on the travails of the period's "marginal man."

> The midnight streets, furnished rooms, low bars, dance halls, precinct offices, rain, heat, shadows, whiskey fumes and cigarette smoke—all the familiar elements of New York *noir's misé en scène*—are the sometimes overstrained vehicles for an imagination fundamentally melodramatic and manichean. . . . They are very much rooted in the experience of the Depression, when the fear (or, in other quarters, hope) arose that capitalism and its incarnation in the modern metropolis had entered some permanent crisis. In Woolrich's fiction the depression has become a sort of eternal unrelieved dark night of body and soul.[41]

This is true not only of Woolrich's prewar fiction but also of the postwar pulp fiction of Jim Thompson and David Goodis. In the latter's case, it is given overt expression in his 1954 novel *The Blonde on the Street Corner;* Goodis reanimates the 1930s marginal man and disavows any remedies for his condition. The story is located in "the year of Our Lord, 1936," which has the effect of anchoring the characters within a set of historically positioned socioeconomic markers, but, as the date is not given until the end of chapter 4, the story's temporal location comes as something of a shock for the reader. Until then, the story of jobless men hanging around on street corners, bumming cheap cigarettes off each other, has appeared contemporaneous to the book's publication date. "Rather than dramatizing the ordeal of change," as Reid and Walker argue, "it would be truer to the mood of these [noir] films [and certainly Goodis' novel] to say they melodramatize the ordeal, or at least the fear, of changelessness."[42] In films of the period, this is symbolized most effectively by the image of the (dead) burlesque dancer.

Dressed in high heels and an evening dress, a woman's limp body lies beneath the word "NAKED" and on top of the word "CITY"; this illustration forms part of an advertisement for Mark Hellinger's 1948 production *Naked City*. The advertisement's copy confirms a metaphoric link between the city and (dead) women: "The Soul of a City. HER GLORY STRIPPED! HER PASSIONS BARED!" The dead woman was a model, but in the films that followed on the heels of *Naked City*'s box-office success, the dead woman—and there was always a dead woman—was more likely to have been a B-girl or burlesque dancer, female types that more explicitly connected naked women to urban exposé.

In his exemplary study of the 1950s cycle of exposé and confidential films—*The Phenix City Story* (1955), *New Orleans Uncensored* (1955), *Kansas City Confidential* (1955), *Las Vegas Shakedown* (1955), *Portland Expose* (1957)—Will Straw noted the narratives were "secondary to their cataloguing of vice, and to the formal organization of these films as sequences of scenes in night-clubs, gambling dens and along neon-lit streets."[43] Simultaneously to their representation in film, these urban spaces were being explored in exposé books and magazines, as well as in Congressional investigations, but what marks this intertextual space, according to Straw, is the proliferation of urban sites: "New York, Chicago and other prominent cities will figure in many of these texts, but as the cycle unfolds there is a dispersion of attention outwards, towards medium-sized cities, regional capitals, and, in a variety of films, fictionalized versions of the mythically corruption-ridden 'wide open' town." The abundance of city locations is explained, in part, in order "that the production of differentiated texts may continue."[44] The proliferation of urban spaces placed under the camera's investigative eye leads to a displacement of a recognizable metropolitan center, whether represented by New York, San Francisco, Chicago, or Los Angeles, a displacement that is rhymed in the development of the suburbs and the consequent evacuation of city spaces.

Emptying out into the postwar suburbs, the nocturnal subterranean urban world represented in films of the 1940s and 1950s is portrayed as the last stand of a once vital and always vulgar American urban vernacular. Other than the policeman or racketeer, the key metropolitan figure of the postwar years was the B-girl ("That's short for shady lady")[45] and

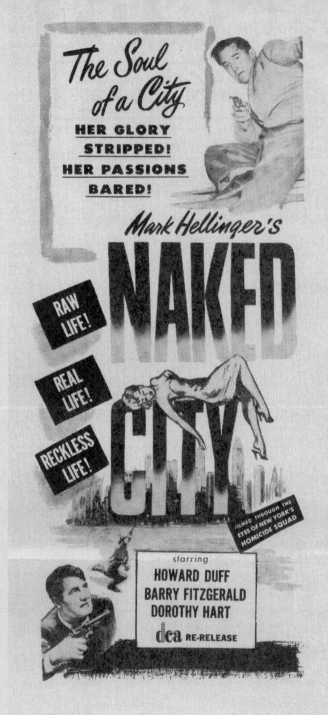

Publicity image for *Naked City* (author's collection)

the burlesque dancer (or stripper) who act out a sexual economy one step removed from the street and prostitution, or as a bartender in *The Big Heat* (Columbia, 1953) explains "there's not much more than a suitcase full of nothin' between them and the gutter." In their filmic representation, the B-girl and burlesque queen function both as tour guides to an urban American underworld and as that which must be surveyed. In a significant number of police procedural films of the period, the body of the burlesque dancer is, literally and figuratively, at the center of the investigation. Whether in motion on stage or laid out on the cooling slab in a mortuary, the burlesque dancer's body is the evidence that must be examined in order to chart, document, and police the underworld. The lost souls in *City That Never Sleeps* (Republic, 1953), a late entry in the cycle of faux-documentary urban narratives inaugurated by *The Naked City,* are characteristic of the types described by Reid and Walker. These include a patrolman's young wife who feels guilty about earning more than her husband. He is on the verge of jacking in his career and taking employment with a shyster lawyer and leaving his wife for a burlesque dancer. Then there is the failed vaudeville magician who is blackmailing the lawyer and having an affair with his wife. She resents the fact that her husband parades her to his friends and associates as someone who once served him coffee in a hash house. In love with the burlesque dancer is another of life's failures, an actor fallen to the lowly level of having to perform a mechanical man routine in the window of the Silver Follies burlesque house. "Is he man or machine?" repeats the recorded voice on the street's PA system. These are the film's representatives of the citizens of Chicago; their stories are told over the course of a single night. The film's locations are similarly representative: hotel room, furnished apartment, penthouse, small offices, boiler rooms, police station, church, abandoned warehouse, burlesque joint, and in the city's streets, back alleys, and on its elevated railroad—dead spaces occupied by characters who are barely conscious of a world beyond their own sense of failure. The Catholic Legion of Decency decried the film for having a "low moral tone." *Variety* labeled it "pulp fiction."[46]

The deserted and neglected warehouse opposite the Silver Follies is wholly emblematic of the slide into decline that characterizes urban spaces in 1940s and 1950s fictions. There is an almost overbearing sense of malaise and an overriding image of ruin and deprivation: "central city . . . abandoned for the suburban fringe."[47] The lurid, sleazy spectacle offered by the burlesque house dominates the city landscape while spaces of production fall into wrack and ruin, becoming picturesque sites for the gangster's final shootout with the law. The filmic city space has become an assemblage of dislocated marginal recesses, nocturnal subterranean joints lit by low-wattage bulbs or lit briefly by a single spotlight pointed toward a body on stage moving mechanically to the rhythm of a barely passable jazz combo. As Straw notes, "As the exposé culture of the 1950s develops, there is a marked shift from an earlier preoccupation with gambling to a fixation on the figure of the prostitute or B-girl." This figure's presence, Straw argues, "poses the question of whether any relationships are possible outside the homosocial bonds of the police force and criminal syndicates who, virtually alone, remain to inhabit the inner city."[48] Straw's argument is supported by a line or two of dialogue spoken by a policeman in the 1954 Columbia picture *Pushover*. Asked why he has not married, the cop responds: "We've seen all kinds since we joined the force—B-girls, hustlers, blackmailers, shoplifters, drunks. You know, I'd still get married if I could find a half decent woman—there must be a few around."

Indeed, this is the essence of the narrative tension in *Scene of the Crime* (MGM, 1949), a run-of-the-mill police procedural starring 1940s matinee favorite Van Johnson.[49] Investigating the shooting of his former partner, officer Mike Conovan (Johnson) works undercover in order to court the attention of Lili (Gloria De Haven), a burlesque dancer and former girl-friend of the chief suspect in the investigation. The downtown world of low bars and burlesque houses is contrasted to Conovan's domestic life. Newly married to an former model, whose framed photographic images cover the walls of their small, neat, modern, and soulless apartment, Conovan seems to have the perfect life: a job he obviously loves and a loving, beautiful wife, who has exchanged public modeling in fashion magazines for the domestic modeling of ostentatious housecoats and nightdresses for her husband's eyes only. The Club Fol-de-Rol (a play on the word "falderal," meaning trinket, gewgaw, trifle, or nonsense) and its two-star attractions (watch out for the pun)—"Lili, in her dance of enchantment" and "Mar.le.ne, in her own famous dance of the dying blond swan"—are introduced by a shot of an advertising poster. The fol-lowing sequence in the club is framed by the grotesque performance of Mar.le.ne, who is clearly past her prime; this image of degeneration is produced as a contrast to Conovan's home and wife. Lili, on the other hand, is young and beautiful, a closer match to Conovan's wife than the more elderly dancer, or so it seems. Early in their courting, Lili prohibits Conovan from watching her dance—she wants, apparently, to maintain the appearance that love between them is possible if it is not sullied by his witnessing her burlesque performance. Nevertheless, the knowledge that she is an "erotic" dancer animates their relationship and sets up a contrast between the two women in his life. His wife, who is rarely shown outside the home, is "fixed" within the domestic while Lili is in "flux," situated in bars, restaurants, furnished rooms, and city streets. Conovan's wife is further fixed in her eroticization through still photography and as a domestic "mannequin" for her apparently inexhaustible supply of nightdresses. Lili, by occupation, is in movement, and not only through her stage appearances.

However legitimate Conovan's objectives, in his masquerade as the lover who promises to "rescue" Lili from a life of degradation he is performing an act of duplicity that is not beyond reproach. The turn of the film's narrative, then, is to reveal Lili as equally duplicitous: she has known all along that he is a policeman and has been using him in order to pass on information to her hoodlum boyfriend. As the deceptions and double crosses are unraveling, Conovan witnesses Lili's act. On a high stage, she engages a vociferous and desiring audience with a song-and-dance routine. The performance moves towards a climax where the revelation is not her naked body but its concealment as ties on her bodice are pulled which release the full skirts of an evening dress. The "strip" ends with Lili more fully clothed than when the dance began. Her costume is visually rhymed with Conovan's wife's outfits, putting into play the suggestion that the difference between the two women is the performance space in which they exist. Robert C. Allen explains that a strip dancer's "exhibition is structured around the tension between her similarity to 'ordinary' women the male audience sees and knows outside the tent [the site of performance] and her fascinating otherness produced by her expressive and displayed sexuality."[50] Lili promises to give her audience "what you'll never see at home" while simultaneously giving them exactly what they do see at home.

The song Lili sings during her strip act underlines the image of female duality enacted in the dance—wife/whore (encoded as lady/woman): "I call myself a lady / Though they say I'm pretending to be . . . my quality shows . . . I'm a lady 'til love makes a woman out of me." When Conovan eventually confronts Lili with her duplicity, she remains defiantly unrepentant: "What'll they throw at me—the book? The book, there's a crime on every page to fit me." The image of flux and movement (relative to the stasis in the depiction of Conovan's wife) was an illusion; there is

Body and Soul

no "outside" or sanctuary for her. She is as trapped in her role as wanton woman as Conovan's wife is in her role as a paragon of domesticity.

In his history of jazz on New York's 52nd Street, Arnold Shaw devotes a chapter to the neighborhood's "stripperies." Lili St. Cyr was the star stripper at the Samoa Club, and she, it was said, "rubbed a bit of much-needed glamour on The Street even in the days of its decline." But by 1952, Lili had gone on to bigger stages and *Variety* had changed the street's label from "Swing Street to Strip Row": "It described the girls as 'flat, flabby and in their forties.' What it objected to more than the sleazy stripping was the tawdry atmosphere and uncouth treatment of customers." For Shaw, the situation was much more serious. The "peelers," club owners, and audiences were a "destructive virus" on the scene's musical culture.[51] By the 1930s, historian of burlesque Robert C. Allen writes, "As in 1869, burlesque was framed in terms of the 'low,' whose contaminating penetration into the heart of the city and its entertainment district had to be opposed on social, moral, and economic grounds."[52] The argument against striptease may have been publicly fought on moral terms, but the real motivating force behind city officials' efforts to drive out the pernicious purveyors of sleaze was the effect they had on business and real estate prices. Noting the city of New York's acts of legislation aimed at removing burlesque companies from city center theaters, Allen writes:

> stores and trades built on servicing middle-class customers drawn to the Times Square area by the legitimate theaters were suffering. Not only did the success of Broadway burlesque not produce the same "spin-off" trade legitimate theaters had in the 1920s, but also it flooded the area with "undesirable" characters whose presence, in turn, further depressed middle-class trade. Property owners saw the value of their investments plummet during the depression, and burlesque was a convenient villain. . . . The problem burlesque presented to the surrounding property interests, an editorial [in the *New York Times*] pointed out, was that "the alleged obscenity of the burlesque shows is exceeded by their external frowziness. The neighborhood of such theaters takes on the character of a slum."[53]

In the *Scene of the Crime,* Lili is represented as a wholly destructive presence, one that eventually must be contained. This "containment" is usually achieved by having the burlesque dancer killed. The dancer Sugar Torch meets just such an end in Samuel Fuller's *The Crimson Kimono* (Columbia/Globe, 1959). After a performance, an assassin chases Sugar

Torch out onto the city streets where she is murdered. The dead body of the dancer lying in the street provides the key image upon which the rest of the film can base its story of racial distrust and urban corruption. *The Female Jungle* (Burt Kaiser Productions, 1955) similarly suggests that a dead female body projects the primary image of an urban malaise. The film begins at night. A neon sign—"cocktails"—flashes on and off, a languid musical motif played on a saxophone is heard on the sound track, and a taxi cab pulls to a halt and a young blonde woman in a strapless satin evening dress steps out. When the cab moves off, she crosses the street; in close-up, two hands appear and close around her neck. Her slack body is dropped into the street whereupon the film's title, "Female Jungle," explodes dramatically on screen from out of her dead body. The victim is Monica Madison, film star, who an investigating policeman suggests has been "slumming" at the Club Can Can.

The Female Jungle suggests how closely linked are images of urban spaces and the dead bodies of female performers. The similarly titled *The Human Jungle* (Allied Artists, 1954) also begins with the murder of a woman: a burlesque dancer strangled in a back alley. Police surveillance focuses on a strip club called the Hut, part of a criminal organization run by an asthmatic chain-smoking letch of an old man, Mr. Ustick. He caters to, and bankrolls, the dregs of society, those whom the banks and capitalism have left behind. The dead body of the burlesque dancer becomes the perfect metonym for the degradation behind this level of human exploitation. This idea had earlier been played out in the public forum of the law courts and New York City's newspapers when, in 1937, following a series of sex crimes, the city's officials used these attacks as an excuse to revoke theatrical licenses granted to burlesque shows.[54] In the film, Jan Sterling, who plays one of the Hut's "Tassle-Tossing Teasers," becomes the bait the police use in order to trap the murderer.

In *Mystery Street* (MGM, 1950), Sterling plays the victim, Vivian Heldon, a B-girl who hangs around in the Grass Skirt saloon that serves drinks accompanied by bad jazz—the beat so slack it seems as if it will never click. Vivian's married lover murders her when she tells him she is having his baby. On the discovery of her body, the scientific resources of the police department are used in order to sift through the evidence. The forensic lab work, rather than being sterile and dull, is wonderfully macabre as they work first to reconstruct Vivian's body to discover her identity and cause of death and then piece together the skeleton of her fetus: crucial evidence that is presented to the investigating officer in a white envelope in an almost comically offhand and banal manner. Ostensibly the scene demonstrates the skill of the pathologist, but more pointedly it provides a particularly horrific image of the urban female performer's inability to produce and nurture children.

In a scene redolent with symbolism, a disenchanted police officer in *City That Never Sleeps* helps a pregnant woman give birth. She is carried from a taxicab and taken behind a brick wall bordering waste ground. With the baby safely wrapped in a blanket, he hands her over to a brusque policeman in the back of a patrol wagon. It is the third birth in two months that he has aided. But he hardly need to bother replying when asked by another officer whether he has children. His excuse for not having kids is his low salary, but his relationship with his wife would not warrant children (he leaves for work as she returns from her job), and, just as significantly, this desolate city is no place to bring children into the world.

The barren female body that echoes the idea of the city as an abandoned space suggests a marked distinction from city narratives produced during the Depression, or if not a distinction, then something of a logical playing out of the city as defined in terms of malaise and degradation. The 1930s narratives of performing women—*Applause, Torch Singer, Show Boat, Blonde Venus, Reckless*—as well as narratives of nonperforming women—*Imitation of Life, Three on a Match, Stella Dallas*—are about trying to hold on to a child, to provide the means for the child's upkeep and welfare against all that a depressed urban environment can throw at them. By the 1950s, this narrative has been lost and the image of the sacrificing mother has given way to an overriding image of the female inhabitants of the city as sterile and unproductive sexual performers. This shift is particularly marked in a comparison of the 1934 and 1959 adaptations of Fannie Hurst's 1933 novel *Imitation of Life.* In the former version, the emphasis is on both the black and the white mother's need to provide economic security for their children in the absence of a patriarchal figure, which is achieved through the production and marketing of a pancake mix. In the latter version, the white mother is transformed from a domestic figure without a husband into an ambitious actress, still a widow but one who now spends much of the narrative fighting off the attentions of numerous suitors. While ostensibly driven by the need to provide for her child, her overriding motivation is to succeed as an actress, success that will mean she is unable to nurture her relationship with her daughter.

The degrading of the maternal in the 1959 version is echoed in the changes made between the two adaptations in the representation of the character of Peora/Sarah Jane, the light-skinned daughter of the white mother's maid. In the 1934 version, Peora runs away from home, her mother, and her race, and finds (temporary) anonymity and employment in a restaurant. In the 1959 version, she "escapes" to New York where her mother discovers her working as a burlesque dancer in a subterranean jazz club. Later she again leaves home and gains employment as a dancer in Los Angeles at the Moulin Rouge nightclub. The distinctly classed and racially figured spaces for female performance—the legitimate theater and the burlesque house—are nevertheless linked in the idea that neither will enable, indeed will actively undermine, the formation of the loving, mutually supportive, couple (the foundation for the desired ideal of a family).

The lack of a strong maternal figure is also at the heart of *Glory Alley* (MGM, 1952), a film that seems to have been produced not from a story idea but from the dominant elements and motifs that were representative of late 1940s and early 1950s urban dramas, linked together by a voice-over narration seeped in a sentimental nostalgia for a rawer, more heroic American street life. The setting is the bars and dives on Bourbon Street in New Orleans (authenticated by cameos from jazz greats Louis Armstrong and Jack Teagarden).[55] The characters are a boxer, a burlesque dancer, her blind father and his helper, Shadow (Armstrong in a particularly demeaning role), and a journalist who narrates the story of "Glory Alley."[56] The boxer, Socks's (Ralph Meeker) backstory is built wholesale from the period's fixation with creating character motivation from childhood trauma (he watched his father beat his mother to death with a tire iron). Just before his title fight, Socks runs out of the ring and refuses to fight; later it is revealed that the stage lights had caused him to flash back to his childhood and memories of local kids laughing at his shaved head and the stitches that held his scalp together. After his father had finished assaulting his mother, he had turned on Socks and split open his head. Branded a coward, he hits the bottle and skid row, but eventually he begins the process of putting his life back together. He seizes the opportunity for restitution that the war in Korea presents and returns home with a Congressional Medal of Honor. But while Bourbon Street greets him as a returning hero, the one man from whom he most wants approval refuses to yield to public opinion—his surrogate father, the judge. The judge is blind and is being looked after by his daughter Angie, Socks's girlfriend. The judge believes she supports him by working nights as a nurse, but she is really working as a dancer in a burlesque house Chez Bozo. Before the judge went blind, he had hoped Angie would become a great ballet dancer, but in her new occupation her skills are not wasted because she is able to mix the two dance forms—burlesque and ballet—to create a high/low cultural hybrid that is echoed in her stage name, Lili L'Anglais. Because Angie is played by the French dancer and actress Leslie Caron, who would later have the lead in *Gigi* (1958), the classical European and the vernacular American attributes of her show are particular resonant. When she eventually tells her father how she earns her living, he will not believe her, not until he experiences her show at Chez Bozo. In front of a set of backdrops painted to represent a run-down city street, Lili L'Anglais/Angie performs a particularly bawdy dance using a lamppost as the principal prop—up and down and around and around this phallus she glides her legs. Gone is any reference to classicism and ballet that had previously featured so strongly in her dances. This is the show that must reveal to her blind father what she has had to sacrifice in order to provide for them both. The scenario presents a generational and partial gender reversal of the situation in *Stella Dallas:* not a self-sacrificing mother attempting to alienate her daughter, but a self-sacrificing daughter alienating her father. The band that backs her performance is led by the great trombonist Jack Teagarden, who ensures that she is given a particularly spirited version of "St. Louis Blues" to sing along and to dance with. W. C. Handy's tune is asked to do much the same work as it had in *Stella Dallas* and elsewhere.

On hearing the song and the audience's reaction, her father recognizes just how blind he has been and gives his blessing to her marriage to Socks. The rebuilding of a family out of the ruins provided by previous generations is now a possibility. More often, though, there is no future for the burlesque dancer; she is figuratively and literally dead. The correlation between the abandoned city, death, and the nonreproductive female performer is repeated in Mickey Spillane's novel *The Long Wait* (1951): the hero describes the stripper he is with as a "lovely zombie."[57] This image of the sexual worker as one of the "living-dead" was repeated in a 1946 edition of the jazz journal *Down Beat,* "Zombies Put Kiss of Death on 52nd St. Jazz" cried the headline to a story on strip acts outnumbering jazz acts in the street's clubs.[58] The metaphor for strippers as the living dead also appeared in Fritz Lang's *Beyond a Reasonable Doubt* (1956), where dancers strutted their stuff at "The Club Zombie."[59] The film is plotted around the murder of burlesque dancer Patty Gray, whose decidedly downbeat stage name conceals her real identity, Emma Blooker. Gray worked with three dancers who are all shading middle age whose coarse New York accents contrast with the urbane tones of novelist Tom Garrett (Dana Andrews).

Garrett is investigating the case so as to incriminate himself for the murder and then, after his trial and sentencing, expose and discredit the processes by which innocent men may be found guilty on circumstantial evidence and still sentenced to death. But this cultured man *is* the killer. Time spent with the dancers, he says by way of explanation to his fiancée, is "research." Intended to uncover evidence for the police that will lead to his conviction for murder, the "research" is simultaneously meant to suggest to the film viewer his innocence. The acts of deception, built on apparently empirical evidence and rational research, have their correlate in the act of striptease that produces not a satisfying conclusion but an ambiguous and profoundly disturbing image of the female body.

The disturbing female body is text and subtext of D. H. Clarke's novel *A Lady Named Lou* (1941). "No other woman could compete with her specialty. . . . The piano player started beating out a sensual rhythm as Lou stepped on stage. He watched her walk into the spotlight, her body picking up the tempo he was playing. And then she went into her act—her very special act. . . ." This is the "scalding, intimate story of how a strip-tease queen got that way," a novel that is presented to the reader in its cover copy as, literally, an "anatomy of a stripper."[60] The cover shot has an image of a tall, lean, large-breasted stripper in a red bikini costume, high stiletto heels, and three-quarter-length sheer net gloves; between her legs hangs a long piece of silk. As animated in any of the burlesque dance sequences discussed in this chapter, the piece of silk is the primary fetish of the strip. Used in the Freudian sense, the fetish is that which masks an absence. The stripper's phallic play with the piece of silk, its apparent substitution for a penis in the masturbatory movements of the fabric between her legs and in front of her groin, staves off the notion of sexual difference as it plays with the possibility (and subsequent fear) of its revelation.

The oscillation between containment and exposure produces the male spectator's sense of arousal and disturbance: fear and desire. As Jean Baudrillard writes in *Symbolic Exchange and Death,* the oscillation between extremes is the necessary precursor to the eroticized image in "fashion, advertising, nude-look, nude theatre, strip-tease: the playscript of erection and castration is everywhere. It has an absolute variety and an absolute monotony."[61] The "playscript of erection and castration" is particularly marked in the adaptation of David Grubb's novel with a Depression setting, *The Night of the Hunter* (novel 1953, film 1957). Preacher Harry Powell has left behind a trail of dead widows; passing through hamlets and small towns in his Model T Ford, he engages in a monologue with the Lord on the duplicitous nature of women. In book and film, he visits a burlesque show. In the film, Powell is figured as voyeur by framing the dancer within an optical iris in the shape of a keyhole. Continuing his monologue as the dancer suggestively gyrates her hips and masturbates her fabric tail, he places his fist with the word HATE tattooed across the knuckles into his jacket pocket, and as the music and dance reach a climax, a little phallic knife blade bursts through the pocket. The scene ends with the hand of an arresting officer placed on his shoulder. The masturbatory play with the knife and the fear of the castrating (and castrated) woman is equally explicit in the novel:

> He would pay his money and go into a burlesque show and sit in the front row watching it all and rub the knife in his pocket with sweating fingers; seething in a quiet convulsion of outrage and nausea at all that ocean of undulating womanhood beyond the lights; his nose growing full of it: the choking miasma of girl smell and the cheap perfume and stogie smoke and man smell and the breath of ten-cent mountain corn liquor souring in the steamy air; and he would stumble out at last into the enchanted night, into the glitter and razzle-dazzle of the midnight April street, his whole spirit luminous with an enraptured and blessed fury at the world these whores had made.[62]

However caricatured, this is the psychic scenario behind the male desires and fears that lead to the "inevitable" (to use pulp writer Mickey Spillane's term) revelation/murder of the burlesque dancers and B-girls.

If burlesque and its representations in the late 1940s and 1950s dealt metaphorically with death, the "true strip" as Allen notes, "was burlesque's last-ditch and ultimately unsuccessful strategy to stay alive. It represents not the symbol of burlesque's golden age—although it is remembered as such—but rather its ultimate failure to sustain a performance medium sufficiently distinct in its appeals from other forms to draw an audience."[63] Burlesque, like the empty city streets it helped produce, was dying, and the repetition of kewpie doll poses in the folios of photographs of burlesque girls suggests not the movement of dance but tableaus of death. Their déshabillé is rendered all the more decomposed by the fetishistic use of furs, skins, and feathers of dead animals.[64] This is in line with Roland Barthes' contention that:

> Contrary to the common prejudice, the dance which accompanies the striptease from beginning to end is in no way an erotic element. It is probably quite the reverse: the faintly rhythmical undulation in this case

exorcizes the fear of immobility. Not only does it give to the show the alibi of Art (the dances in strip-shows are always "artistic"), but above all it constitutes the last barrier, and the most efficient of all: the dance, consisting of ritual gestures which have been seen a thousand times, acts on movements as a cosmetic, it hides nudity, and smothers the spectacle under a glaze of superfluous yet essential gestures, for the act of becoming bare is here relegated to the rank of parasitical operations carried out in an improbable background.[65]

The "hiding of nudity" was an idea Mickey Spillane no doubt had in mind when he described a burlesque dance in the following manner:

No matter which way she stepped you'd see almost all the inside of a lovely tanned leg that was a tantalizing flash in the amber spotlight. She started off the song with little steps that got larger and more critical and had everyone forgetting their chow waiting for the inevitable.

The song was about three bars too short and the inevitable stayed hidden.[66]

Never revealing that which is promised also underscored the manner in which films, due to the production code, could represent the strip act. Film companies could neither use the word "strip-tease" nor overtly represent such a dance. The following quotation from the PCA represents a typical edict: "The indication on these two pages that the girl on the stage is doing a strip-tease is completely unacceptable and could not be approved in your finished picture. As you know, we cannot approve any inference whatever of strip-tease."[67] Like prostitutes in a filmic western saloon, the dancer had to become something else.[68] Sally (Angel Face) Connors in *City That Never Sleeps* was characterized in the story summary submitted with the PCA's "Analysis of Film Content" as a "Honky-Tonk dancer." The trade press generally played along with these acts of sophistry: *Motion Picture Daily* and *Variety* (Daily) both repeated this description of her.[69] *Variety* (Weekly), however, called her a "cheap saloon dancer," while *Hollywood Reporter* described her as a "pretty cabaret dancer."[70] Like the strip act that promises to show the "whole" woman but in fact conceals more than it reveals, these acts of name changing signal a profound uncertainty around female identity.

Fascination with dissembling female identity is central to the concerns of *The Narrow Margin* (RKO, 1952). Two Los Angeles policemen travel to Chicago by train. The younger cop is hard-boiled, cynical, and the older cop is sentimental, trusting; he won't live long. Their assignment is to escort a mobster's widow back to Los Angeles where she will testify against organized crime in front of a grand jury; her husband's cronies want to stop her. In a taxi, the two policemen discuss what Mrs. Neal is like. The younger cop, Walter Brown (Charles McGraw), thinks she will be a "dish . . . 60 cent special, cheap, flashy, strictly poison under the gravy. . . . What kind of dame would marry a hood?" he asks rhetorically. "All kinds," replies his partner. They have a $5 wager on who is right. Their first impression of Mrs. Neal (Marie Windsor) is gained as they walk up the staircase of a worn-out apartment house and are greeted by the sound of hot jazz leaking from an upstairs room. The music is coming from a portable phonograph owned by Mrs. Neal, and the music, her demeanor, trashy clothes, cheap dress jewelry, and overrouged lips suggest she compares well with Brown's sixty-cent dish.

Before Brown can collect on the bet, his partner is killed. However, had the older policeman lived to pay the wager and to help escort Mrs. Neal back to L.A., he would have been justified in asking for the return of the five bucks. Under the gravy, Mrs. Neal is a policewoman working as a decoy for the real Mrs. Neal and for the Internal Affairs Division as part of a nationwide investigation into police graft. The policewoman's obsessive playing of jazz records gives her away to the gangsters, who kill her. The killers search for a list of names among their victim's possessions and reveal her true identity, which furthers an already established link between female sexuality and phonograph records. Hidden under the turntable in her portable phonograph is not a list of names but her police badge. If Officer Brown had been able to recognize different popular music genres, he would never have mistaken Mrs. Neal for a slut. In 1952, the year of the film's release, the kind of hot Dixieland-style jazz she played on her phonograph should have signaled that she was not all she appeared. Genuine sluts, like Kitty March (Joan Bennett) in *Scarlet Street* (Universal, 1945), for example, are not interested in revivalist jazz but in sickly sentimental ballads like "My Melancholy Baby."

Against this backdrop of deception, desolation, and death, one set of films stand out: *Pick Up on South Street* (1953), *Crimson Kimono* (1959), *Underworld USA* (1961), *Naked Kiss* (1964) and *Shock Corridor* (1963), all written, directed, and, with the exception of the first title, produced by Samuel Fuller. Released several years after the rush of movies featuring burlesque sequences, *Shock Corridor* relies on the viewer's familiarity with striptease's conventions to both confirm and undermine the "playscript of erection and castration." The striptease sequence in the film confounds the male spectator's hoped-for sense of arousal, which Fuller achieves in the manner of both the performance of the strip and in a register that bequeaths subjectivity and desire not to the male viewer but to the dancer. According to Barthes, it is the idea of novelty against a backdrop of conformity and convention that gives striptease the superficial "alibi of Art." Making "art" with her main prop, a long feather boa, Cathy (Constance Towers) runs through all the ritualized movements of a strip as detailed by Joseph Mitchell in his 1930s dispatches from burlesque's front line: the "bump" is a "movement in which the knees are bent and the hips are thrown backward and forward with, in some girls, an almost startling rapidity . . . [and] the grind . . . is, of course, a rotary motion of the hips something like the hootchy-kootchy."[71] Yet these conventions of the strip are disturbed by the striking opening image: the camera pans up Cathy's legs and reveals her torso and head completely wrapped in feathers. As Cathy begins to sing, her breath causes the feather down to tremble slightly, opening and closing where her mouth should be. She resembles nothing so much as a slightly benign version of surrealist Max Ernst's "La Toilette de la mariée" with its disturbing hybrid figure of a naked female and bird of prey.[72] There is no audience present, and her dance, performed in front of an incomplete stage set, is interrupted by cuts to backstage scenes of girls preparing for, and discussing, their acts. Continuity is maintained across the edits by the overlapping music used to accompany Cathy's dance. The music, however, does not conform to an orthodoxy of sleazy blues; rather, Cathy sings a slow sentimental number about her unfulfilled desire for her lover while the name of her estranged boyfriend echoes on the sound track. The combined effect of the alibi of art—novelty set against conformity, the revealing of the means of production, and the incongruity of the romantic song—highlight Cathy's subjectivity—her desire—against the counterclaim for her as object and figure of desire.

But whatever claims made in defense of Cathy's subjectivity (she strips so she can eventually afford to lead a "normal" married life) and the consequent recognition of the economic imperative that comes with her consciousness of what her role entails (she can earn more money stripping than taking shorthand or working as a typist), the film also highlights the duplicity involved in constructing an alibi of art for Cathy's act and how dependent and conditional her subjectivity is on her positioning by others, most particularly her boyfriend Johnny (Peter Preck). A promotional item for the film describes Cathy as a "WILD STRIP TEASER! Claims she does it only because of high pay. But disproven by her avid reactions to excitement of male audiences! Diagnosis: Manic sensualist." In this light, it is best to remember the wise words of a young student to his professor (played by Ronald Reagan) in *She's Working Her Way Through College* (Warner Bros., 1952). In reply to the latter's claim that "Burlesque originated from *commedia dell'arte,* it's still a definite art form," the student responds wryly, "It's become more form than art, professor."

Now a certified American film classic, on its original release *Shock Corridor* was marketed and received in America as a "sexy sensational" exploitation programmer destined for double-billing in neighborhood grind houses. Promotional material for the film makes this abundantly clear. Using the format of a tabloid newspaper—*Daily Express News*—screaming headlines promise the "SHOCKING WORLD OF PSYCHOS AND SEX-MADDENED WOMEN EXPOSED!" "Shock Corridor begins where other pictures leave off! Bares provocative scenes they don't dare show!" "THE MEDICAL JUNGLE DOCTORS DON'T TALK ABOUT . . . 'SHOCK CORRIDOR'" and "The snake-pit world revealed in all its outrages!" "Stripper bares strange love obsessions!" "Trapped in the ward of sex-maddened women!"[73] *Variety* thought the film a "tasteless, tedious quagmire of shock and sensation," and *Cue* thought much the same: it is "swamped by a predilection for tossing shocking features . . . for the sake of shock." The *Los Angeles Times* feared for the "spectator-listener [who] is assailed by so much sound and fury that he emerges after 101 minutes feeling groggy and, I am afraid, largely unconvinced." *Film Quarterly* considered it to be "one of the most preposterous and tasteless films of all time," and the *Herald Tribune* warned that it "hasn't got the decency to qualify as a lower B-level film. It's coated with sexual jargon, psychiatric and political palaver and pathetic photographic effects . . . but nothing can hide the film's infintile [*sic*] pretensions and drooling preoccupations."[74]

The British Board of Film Censors appeared to agree with these American critics. After twice viewing the film, they decided not to issue a certificate on the grounds that it might upset viewers with mentally ill relatives, and that it "would have a bad, and possibly dangerous, effect on viewers with any degree of mental disturbance." However, the overriding reason for denying the film access to British cinemas was the suggestion "that a sane person could secure admission to a mental hospital by putting on an act and convincing qualified medical men that he is mentally disturbed, and equally irresponsible to suggest that residence as an inmate of a mental hospital could make a sane person insane."[75] Fuller's allegorical pretensions obviously held no sway over the British cultural guardians, because what was really at stake for John Trevelyan, the secretary of the BBFC, I would argue, was the film's omission of an explanatory context that obeyed the principles of narrative realism and, above all else, any notion of good taste. This was certainly a position held by the reviewer for *Film Daily* who was concerned with the fact that the picture "sacrifices sincerity for the sake of exploitation values."[76]

Fuller's assault on good taste determined much of the American critical establishment's disbelief at the European valorization of his work. Robert G. Dickson writing in *Film Quarterly* sardonically noted in his review that Fuller was "currently the subject of much fatheaded adulation in France and England" and that, no doubt, *Shock Corridor* would soon be "hailed, by the *Cahiers/Movie* mob, as 'Fuller's Testament' or 'A Masterpiece—symptomatic of our age'" when, "in fact," it is "a cheap, nasty, lurid melodrama with artistic pretensions."[77] Discussing *The Naked Kiss,* made in the following year, the reviewer for *Cosmopolitan* wrote, "If it is true that the French New Wave of film-makers dotes on Fuller's underdone cinematics (they are said to consider his *Shock Corridor* an American classic), then all one can say is that fifty million Frenchmen can be wrong. The words *low budget* would upgrade this low-budget melodrama."[78] In their favor, most of the American reviews did note that the film had a social agenda. For example, *Variety* wrote, "Fuller apparently is trying to say something significant about certain contemporary American values." The reviewer isolates what he feels are the film's three key points:

> A Communist—brainwashed and subsequently disgraced Korean war vet (James Best) is the mouthpiece through which Fuller pleads for greater understanding of such unfortunate individuals. Likewise, a Negro (Hari Rhodes), supposed to have been the first to attend an all-white Southern university serves to make the point that it takes enormous emotional stamina to play the role of the martyr in social progress. And the character of a renowned physicist (Gene Evans) whose mind has deteriorated into that of a six-year-old enables Fuller to get in some digs against bomb shelters and America's participation in the space race.

But all this is qualified by their context. The "points are sound and have merit. But the melodrama in which he has chosen to house these ideas is so grotesque, so grueling, so shallow and so shoddily sensationalistic his message is totally devastated."[79] On the other hand, the cineastes in Britain and France could validate Fuller precisely because he did not house his vision within a world of comfortable middle-class notions of good taste. Fuller's critique of American complacency and self-righteousness was harder hitting, was more effective, because it was not couched in the language of the complacent and self-righteous. This is why radical American critics such as Andrew Sarris and Manny Farber were right to hail him as an American primitive, and why Farber was so astute in his seminal analysis of Fuller's oeuvre. Farber called Fuller's aesthetic an *art brut* styling that rejected the "realm of celebrity and affluence" and instead embraced or, rather, "burrowed" like a "termite" into the "nether world of privacy." Fuller's films lacked a pretentious appeal to the call of high art (whatever I or others may have ascribed to it subsequently) but instead engaged in the horizontal, which is to say democratic, mobility of both "observing and being in the world."[80] In forsaking any pretentious assertion to being involved in making great art, Sam Fuller, like his friend and contemporary Jim Thompson, can be reclaimed by later generations of critics as uncorrupted by middle- or highbrow values and instead celebrated as a cipher for an authentic American culture.[81] Fuller's best films, then, follow the line described by Lawrence Levine in his essay on jazz and American culture that recognized "in the various syncretized cultures that became so characteristic of the United States not an embarrassing weakness but a dynamic source of strength."[82] Fuller's representative American heroes are tabloid journalists, pickpockets, B-girls, prostitutes, and strippers, and his emblematic American couple is the mixed-race lovers in *The Crimson Kimono.* This is to say that the best of American culture is a miscegenated gutter art. Mitchell's image of minstrelsy and the strip act as definitive American forms suggest as much, as do *The Jazz Singer,* "Frankie and Johnny" and "St. Louis Blues," torch singers, burlesque dancers, and Samuel Fuller's movies.

Conclusion

Well, I'm so glad I'm livin' in the U.S.A.
Yes, I'm so glad I'm livin' in the U.S.A.
Anything you want, we got right here in the U.S.A.
—Chuck Berry, "Back in the U.S.A."

A product of the historical forces of immigration and modernization, Hollywood represented an image of American culture that sought to repair the fissures these social shifts had engendered. Hollywood attempted to replace the vanishing culture of the old America with a vision of the New World, one more amenable, more open, to immigrant cultures. The price of entry was to lose one's inherited characteristics and replace them with a new American identity. In this context, *The Jazz Singer* is a unique contribution to Hollywood's identity politics because it offered the image of something akin to the continuous interplay between Old World and New World identities, achieved through the mediation of minstrelsy. Minstrelsy is not left safely in the past, as it is in *Show Boat,* but is instead shown to be a crucial element in the praxis of making the idea of a modern "American" into a reality. Jakie Rabinowitz/Jack Robin holds on to his dual identity by embracing and subjugating a third party: the African American. The desire for, and fear of, blackness governs Hollywood's image of American culture: against blackness, whiteness defines itself. This process of definition based on revealing that which the self is not paradoxically gives presence and importance to that which the self wants to disclaim.

The films discussed in this book all dramatize this process of revelation and concealment.

Eventually the occluding of black American culture could no longer be maintained. As W. T. Lhamon Jr. explains, by the mid-1950s "new forces" had "breached the exclusive club said to determine American myths."[1] This new force was called rock and roll, and its standard bearers were black Americans—Fats Domino, Ray Charles, Little Richard, and Chuck Berry— or white Americans who aped black culture yet forsook the demeaning mask of minstrelsy, such as Elvis Presley. These performers penetrated mainstream culture in a more embracing and seditious manner than had hitherto been achieved. Aided in no small part by the new media of 45 rpm phonograph records, transistor radios, and television, black culture begun to find a home in white suburbia; Chuck Berry, writes Lhamon, "represented a man from nowhere entering history. He thought of his roots as nowhere, suburbia as somewhere, and his leap between the two as historic. He tried at first to leap beyond black culture, but in pulling himself into the consciousness of Americans he pulled black culture in, too, like a black Trojan horse."[2] As Lhamon notes, elsewhere the black presence in America was similarly felt in ways never experienced before. The news of Emmett Till's murder and the outcry over the not-guilty verdict given his white racist killers was a symbol of what was at stake for the civil rights movement, as much as Rosa Parks' refusal to give up her bus seat became a symbol of what the movement could hope to achieve. As Lhamon summarizes, "The emergence of black culture into American prominence greatly altered the course of American art, balancing and lending it a completeness it had lacked."[3]

Only a bigot would try to deny the centrality of black experience and culture within a broad understanding of what constitutes American identity, just as only a romantic would argue that control over that identity has shifted from the white mainstream. Where American films had once played a dominant role in the formation of an American identity, just as vaudeville and blackface minstrelsy had previously done, Hollywood in the 1950s had to contend with competing media technologies in a way it never had before. The print media, television, radio, and the phonograph record industries competed much more effectively for the public's attention. And they did this as the oligopoly of the studio era waned following the 1948 Paramount decree that demanded the separation of exhibition, production, and distribution. Antitrust action created a period of intense independent production activity that also weakened the centralized self-censoring body that the studios had used so effectively. In the absence of any effective central control, the tolerance for more "progressive" ideas about the state of the American body politic ensured that there was, for a limited period, a space available for liberal filmmakers like Fuller to exploit. This exploitation was only economically expedient when linked with sex-sensational ideas, particularly those that suggested acts of transgression—and what was more transgressive in American culture than the act of miscegenation? But while the financial benefits of this newly found freedom for independent producers are obvious, so was Fuller's desire in films such as *The Crimson Kimono* to portray an America where the mixing of races was not a punishable offense. Before they became art-house fodder, Fuller's best films—*The Naked Kiss, Shock Corridor*—were produced for the grind house circuit of cinemas, run-down fleapits just a sidewalk away from the gutter.

Will Straw draws a comparison between the dissolution and dispersion of fixed urban centers in popular American crime fictions of the 1950s and the breakup of the Hollywood studio system across the same time period, noting the shift to "regionalist" and "exploitative filmmaking practices" and the consequent diminishing of mainstream Hollywood production values.[4] The decline of a centralized film production culture saw a commensurate decline in the upkeep of urban sites of exhibition. Despite film noir's representational concern with empty city streets, the inner cities were simply not being "abandoned" in the years following the close of World War II, but were, in counterpoint to the images propagated in the films, being filled to overflow. Between 1940 and 1970, 5 million Americans migrated from the rural South, relocating in the industrial cities of the North and West. Social historian Nicholas Lemann writes, "In 1940, 77 per cent of black Americans still lived in the South—49 per cent in the rural South. . . . Between 1910 and 1970, six and a half million black Americans moved from the South to the North; five million moved after 1940 . . . In 1970, when migration ended, black America was only half Southern, and less than a quarter rural; 'urban' had become a euphemism for 'black.'"[5] The real story of postwar urban America is not its abandonment, however representative that may be of middle-class fears and anxieties, but its repopulation by black American migrants and the subsequent making of a new underclass of disenfranchised, undereducated, and underemployed urban citizens. If the mainstream crime film of the 1940s and 1950s failed to represent the enormity of this demographic shift—which it did—it nevertheless laid the groundwork for the cycle of films produced in the early to mid-1970s that did represent a black urban milieu, in particular that group of films known as blaxploitation: *Shaft* (MGM, 1971), *Black Gunn* (Columbia, 1971), *Come Back Charleston Blue* (Warner Bros., 1972), *Slaughter* (AIP, 1972), *Across 110th Street* (UA, 1972), *Black Caesar* (AIP, 1973), *Run Nigger Run* (BIP, 1973), *The Slams* (MGM, 1973), *Trick Baby* (Universal, 1973), *Hell Up in Harlem* (AIP, 1973), *The Mack* (CRC, 1973), *Slaughter's Big Rip-Off* (AIP, 1973), *Coffy* (AIP, 1973), *Foxy Brown* (AIP, 1973), *Black Samson* (Warner Bros., 1974), *Black Belt Jones* (Warner Bros., 1974).

Between 1971 and 1975, the high-water mark for the production of blaxploitation films, the film industry, according to Richard Maltby, retrenched after a period of escalating production costs and overproduction of films that saturated an unresponsive theatrical market. The mainstream industry had shown a marked reluctance to abandon the concept of the universal, undifferentiated audience that had characterized production, marketing, and exhibition under the studio system. The dwindling urban audience for the studios' core product, the effect of the new ratings system, and new sites of film exhibition located in suburban shopping malls, however, contributed to the organization of production based on a projection of differentiated audiences.[6]

The new suburban film theaters attracted a young audience whose tastes were catered to by the rising stars of Hollywood's "renaissance" such as Stephen Spielberg, Brian DePalma, George Lucas, Francis Ford Coppola, William Friedkin, and others. Their sensationalist offerings—*The Godfather* (Paramount, 1972), *The Exorcist* (Warner Bros., 1973), *American Graffiti* (Universal, 1973), *Jaws* (Universal, 1975), and *Carrie* (UA, 1976)—were big budget reworkings of the kind of juvenile material that had previously been the exclusive concern of independent film companies that served the drive-in market. "The shift in content to exploitation genres was, like the use of saturation booking and the relocation of the site of movie going," argues Maltby, "part of what Thomas Doherty has called the 'juvenilization' of American cinema, and ultimately a consequence of the juvenilization of its primary audience."[7]

While the movie brats played to the new youthful suburban audience, what of the inner-city filmgoer and the long-established theaters? One consequence of the 1948 Paramount decree (that sought the breakup of the major studios' grip over all aspects of the industry) was that the major exhibition chains "were not permitted to acquire theaters without court permission, which was regularly refused when they proposed closing a downtown movie theater and replacing it with one in the suburbs."

Unable to shift their sites of exhibition, the major chains needed film product that would appeal to its principal inner-city audience of young black consumers, furthering Hollywood's differentiation of films along generational *and* racial lines. The blaxploitation film cycle recognized and played to this newly targeted constituency. Film historian Douglas Gomery writes:

> by the late 1960s the black only theatre—by law—was a thing of the past. However, as downtown and inner-city theatres in large cities were abandoned by whites, a large number of blacks patronized the theatres. *Variety* reported that although blacks were only 10 to 15 percent of the population, they represented a third of movie ticket buyers, especially in major cities. . . . By the early 1970s, the former picture palaces and neighborhood houses that during the 1930s and 1940s had provided Hollywood with all its gold were servicing only African-Americans. Chicago was typical. In the early 1970s the former picture palaces in Chicago's loop programmed action films exclusively. The changeover in Chicago took place in the years after that city's urban riot. The owners of the theatres actually welcomed the transformation because targeting black teens precipitated the first boost in patronage since the flight to the suburbs had begun in earnest two decades earlier.[8]

Hollywood's images of America's inner cities in the early years of the 1970s hardly matched the reality, but it did finally register the racial composition of urban centers, and it specifically played on the white fear of street crime. Many films produced during Hollywood's renaissance—*Midnight Cowboy* (UA, 1969), *The French Connection* (Twentieth Century Fox, 1971), *Dirty Harry* (Warner Bros., 1971), *Serpico* (Paramount, 1973), *Death Wish* (Paramount, 1974), *Taxi Driver* (Columbia, 1976), and *Cruising* (Lorimar, 1980)—pandered to their principally white suburban audience by playing on their fears and prejudices of American inner cities aroused by news stories of race riots, rising crime rates, police corruption, the ranking of cities according to the number of murders committed within their borders, an escalating drug problem, and endemic poverty.[9]

While the fictional city streets of American film in the first half of the 1970s register black experiences, these films also limit those experiences to a world exclusively defined by and confined to the streets. If the city had to be reconfigured by America's filmmakers, albeit on the borrowed terrain of earlier crime films, what better way to display and re-map this space than through the "savages" of the modern city—detectives, drug dealers, pimps, and gangsters—tour guides drawn from the streets and underworld. And while these character types hardly represent a progressive vision of a more democratic and inclusive United States, the central role given to urban blacks suggests a more vital, lively, and charismatic figuration than the generally symbolic role he or she was assigned in the white cast imaginary of Hollywood's earlier representational strategies. Yet what was gained in the promotion and recognition of film images of black urban life was at the cost of representing a female engagement with black musical forms. Blaxploitation is excessively concerned with appealing to a male sensibility in contrast to the films essayed in this book's earlier chapters. Left behind was the previously dominant image of jazz and blues' evocation of a low-class, black, sexualized, female subjectivity.

Despite its basic exploitation of contemporary urban fears and desires and the "loss" of a feminine address, what was singular about blaxploitation was its particular mix of film and popular black musical forms. The funk and soul sound tracks provided by James Brown, Isaac Hayes, Marvin Gaye, Donny Hathaway, Booker T. and the MGs, and Curtis Mayfield, to name only the most notable, gave prominence to black music and film. This laid the groundwork for the critically more respected hip hop movies of the 1980s and 1990s; as rock critic Dave Marsh attested in 1973, the soul stars that created the sound tracks "insured black rhythm music's place in the pop mainstream," and they did so by highlighting, not hiding, the music's political charge. For the first time, writes Marsh, black music was "fully, proudly conscious of its blackness."[10]

Perhaps not surprisingly given the long history of Hollywood's racial masquerade, the most fulsome articulation of pride through the performance of black music does not occur in the black-centric films of the 1990s (which like the previous blaxploitation cycle were overdetermined by the tropes of the crime/thriller genre) but in *8 Mile* (Universal, 2002) starring the white rapper Eminem. As in *The Jazz Singer,* this film suggests that race mixing allows for the true expression of the heartfelt; moreover, unlike the vast majority of contemporary films, *8 Mile* forsook an easy celebration of a white, middle-class, family-oriented morality and consumerism (no brand names are displayed on the characters' clothes or elsewhere). Instead it engaged with a working-class, mixed-raced existence as an expression of an authentic American accent. "What is that?" It is, to paraphrase the answer to the same question asked about the dancer in *Gangs of New York,* the rhythm of the Dark Continent of the white imagination tapped out in a fine American mess.

When I die don't bury me at all,
Just nail my bones up on the wall
Beneath these bones let these words be seen
"The running gears of a boppin' machine."

—Ronnie Dawson, "Rockin' Bones" (1958)

Notes

Introduction

1. *Martin Scorsese's Gangs of New York: Making the Movie* (London: Headline Books, 2002).

2. Jennifer DeVere Brody, *Impossible Purities: Blackness, Femininity, and Victorian Culture* (Durham, N.C.: Duke University Press, 1998).

3. W. T. Lhamon Jr., *Raising Cain: Blackface Performance from Jim Crow to Hip Hop* (Cambridge, Mass.: Harvard University Press, 1998), 3–4.

4. Lawrence W. Levine, "Jazz and American Culture," in *The Unpredictable Past: Explorations in American Cultural History* (New York: Oxford University Press, 1993), 172–88. The movie *Four Daughters* (Warner Bros., 1938) offers a particularly rich example of an American culture caught between the polarities of high and low musical forms.

5. Brody, *Impossible Purities,* 1, 66–67.

6. Joseph Mitchell, *My Ears Are Bent* (New York: Pantheon Books, 2001), 55.

7. Robert C. Allen, *Horrible Prettiness: Burlesque and American Culture* (Chapel Hill: University of North Carolina Press, 1991), 225–36.

8. Marcus Klein, *Foreigners: The Making of American Literature, 1900–1940* (Chicago: University of Chicago Press, 1981), x.

9. Dan Morgenstern, booklet with the compact disc set *The Commodore Story* (BMG, CMD 24002, 1997). "A Selection from the Gutter" also appears on *Commodore Piano Anthology* (GRP, 543 273-2, 2000). Some of the sides Hodes cut in the 1940s can be found on the *Hot Jazz on Blue Note* anthology (Smithsonian Institution/Capital Records, CDP 7243 8 35811 2, 1996).

10. Art Hodes and Chadwick Hansen, eds., *Selections from the Gutter: Portraits from the Jazz Record* (Berkeley: University of California Press, 1977). Art Hodes

and Chadwick Hansen, *Hot Man: Life of Art Hodes* (Urbana: University of Illinois Press, 1992).

Chapter 1: An Octoroon in the Kindling

1. Robert C. Allen, *Horrible Prettiness: Burlesque and American Culture* (Chapel Hill: University of North Carolina Press, 1991), 158–78: "Burlesque, the melting pot of show business, recruited performers from everywhere, from honka tonks, vaudeville, carnival." Beth Brown, *Applause* (New York: Grosset and Dunlap, 1928), 40. For an overview of the history of minstrelsy, see Robert C. Toll, *Blacking Up: The Minstrel Show in Nineteenth Century America* (New York: Oxford University Press, 1974).

2. Henry Jenkins, *What Made Pistachio Nuts? Early Sound Comedy and the Vaudeville Aesthetic* (New York: Columbia University Press, 1992), 153–84.

3. Michael Rogin, *Blackface, White Noise: Jewish Immigrants in the Hollywood Melting Pot* (Berkeley: University of California Press, 1996).

4. David R. Roediger, *The Wages of Whiteness: Race and the Making of the American Working Class* (London: Verso, 1991).

5. Dale Cockrell, *Demons of Disorder: Early Blackface Minstrels and Their World* (Cambridge: Cambridge University Press, 1997), 141.

6. W. T. Lhamon Jr., *Raising Cain: Blackface Performance from Jim Crow to Hip Hop* (Cambridge, Mass.: Harvard University Press, 1998), 179.

7. Ibid., 107.

8. Ibid., 107.

9. Chip Rhodes, *Structures of the Jazz Age: Mass Culture, Progressive Education, and Racial Disclosures in American Modernism* (London: Verso, 1998), 177.

10. Lhamon, *Raising Cain,* 114–15.

11. Ibid., 104.

12. Ibid., 108.

13. Herbert G. Goldman, *Jolson: The Legend Comes to Life* (New York: Oxford University Press, 1988), 87.

14. Ibid., 110–11.

15. Nick Tosches, *Dino: Living High in the Dirty Business of Dreams* (London: Secker and Warburg, 1992), 28.

16. Lhamon, *Raising Cain,* 112–13.

17. Samson Raphaelson, *The Jazz Singer* (New York: Brentano's, 1925), 9–10, cited in *The Jazz Singer,* ed. Robert L. Carringer, Wisconsin/Warner Bros. Screenplay Series (Madison: University of Wisconsin Press, 1979), 23.

18. Marinetti quoted in Umbro Apollonio, *Futurist Manifestos* (Boston: MFA Publications, 2001), 19–24.

19. Ann Douglas, *Terrible Honesty: Mongrel Manhattan in the 1920s* (London: Picador, 1996), 4.

20. Robert Cantwell, *Bluegrass Breakdown: The Making of the Old Southern Sound* (New York: Da Capo, 1992), 141.

21. Bernard Gendron, *Between Montmartre and the Mudd Club: Popular Music and the Avant-Garde* (Chicago: University of Chicago Press, 2002), 106.

22. Ibid., 97. In his introduction to the Belgian jazz critic Robert Goffin's *Jazz* (London: Musicians Press, 1946), Englishman Ray Sonin writes, "European composers, European poets, European critics were all quick to realize that the music that reached out from Storyville in New Orleans was more than the cacophony many would have the world believe" (ii).

23. Lhamon, *Raising Cain,* 108–9.

24. "Toot, Toot, Tootsie!" is best heard on the compact disc *Let Me Sing and I'm Happy: Al Jolson at Warner Bros. 1926–1936* (Rhino R272544, 1996). The source is a second-generation Vitaphone disc that is brighter and louder than the muddy optical sound track heard on the film. Ian Whitcomb, the CD's producer, also documents the musicians who played on this session; none are known "jazz" musicians.

25. Goldman, *Jolson,* 44.

26. Roediger, *The Wages of Whiteness,* 118.

27. Ibid., 218.

28. Ibid., 211.

29. Ibid., 231.

30. Quoted in Thomas Cripps, *Slow Fade to Black: The Negro in American Film, 1900–1942* (New York: Oxford University Press, 1977), 113.

31. Letter dated Oct. 17, 1935, in PCA file on *Show Boat,* Margaret Herrick Library of the Academy of Motion Picture Arts and Sciences (AMPAS), Beverly Hills, Los Angeles, California.

32. See also the Marx brothers performance in blackface played out against a cast of African American dancers and singers in *A Day at the Races* (MGM, 1937).

33. Linda Williams, *Playing the Race Card: Melodramas of Black and White from Uncle Tom to O. J. Simpson* (Princeton: Princeton University Press, 2001), 176.

34. Barris was a former member of the Rhythm Boys, alongside Al Rinker and Bing Crosby.

35. The show starring her daughter that Magnolia attends was originally intended to trace the "development of jazz dance from southern plantation to modern times." The stills from the cut scenes are reproduced in Miles Kreuger, *Show Boat: The Story of a Classic American Musical* (New York: Da Capo, 1977), 148–50.

36. Edna Ferber, *Show Boat* (New York: Signet Classic, 1994), 275.

37. Ibid., 275.

38. Ibid., 297.

39. Ibid., 299.

40. Charles Hamm, *Yesterdays: Popular Song in America* (New York: Norton and Co., 1983), 271. For a more detailed analysis of the distinction between antebellum and postwar nostalgia in the minstrel song, see Lee Glazer and Susan Key, "Carry Me Back: Nostalgia for the Old South in Nineteenth Century Popular Culture," *Journal of American Studies* 30, no. 1 (Apr. 1996): 1–24.

41. Hamm, *Yesterdays*, 321.

42. Robert Lawson-Peebles, ed., *Approaches to the American Musical* (Exeter: University of Exeter Press, 1996), 2.

43. Complete lyrics quoted in Eric Lott, *Love and Theft: Blackface Minstrelsy and the American Working Class* (New York: Oxford University Press, 1995), 204.

44. The recording can be heard on the Canadian compact disc set *American Pop: An Audio History* (West Hill Audio Archives, 1998).

45. Paul Oliver, *Songsters and Saints: Vocal Traditions on Race Records* (Cambridge: Cambridge University Press, 1984), 47–77.

46. Ferber, *Show Boat*, 243.

47. Peter Stanfield, *Hollywood, Westerns, and the 1930s: The Lost Trail* (Exeter: University of Exeter Press, 2001), 33–40, 208–12.

48. Allen, *Horrible Prettiness*, 73–78.

49. Mary Beth Hamilton, *The Queen of Camp: Mae West, Sex, and Popular Culture* (London: Pandora, 1996), 24.

50. Ibid., 24. On Mae West's claims to have invented this dance, see Marshall and Jean Stearns, *Jazz Dance: The Story of American Vernacular Dance* (New York: Da Capo Press, 1994), 104–5.

51. Lott, *Love and Theft*, 18. For the fullest account of Rice's life and work, see W. T. Lhamon Jr., *Jump Jim Crow: Lost Plays, Lyrics, and Street Prose of the First Atlantic Popular Culture* (Cambridge, Mass.: Harvard University Press, 2003).

52. Quoted in Francis Davis, *The History of the Blues: The Roots, the Music, the People from Charlie Patton to Robert Cray* (London: Secker and Warburg, 1995), 25–26.

53. Hamilton, *The Queen of Camp*, 134.

54. Ibid., 15.

55. Rosetta Reitz, sleeve notes to *Mae West Sings Sultry Songs* (Rosetta Records, CD RRCD 1315, 1990). For a useful description of the distinction between minstrel "Mammys" and blues "Mamas," see Rogin, *Blackface, White Noise*, 111. The best compact disc collection of Mae West's recordings is *I'm No Angel* (Jasmine, JASCD 102, 1996) that compiles her only commercial phonograph recordings alongside dubs from her movies.

56. Angela Y. Davis, *Blues Legacies and Black Feminism: Gertrude "Ma" Rainey, Bessie Smith, and Billie Holiday* (New York: Pantheon, 1998), 119.

57. Collected on *Ethel Waters, featuring Benny Goodman and Duke Ellington, 1929–1939* (Timeless Records, CBC 1-007, 1992).

58. For an account of the construction of the Irish as "black," see Roediger, *The Wages of Whiteness*, 133–56.

59. Ian Whitcomb, *Irving Berlin and Ragtime America* (New York: Limelight Editions, 1988), 106, and Oliver, *Songsters and Saints,* 49. "Frankie and Johnny" was also said to have been first performed by "Mammy Lou": see Vance Randolph, *Ozark Folksongs,* vol. 2, *Songs of the South and West* (Columbia: University of Missouri Press, 1980), 126.

60. Allen, *Horrible Prettiness,* 131.

61. See correspondence and notes in *The Bowery* PCA file, Margaret Herrick Library, AMPAS.

62. Memo from W. Hays, Jan. 13, 1935, in *Barbary Coast* PCA file, AMPAS.

63. Letter from J. Breen to W. Hays, Feb. 5, 1935, in *Barbary Coast* PCA file, AMPAS.

64. Letter to Breen, Mar. 12, 1935, in *Barbary Coast* PCA file, AMPAS.

65. Matthew J. Bruccoli, ed., *San Francisco: A Screenplay by Anita Loos* (Carbondale: Southern Illinois Press, 1979), 3.

66. Ibid., 33, 34.

67. Ibid., 137.

68. Letter from Breen to Hays, Aug. 31, 1935, in *Barbary Coast* PCA file, AMPAS.

69. Stanfield, *Hollywood, Westerns, and the 1930s,* 173–80.

70. See Tino Balio, *Grand Design: Hollywood as a Modern Business Enterprise, 1930–1939* (Berkeley: University of California Press, 1993), 179.

71. Cripps, *Slow Fade to Black,* 366.

72. For example, consider how "nigger" is used in the dialogue spoken in private by Red agents in *I Was a Communist for the FBI* (1951). The film's producers obviously hoped to elicit an emotional response from viewers to further help discredit the Commies' egalitarian public rhetoric. The sense of implied outrage in this deployment of a racial epithet suggests a significant movement away from its more casual and often comically intended usage in early 1930s movies.

73. Cripps, *Slow Fade to Black,* 3.

74. Ibid., 376.

Chapter 2: This Extremely Dangerous Material

1. Shields would have a small role in Al Jolson's early stage career; see Herbert G. Goldman, *Jolson: The Legend Comes to Life* (New York: Oxford University Press, 1988), 35–36.

2. John A. Lomax and Alan Lomax, *American Ballads and Folk Songs* (New York: Macmillan, 1934), 103.

3. The following texts helped to construct this account of the origins and intertexts of the ballad and provided most of the quoted lyrics: Peter Van Der Merwe, *Origins of the Popular Style The Antecedents of Twentieth-Century Popular Music* (Oxford: Clarendon Press, 1992), 184–97; Vance Randolph, *Ozark Folksongs,* vol. 2, *Songs of the South and West* (Columbia: University of Missouri

Press, 1980), 124–36; Peter Grammond, *The Oxford Companion to Popular Music* (Oxford: Oxford University Press), 207; John A. Lomax and Alan Lomax, *American Ballads and Folk Songs* (New York: Macmillan, 1934), 103–11; Bruce R. Buckley, "Frankie and Her Men: A Study of the Interrelationships of Popular and Folk Traditions" (PhD diss., Indiana University, 1961); and John Russell David, "Tragedy in Ragtime: Black Folk Tales from St. Louis" (Ph.D. diss., St. Louis University, 1976).

4. Carl Sandburg, *American Songbag* (New York: Harcourt Brace, 1955), 75.

5. John Huston, *Frankie and Johnny* (New York: Albert and Charles Boni, 1930), 111. See also Paul Oliver, *Songster and Saints: Vocal Traditions on Race Records* (New York: Cambridge University Press, 1984), 235.

6. Huston, *Frankie and Johnny,* 106–7.

7. David, "Tragedy in Ragtime."

8. Ibid., 202.

9. Sigmund Spaeth, *A History of Popular Music in America* (New York: Random House, 1948), 206.

10. John Held Jr., *The Saga of Frankie and Johnny* (New York: Clarkson N. Potter, 1972).

11. David, "Tragedy in Ragtime," 204–5.

12. A 1945 recording is available on compact disc (Koch, KIC 7367).

13. The concerto was first performed on Bing Crosby's radio show in 1941 and later recorded as a V-Disc for the armed forces during World War II.

14. Gerald Bordman, *American Theatre: A Chronicle of Comedy and Drama, 1930–1969* (New York: Oxford University Press, 1996), 7.

15. This and the following quotations that relate to censorship are from the *Her Man* PCA file, AMPAS.

16. *Variety,* Sept. 17, 1930.

17. Milt Gross, *He Done Her Wrong: The Great American Novel And Not a Word in It—No Music, Too* (New York: Dover Publications, 1971). In 1927 Covarrubias contributed eight half-tone illustrations and several drawings to W. C. Handy's *Blues: An Anthology* (1926; New York: Da Capo, 1990), which formed the basis of his *Negro Drawings* (n.p., 1927). Meyer Levin, *Frankie and Johnnie* (New York: John Day, 1930), was republished as *The Young Lovers* (New York: Signet, 1952).

18. Ma Rainey sung "Stack O'Lee" to the tune of "Frankie and Johnny" (as did Johnny Dodds and His Chicago Boys in their 1938 recording "Stack O'Lee Blues"), but she still managed to get in the line "He was her man, and he was doing her wrong."

19. Crumit's version is best heard alongside contemporary blues, jazz, and country cuts on the compact disc collection *When the Sun Goes Down: The Secret History of Rock and Roll,* vol. 1, *Walk Right In* (Bluebird/RCA Victor, 2002).

20. While Autry's risqué version reveals the "truth" that underlies all versions of the ballad, what makes it an extraordinary version is that it is Autry who is singing it. John Paddy Browne, who passed on a copy of the recording,

writes that Autry's "public image is so far removed from the *mise en scene,* as it were, of the ballad that we are shocked by the juxtaposition of the ballad and singer. The song, in this instance, has the power to convince us, finally, that nothing is ever as it seems" (letter to the author, Apr. 19, 2003). As far as I'm aware, no commercial copies have been made available of this version, nor of the other dozen or so bawdy songs, "Goodbye Cherry" among them, that Autry recorded for the private contemplation of gentlemen.

21. Other prewar country recordings of the ballad are by Clayton McMichen's Georgia Wildcats, by Riley Puckett, and on a radio transcription disc by the Carter Family.

22. Oliver, *Songsters and Saints,* 237–38.

23. Huston, *Frankie and Johnny,* 150.

24. Sterling A. Brown, *The Collected Poems of Sterling A. Brown* (New York: Harper and Row, 1980), 44.

25. James H. Dormon, "Shaping the Popular Image of Post-Reconstruction American Blacks: The 'Coon Song' Phenomenon of the Gilded Age," *American Quarterly* 40, no. 4 (1988): 440–77.

26. *Variety,* Sept. 17, 1930.

27. Huston, *Frankie and Johnny,* 85.

28. Fergus Cashin, *Mae West: A Biography* (London: W. H. Allen, 1981), 80.

29. The film is discussed at some length by Nick Roddick, *A New Deal in Entertainment: Warner Bros. in the 1930s* (London: British Film Institute, 1983), 169–71.

30. *Red Headed Woman* PCA file, AMPAS.

31. *Life Begins* PCA file, AMPAS.

32. Lea Jacobs, *The Wages of Sin: Censorship and the Fallen Woman Film, 1928-1942* (Berkeley: University of California Press, 1997), x.

33. Ibid., 35.

34. Richard Maltby, "The Production Code and the Hays Office," in *Grand Design: Hollywood as a Modern Business Enterprise, 1930–1939,* ed. Tino Balio (University of California Press, 1995), 40.

35. Jacobs, *The Wages of Sin,* 35.

36. *New York Times,* Oct. 6, 1930.

37. *Motion Picture* 40, no. 5 (Dec. 1930): 63.

38. *Picture Play* 33, no. 5 (Jan. 1931): 24–25, 65.

39. *Exhibitors Herald World,* Sept. 13, 1930.

40. *Film Daily,* Sept. 21, 1930.

41. *Motion Picture News,* Sept. 27, 1930, and *Variety,* Sept. 17, 1930.

42. *Exhibitors Herald World,* Oct. 11, 1930.

43. *Variety,* Sept. 17, 1930.

44. John Andrew Gallagher, "Rediscovering *Her Man," Films in Review* 46, no. 9/10 (Nov./Dec. 1995): 36–45.

45. Ruth Vasey, *The World According to Hollywood, 1918-1939* (Exeter: University of Exeter Press, 1997), 107.

46. Richard Maltby, "Spectacle of Criminality," in *Violence and American Cinema,* ed. J. David Slocum (New York: Routledge, 2000), 117–52.

47. Jacobs, *The Wages of Sin,* 66–70.

48. *Exhibitors Herald World,* Sept. 13, 1930, 38.

49. *Her Man* PCA file, AMPAS.

50. Giuliana Muscio, *Hollywood's New Deal* (Philadelphia: Temple University Press, 1997), 113.

51. See Vasey, *The World According to Hollywood,* 118, 123, 211.

52. *Variety,* Sept. 17, 1930.

53. Quoted in Gallagher, "Rediscovering *Her Man*"; he also gives more details of the censor's cuts and edits.

54. *Motion Picture Herald,* May 23, 1936, 45.

55. *New York Times,* May 25, 1936.

56. *Variety,* May 27, 1936.

57. *Motion Picture Herald,* May 30, 1936.

58. Helen Morgan's vocal recording was given a commercial phonograph record release and has subsequently been collected on the compact disc *The Glory of Helen Morgan* (MCI Presents, MPMCD 003, 1998).

59. Jacobs, *The Wages of Sin,* 148.

60. Letter from Breen to Ben Goetz, Consolidated Film Laboratories [Republic Pictures], Oct. 8, 1934, PCA files, AMPAS. For the record, the specific revisions demanded from the first cut of the film are as follows:

> The predominant background of a brothel and the attendant evidences of prostitution. The theme, which portrays sin and immorality without compensating moral values. An illicit love affair is justified and condoned. This immoral behavior is not clearly shown to be wrong, but is actually shown to be right and permissible. The specific objections to indecent over-exposure are frequently violated. Various minor characters are exposed for the sake of exposure solely. All uses of "Frankie and Johnny" song throughout the picture must be deleted. The title should not mention Jack Kirkland's original play *Frankie and Johnny.* Opening shot of woman coming out of the door smiling at man following her. The dialogue, "Carriage for Madame Lou." "Gentlemen have no illusions about." "In their own bed—let them lay in it." Backdrop in cabaret. Statue on side of stage. Costume of chorus. "Pearls are not so expensive in the long run." "After all, a woman's only a woman." Shot of girl at table showing her breasts. "One of my girls goes out into the world." Girl taking off garter. "May I ask which of the men is the happy bridegroom?" Shot of the girl with legs bare at Johnny's entrance. Picture on wall. . . . lady with shoes on before. ". . . play around for a quarter." Frankie and Johnny music when they are introduced to each other. "Well I'll be a—" Singing of Frankie and Johnnie song, "Johnnie came up on the steamboat." Girls running to Johnny after announcement of winning money. "He looks old enough to me." "With a few lessons I could teach you lot about dancing." "When do we start?" "Right now" (and kiss). "What were you thinking about when you were

staring about?" "That you and me ought to get together." "Women like you know their place." Shot of sheriff. "Somebody get shot?" "Bring two more." "I'll show you how to get out of here—come on." (entering her room). "That's been lasting longer than I thought it would." "I can't see what you wanted to leave the Mansion House for." Singing song in empty Mansion House of "Frankie and Johnny." "I paid for it didn't I?" "You paid for it—Frankie paid for it." "After that first night I know you was no farm boy." "To elevate my girls to a broader understanding of their functions." "I figured it was a one night stand." Frankie's entrance to house without key. Frankie going into bedroom to take off her hat and scarf. Kiss on neck in Johnny's house. "It's a great shame for a town to harbor such creatures." "You wouldn't do anything to hurt Little Miss Elsie—not after Saturday night." "You leave my girls alone—my girls are honest." Men accosting Frankie on way to Mansion House. Frankie looking for Johnny in his house. Johnnie kissing Nellie on the couch and shot of cupids, cherubs, etc. "Frankie and Johnny were sweethearts, said they would love 'til they died. Frankie was sure that he loved her but he loved Nellie Bly." Frankie listening from balcony to song. Shot of sign on Frankie's door. Frankie entering, shot of Frankie coming out of her room. Shot of man drawing guns on Johnny. Shooting of Johnny. After Johnny's death the singing of "Frankie and Johnny" song. Scene in carriage with sheriff. "She won't be alone for long." Tag of Frankie going off with Curly.

61. Gaylyn Studlar, *This Mad Masquerade: Stardom and Masculinity in the Jazz Age* (New York: Columbia University Press, 1997), 151–52.

62. *Screen Romances Album* 1, no. 1 (Feb. 1931): 13.

63. Sandburg, *American Songbag,* 75.

64. *Ziegfeld Follies* PCA file, AMPAS and quoted in Hugh Fordin, *The World of Entertainment: Hollywood's Greatest Musicals* (New York: Doubleday, 1975), 121–22.

65. Sandburg, *American Songbag,* 75.

66. MPAA turned down the registration of the title "Frankie and Johnny" on a number of occasions towards the end of the 1930s. See letter from Milliken to Edward Small Productions, May 2, 1939. Letter from Milliken to John H. Whitney, Pioneer Pictures New York, June 14, 1940: "Pursuant to the actions of the Board of Directors at their meeting of December 10, 1930, it is suggested that the above title be not registered" (*Frankie and Johnnie* PCA file, AMPAS). Letter to Milliken from Breen, Dec. 18, 1939:

> Lou Edelman, a producer at Warners, told me Saturday afternoon about an idea he has to write a story for Bette Davis and Jimmy Cagney on what he calls the "Frankie and Johnny formula."
>
> We had some discussion about it, and his idea as far as we are concerned it is not as bad as might appear at first sight. The theme with the story—he has nothing concrete as yet—will not be the theme which is probably associated in the public's mind with the song Frankie and Johnny, and will, of course, be acceptable under the provisions of the production code.

In the course of our conversation Mr. Edleman asked me if I thought you'd approve the title, "Frankie and Johnny," and I told him, in reply, that we had no thought in this office concerning titles of any kind, pointing out to him that the question of titles was not within the responsibility of the production code.

I ventured to tell him, as my personal viewpoint, however, that I thought he would have difficulty with the title, "Frankie and Johnny," even though his picture might be perfectly acceptable otherwise. I gave it as my personal opinion that your title committee would hesitate to approve such a title, because the expression "Frankie and Johnny" is associated in the public mind with a very definite fault, which is not good.

I pass along this information against the possibility that you may hear from Warners about the matter, as far as the story goes, we have made no commitment. We did say, that we shall be very glad to read a treatment of the story and render a decision upon it, immediately Mr. Edleman gets something down on paper.

Cordially Yours, Joseph I Breen.

From *Gal Who Took the West* PCA file, AMPAS.

67. Maria Leach, ed., *Funk and Wagnall's Standard Dictionary of Folklore Mythology and Legend* (London: New English Library, 1975).

68. For example, Tom Glazer, *A New Treasury of Folk Songs* (New York: Bantam, 1961). For an exemplary history of the folk revival, see Robert Cantwell, *When We Were Good: The Folk Revival* (Cambridge, Mass.: Harvard University Press, 1996).

Chapter 3: An Excursion into the Lower Depths

1. Carl Sandburg, *The American Songbag* (New York: Harcourt Brace Jovanovich, 1990), 204–6.

2. Quoted in Hugh Fordin, *The World of Entertainment: Hollywood's Greatest Musicals* (New York: Doubleday, 1975), 121–22.

3. Spaeth, *A History of Popular Music in America,* 441. In 1934, Paramount Pictures produced a film starring George Raft under the title *Limehouse Blues.*

4. Henry Cohen, ed., *The Public Enemy* (Madison: University of Wisconsin Press, 1981), 73.

5. Jelly Roll Morton also claimed authorship of "Hesitating Blues." His risqué version is heard on *The Library of Congress Recordings,* vol. 1 (Rounder, CD1091, 1993).

6. According to one of her biographers, "St. Louis Blues" was playing on the radio when sixteen-year-old Harlean Harlow Carpenter (Jean Harlow) married Charles McGrew II. Perhaps it did happen. . . . (David Stein, *Bombshell: The Life and Death of Jean Harlow* [New York: Doubleday, 1993], 26).

7. Gary Giddins considers "St. Louis Blues" to be the "most frequently re-corded song in America during the quarter century between the two world wars" in *Visions of Jazz: The First Century* (Oxford: Oxford University Press, 1998), 29.

8. Ethel Waters, *His Eye Is on the Sparrow* (London: Jazz Book Club, 1958), 72. Charles Anderson is one of the many "lost" performers in a history of African American vaudeville that is still to be written. He recorded three sessions for the Okeh label in 1923, 1924, and 1928. He specialized in novelty yodel numbers (a mainstay of blackface vaudeville performers), mimicking contemporary female sopranos. He recorded "St. Louis Blues" in his final session, but it remains unissued. His issued sides can be heard on "Eddie Heywood and the Blues Singers" (Document, DOCD-5380, n.d.) and "Male Blues of the Twenties" (Document, DOCD-5532, n.d.); they do not make for easy listening. Despite a much more productive and commercially successful recording career, Ethel Waters did not record the song until 1942. For full discographies of both artists, see Robert Dixon, John Goodrich, and Howard Rye, *Blues and Gospel Records 1890–1943,* 4th ed. (Oxford: Oxford University Press, 1997).

9. Arthur Kempton, *Boogaloo: The Quintessence of American Popular Music* (New York: Pantheon Books, 2003), 17.

10. See W. C. Handy, *Father of the Blues: An Autobiography* (1941; New York: Da Capo Press, 1991), 195–97. Virtually undocumented, Bernard's discography covers nearly all the period's significant blues and jazz standards: he recorded one of the first versions of "Frankie and Johnny" backed by Handy's "Memphis Blues" for Brunswick in 1920 and a version of "Hesitation Blues" in 1927 accompanied by the Goofus Five.

11. Al Bernard's recording of St. Louis Blues with the ODJB can be heard on *The Original Dixieland Jazz Band: The Seventy-fifth Anniversary* (BMG, ND90650, 1992); Emmett Miller's version and the parody is on *The Minstrel Man from Georgia* (Columbia, 483584 2, 1996); the Cotton Pickers' "St. Louis Gal" is on *The Original Memphis Five/Napoleon's Emperors/The Cotton Pickers 1928–29* (Timeless, CBC 1–049 Jazz, 1998). Yet another blackface minstrel recording was by Roy Evans and is featured on *Blue Yodelers with Red Hot Accompanists* (Retrieval, RTR 79020, 1999). The recording is apparently a sound track to a 1929 MGM short. Other than the minstrel parodies, variations on the theme of "St. Louis Blues" were common currency in the late 1920s and 1930s, notably Mae West's performance of Johnson and Coslow's "When a St. Louis Woman Comes Down to New Orleans" as seen in *Belle of the Nineties* (Paramount, 1934).

12. "A Negro from the London docks sings the 'Black Out Blues' . . . I hate to see the evenin' sun go down . . . because the German he done bomb this town." I am in debt to Frank Krutnik who discovered this gem on the Internet. For a listing of jazz performances of "St. Louis Blues," see Brian Rust, *Jazz Records 1897–1942,* 5th ed. (Chigwell, Essex: Storyville Pubs., 1983).

13. Brian Peerless, notes accompanying the compact disc Louis Armstrong, *St. Louis Blues* (Columbia, CK46996, 1991); David Schiff, *Gershwin: Rhapsody in Blue* (Cambridge: Cambridge University Press, 1997), 41.

14. For example, see Gunther Schuller, *Early Jazz: Its Roots and Musical Development* (1968; New York: Oxford University Press, 1986), 237. Alyn Shipton, *A New History of Jazz* (New York: Continuum, 2001), 134. Laurence Bergreen writes: "Their performance *is* the blues—straight, no chaser—and this recording became an indisputable classic." *Louis Armstrong: An Extravagant Life* (New York: Broadway Books, 1997), 252.

15. Unless otherwise noted, all lyric transcriptions are taken from W. C. Handy, *Blues: An Anthology* (New York: Da Capo, 1990), 82–85.

16. Ian Whitcomb, *Irving Berlin and Ragtime America* (New York: Limelight Editions, 1988), 205.

17. Alan Lomax, *Mister Jelly Roll* (London: Pan Books, 1959), 215.

18. For example, see J. Martin Favor, *Authentic Blackness: The Folk in the New Negro Renaissance* (Durham, N.C.: Duke University Press, 1999), 1–24, 69–74.

19. Handy, *Blues*, 77.

20. Ibid., 119–21.

21. Ibid., 28–29.

22. Ibid., 118.

23. Ibid., 119.

24. Cited in Burton W. Peretti, *The Creation of Jazz: Music, Race, and Culture in Urban America* (Urbana: University of Illinois Press, 1994), 168.

25. H. O. Brunn, *The Story of the Original Dixieland Jazz Band* (London: Jazz Book Club, 1963), 135.

26. Nathan Irvin Huggins, *Harlem Renaissance* (Oxford: Oxford University Press, 1971), 100.

27. Quoted in Alyn Shipton, *A New History of Jazz* (New York: Continuum, 2001), 257.

28. Armstrong's three 1929 takes of "St. Louis Blues" are collected together on *St. Louis Blues* (Columbia, CK 46996, 1991); April 1934 is on *The Complete RCA-Victor* Recordings (BMG Bluebird, 09026–63846–2, 2001); the Paris recordings are on *Louis Armstrong and Friends* (Universal, 013 979–2, 2001). Armstrong next recorded the song for his collection of W. C. Handy compositions in 1954, and then as a concerto grosso with Leonard Bernstein conducting the Lewisohn Symphony Orchestra in 1956. Armstrong also played "St. Louis Blues" on-screen alongside Danny Kaye in *Five Pennies* (Paramount, 1959). In order to capitalize on the boogie-woogie craze, Handy copyrighted an Earl Hines arrangement, "Boogie-Woogie on St. Louis Blues," which is included in W. C. Handy, ed., *Blues,* 167–71. Hines' recording is collected on *A Left Hand of God: Boogie Woogie* (Nostalgia, NOS 3682).

29. Nick Tosches, *Country: The Twisted Roots of Rock 'n' Roll* (New York: Da Capo Press, 1996), 251.

30. Ibid.

31. Nick Tosches, "Emmett Miller: The Mystery Solved," *Journal of Country Music* 18, no. 3 (1996): 34–35.

32. Cockrell, *Demons of Disorder,* 141. For a discussion of minstrelsy and whistling, see Lhamon, *Raising Cain,* 111–15.

33. For more on the relationship between white singers and black music from this period, see Roger Hewitt, "Black through White: Hoagy Carmichael and the Cultural Reproduction of Racism," *Popular Music* no. 3 (1983): 33–50. On blackface and jazz, see Berndt Ostendorf, "Minstrelsy and Early Jazz," *Massachusetts Review* 20 (Autumn 1979): 574–602. For a review of jazz biopics, which inevitably highlight the white influence on the development of the idiom, see Krin Gabbard, *Jammin' at the Margins: Jazz and the American Cinema* (Chicago: University of Chicago Press, 1996), 64–100. "Black Moonlight" is on *Bing Crosby 1927 to 1934* (BBC, CD 648, 1986) and "Mississippi Mud" is on *Bix Beiderbecke,* vol. 2, *At the Jazz Band Ball* (CBS, 466967 2, 1990).

34. Gabbard, *Jammin' at the Margins,* 160–203.

35. The Crosby/Ellington versions of "St. Louis Blues" are discussed in detail by Gary Giddins, *Bing Crosby: A Pocketful of Dreams, The Early Years 1903–1940* (New York: Little, Brown, 2001), 275–76. They are collected on Duke Ellington, *It Don't Mean a Thing if It Ain't Got That Swing* (Naxos, 8120526, 2001).

36. The two earlier versions of "St. Louis Blues" are collected on the essential and monumental Bear Family box set *San Antonio Rose* (BCD, 15933 LL, 2000). The 1954 version is on the equally essential *Boot Heel Drag: The MGM Years* (Mercury, 088 170 206–2, 2001). The exclusive 1946 two-part recording for radio is on *Tiffany Transcriptions,* vol. 9 (Rhino, R2 71477, 1990). Milton Brown's version is on *Western Swing Chronicles,* vol. 1 (Origin Jazz Library, OLJ-1000, 2001):

> Oh play them blues, man. Play 'em . . .
>
> Come here and tell me baby, whose muddy shoes are these?
> Come here and tell me baby, whose muddy shoes are these?
> 'Cos they are sitting right here, where my shoes ought to be.
>
> I woke up this morning, between midnight and day
> I woke up this morning, between midnight and day
> You ought to see me grab that pillow, where my sweet mama used to lay.
> —Milton Brown and His Musical Brownies, "St. Louis Blues" (1935)

37. Furthermore, though this is clearly relative, Al Bernard, Bob Wills, and Bing Crosby's dissembling of a black female subjectivity is a cultural rendering of the economic "theft of the body" of black females. The white male's performance of gender and racial crossings has an effect similar to that which Hortense J. Spillers has argued occurs under slavery: "the captive body becomes the source of an irresistible, destructive sensuality," which in "stunning contradiction" objectifies the body, reducing it to a "thing." This in

turn produces a lack of "subject position, the captured sexualities provide a physical and biological expression of 'otherness,'" that then translates into the potential for pornotroping and embodies "sheer physical powerlessness that slides into a more general powerlessness." This project of "othering" is continued in Hollywood's more general representation of blackness and in the "darkening" of white women through their proximity to, or use of, recordings and performances of songs such as "St. Louis Blues" (Hortense J. Spillers, "Mama's Baby, Papa's Maybe: An American Grammar Book" in *Feminisms: An Anthology of Literary Theory and Criticism,* ed. Robyn R. Warhol and Diane Price Herndl, rev. ed. [New Brunswick, N.J.: Rutgers University Press, 1997], 384–405).

38. The longest version I've encountered is by Louis Armstrong—close to nine minutes—on *Louis Armstrong Plays W. C. Handy* (1956) with the vocals sung by Velma Middleton and Armstrong, but even this doesn't contain all the stanzas from Handy's original and substitutes a number of stanzas unique to this version.

39. Waters, *His Eye Is on the Sparrow,* 73.

40. Gabbard, *Jammin' at the Margins,* 166.

41. For the fullest account of the film's production, see Thomas Cripps, *Slow Fade to Black: The Negro in American Film, 1900–1942* (New York: Oxford University Press, 1977), 204–7. The film's sound track can be heard on Bessie Smith, *The Final Chapter: The Complete Recordings,* vol. 5 (Columbia/Legacy, C2K 57546, 1996). The film has been released on video as part of Kino Video's *The Paramount Musical Shorts, 1927–1941.*

42. Gabbard, *Jammin' at the Margins,* 166.

43. Angela Y. Davis, *Blues Legacies and Black Feminism: Gertrude "Ma" Rainey, Bessie Smith, and Billie Holiday* (New York: Pantheon, 1998), 119.

44. Ibid., 61.

45. In 1939, the song was again used in an "all-colored" production: in *Moon Over Harlem* (directed by Edgar G. Ulmer and featuring the great clarinetist Sidney Bechet), a young woman tries to explain to two friends how it feels to be half girl/half woman. The womanly side is described by singing the two opening lines from "St. Louis Blues."

46. James Naremore, "Uptown Folk: Blackness and Entertainment in *Cabin in the Sky,*" 169–92, and Adam Knee, "Doubling, Music, and Race in *Cabin in the Sky,*" 193–204, in *Representing Jazz,* ed. Krin Gabbard (Durham, N.C.: Duke University Press, 1995).

47. Naremore, "Uptown Folk," 170.

48. Knee, "Doubling, Music, and Race," 196.

49. Jennifer DeVere Brody, *Impossible Purities: Blackness, Femininity, and Victorian Culture* (Durham, N.C.: Duke University Press, 1998), 57.

50. Quoted in Susan Gubar, *Racechanges: White Skin, Black Face in American Culture* (New York: Oxford University Press, 1997), 16–17.

51. Chip Rhodes, *Structures of the Jazz Age: Mass Culture, Progressive Education, and Racial Disclosures in American Modernism* (London: Verso, 1998), 188–89.

52. Quoted in Chip Rhodes, *Structures of the Jazz Age: Mass Culture, Progressive Education, and Racial Disclosures in American Modernism* (London: Verso, 1998), 188.

53. For further discussion on Stanwyck's early to mid-1930s star persona, see Lea Jacobs, *The Wages of Sin: Censorship and the Fallen Woman Film, 1928–1942* (Berkeley: University of California Press, 1997), and Richard Maltby, "Baby Face, or How Joe Breen Made Barbara Stanwyck Atone for Causing the Wall Street Crash," *Screen* 27, no. 2 (Mar./Apr. 1986): 22–45.

54. See press clippings in *Banjo on My Knee* PCA file, AMPAS.

55. Letter dated Aug. 24, 1936, *Banjo on My Knee* PCA file, AMPAS.

56. *Stella Dallas* is a key film in the debates on women and melodrama, see, for example, Linda Williams, "'Something Else besides a Mother': *Stella Dallas* and the Maternal Melodrama," *Cinema Journal* 24, no. 1 (Fall 1984): 2–27; Jacobs, *The Wages of Sin*, 132–49; Anna Siomopoulos, "'I Didn't Know Anyone Could Be So Unselfish': Liberal Empathy, the Welfare State, and King Vidor's *Stella Dallas*," *Cinema Journal* 38, no. 4 (1999).

57. In the *Lux Radio Theatre* adaptation of *Stella Dallas,* broadcast on Oct. 11, 1937, "St. Louis Blues" is used in the equivalent scene; its significance is underscored by the absence of the visual in detailing Stella's masquerade.

58. Quoted in Friedrich A. Kittler, *Gramophone, Film, Typewriter* (Stanford: Stanford University Press, 1999), 81.

59. The song is collected on *Ethel Waters 1929–1939* (Timeless, CBC 1-007, 1992).

60. Collected on *Blues Yodeler and Steel Guitar Wizard* (Arhoolie, CD 7039, 1996).

61. Collected on *The King R&B Box Set* (King Records, 1995).

62. For more on Johnson and his "Phonograph Blues," see Greil Marcus, *Mystery Train: Images of America in Rock 'n' Roll Music,* 4th ed. (New York: Plume, 1997), 23. The connection between sex and the phonograph was still being made during the soul era. Joyce Kennedy's "My Hi-Fi Albums and I" recorded for the Blue Rock label circa 1966 is an emotional tour de force: "no one's home just my Hi-Fi, my albums, and I." New York's postpunk scuzz rockers Pussy Galore penned and recorded the immortal "Sweet Little Hi-Fi" in 1988: "I fell in love with my sweet little hi-fi, stereo, bass, treble, in-put and out-put." But by that point the compact disc was turning the phonograph into dust, although no one, to my knowledge, has yet recorded a song extolling the metaphoric sexual delight of the compact disc player.

63. Walter Benjamin, "The Work of Art in the Age of Mechanical Reproduction," in *Film Theory and Criticism: Introductory Readings,* ed. Gerald Mast and Marshall Cohen, 3rd ed. (New York: Oxford University Press, 1985), 675–94.

64. Vera Caspary, *Laura* (New York: Ibooks, 2000), 66.

65. Ibid., 77.

66. Greil Marcus, "Real Life Top Ten" *Salon.com,* July 8, 2002. http://www.salon.com/ent/col/marc/2002/07/08/72/index1.html.

67. Theodor W. Adorno, "On Popular Music," in *On Record: Rock, Pop, and the Written Word,* ed. Simon Frith and Andrew Goodwin (London: Routledge, 1990), 301–14.

68. Quoted in Ruth Brandon, *Surreal Lives* (London: Macmillan Press, 1999), 261.

69. Adorno, "On Popular Music," 301–14.

70. Spaeth, *A History of Popular Music in America,* 538.

71. "St. Louis Blues" was also featured in *Dancers in the Dark* (Paramount, 1932), starring Miriam Hopkins and Jack Oakie; David Meeker, *Jazz in the Movies: A Guide to Jazz Musicians 1817–1977* (London: Talisman Books, 1977) records the use of the song in twenty short films between 1929 and 1952. During the 1940s, the song was featured in *The Birth of the Blues* (Paramount, 1941) starring Bing Crosby and apparently based on the story of the ODJB; *Is Everybody Happy* (Columbia, 1943) starring the Ted Lewis band; *So's Your Uncle* (Universal, 1943); *Jam Session* (Columbia, 1944), which features Louis Armstrong; in the Tom Tyler series Western *Sing Me a Song of Texas* (Columbia, 1945), it is played by the Hoosier Hot Shots; *Do You Love Me* (Twentieth Century Fox, 1946); and *For Heaven's Sake* (Twentieth Century Fox, 1950). The song's racial cast is further confirmed by its use in *Bataan* (MGM, 1943): as American troops prepare to blow up a bridge, a Negro soldier (Kenneth Spencer) calms his nerves by humming "St. Louis Blues."

72. Apart from the Bessie Smith short, two other films were titled after the song, both made by Paramount: the first was made in 1939 and starred Dorothy Lamour and Lloyd Nolan, the second in 1958 was a biopic of Handy starring Nat King Cole. The latter all but denies the song's origins as it moves with relentless pace from vulgarity to refinement—from a squeaky clean honky-tonk to a concert hall. Outside of Hollywood, "St. Louis Blues" could still resonate as a signifier of black urban vernacular. Chester Himes uses the couplet "Black gal make a freight train jump de track / But a yaller gal make a preacher Ball de Jack" among other allusions to a black musical vernacular—spirituals, blues, jazz, rock 'n' roll, the latter heard emanating from "nightmare-lighted juke-boxes"—in *A Rage in Harlem* (1957; Edinburgh: Payback Press, 1996), 129.

Chapter 4: Voices of Smoke and Tears

1. Letter dated Oct. 24, 1932, *Torch Singer* PCA file, AMPAS.

2. Linda Williams, *Playing the Race Card: Melodramas of Black and White from Uncle Tom to O. J. Simpson* (Princeton: Princeton University Press, 2001), 176.

3. Her "name is magic in theater circles, Miss Morgan, who was recently acquitted on a charge of selling intoxicants at her nightclub, is lucky in more

ways than one." Unidentified newspaper clipping dated May 27, 1929, Helen Morgan files, AMPAS. Unfortunately the only biography of the torch singer is poet Gilbert Maxwell's poorly researched and anecdotal *Helen Morgan: Her Life and Legend* (New York: Hawthorn, 1974).

4. Miles Kreuger, *Show Boat: The Story of a Classic American Musical* (New York: Da Capo, 1977), 44.

5. The scandal surrounding the death of Reynolds has insured a continued interest in Holman. Three biographies have been published, and all focus on her relationship with Reynolds: Jon Bradshaw, *Dreams That Money Can Buy: The Tragic Life of Libby Holman* (New York: William Morrow, 1985); Hamilton Darby Perry, *Libby Holman: Body and Soul* (New York: Little, Brown, 1983); and Milt Machlin, *Libby* (New York: Tower Books, 1980). Their story had provided the inspiration for *Brief Moment* (Columbia, 1932); *Sing Sinner* (Majestic, 1933); and *Reckless* (1935).

6. Bradshaw, *Dreams That Money Can Buy,* 294.

7. Angela Y. Davis, *Blues Legacies and Black Feminism: Gertrude "Ma" Rainey, Bessie Smith, and Billie Holiday* (New York: Pantheon, 1998), xv.

8. Bradshaw, *Dreams That Money Can Buy,* 73; ibid., 71.

9. Ibid., 71. Apart from being portrayed as grotesquely overweight, Clifton Webb's characterization of Waldo Lydecker was already fully formed in the film's source novel, published in 1942: "He drank his coffee in silent disapproval, watching as I unscrewed the carnelian cap of the silver box in which I keep my saccharine tablets. Although I spread butter lavishly on my brioches, I cling religiously to the belief that the substitution of saccharine for sugar in coffee will make me slender and fascinating. His scorn robbed my attitudes of character" (Caspary, *Laura,* 11).

10. *Motion Picture* 39, no. 1 (Feb. 1930), 67.

11. From unidentified newspaper clippings, Helen Morgan file, AMPAS.

12. Spaeth, *A History of Popular Music in America,* 472.

13. Bradshaw, *Dreams That Money Can Buy,* 85. In an echo of Holman's "mulatto" numbers, Joan Crawford appears in blackface in *Torch Song* (MGM, 1953) singing "Two-Faced Woman," which was written by Howard Dietz and Arthur Schwartz, the principle song writers for *The Little Show* and *Three's a Crowd.*

14. Luc Sante, "Mean Streets," *New York Review of Books* (Dec. 20, 2001), 84–85.

15. Donald Crafton, *The Talkies: American Cinema's Transition to Sound 1926–31* (New York: Charles Scribners, 1997); Scott Eyman, *The Speed of Sound: Hollywood and the Talkie Revolution 1926–1930* (New York: Simon and Schuster, 1997); Richard Barrios, *A Song in the Dark: The Birth of the Musical Film* (New York: Oxford University Press, 1995).

16. Tom Milne, *Mamoulian* (London: Thames and Hudson, 1969). Mamoulian, however, is notably absent from Peter Wollen's "Pantheon Directors" that appeared exclusively in the first edition of *Signs and Meaning in the Cinema* (London: Secker and Warburg, 1969); both books belong to the "Cinema One" series sponsored by the British Film Institute.

17. Beth Brown, *Applause* (New York: Grosset and Dunlap, 1928), 142.

18. Milne, *Mamoulian*, 23.

19. A similar experience of meeting modernity for the first time is described by bluesman Muddy Waters, who in 1943 left the Mississippi plantation on which he had spent most of his life and moved to Chicago: "I got off the train and it looked like this was the fastest place in the world—cabs dropping fares, horns blowing, the people walking so fast. And then trying to get in a taxicab, and he whooshes up and drives fast, and big buildings. I made him pull up and I wouldn't let him leave till I see do my sister and her husband Dan live in this house. All the buildings on the South Side then looked just alike" (Robert Palmer, *Deep Blues: A Musical and Cultural History of the Mississippi Delta* [New York: Penguin Books, 1982], 14).

20. W. T. Lhamon Jr., *Raising Cain: Blackface Performance from Jim Crow to Hip Hop* (Cambridge, Mass.: Harvard University Press, 1998), 111.

21. "Flying High" was written by De Sylva, Brown, Henderson, and Mc-Gowan; "What Wouldn't I Do For That Man" by Gurney and Harburg.

22. Milne, *Mamoulian*, 20.

23. *Applause* PCA file, AMPAS.

24. Letter, New York, Sept. 18, 1929, PCA file, AMPAS.

25. *Film Daily,* Oct. 13, 1929.

26. Mordaunt Hall, *New York Times,* Oct. 8, 1929.

27. *Film Daily,* Oct. 13, 1929.

28. *Photoplay* 37, no. 3 (Feb. 1930), 8.

29. *Film Daily,* Oct. 13, 1929.

30. *Variety,* Oct. 9, 1929.

31. Mimeographed publicity material, *Applause* PCA file, AMPAS.

32. *New Republic,* Oct. 30, 1929.

33. Milne, *Mamoulian*, 13.

34. *Motion Picture* 38, no. 7 (Aug. 1929), 61.

35. Matthew Bernstein, *Walter Wanger: Hollywood Independent* (Berkeley: University of California Press, 1994), 233. Gary Giddins, *Bing Crosby: A Pocketful of Dreams, The Early Years* (New York: Little, Brown, 2001), 241.

36. Patrick McGilligan, *Fritz Lang: The Nature of the Beast* (London: Faber and Faber, 1997), 383.

37. Readers looking for arcane knowledge on the history and prehistory of "Gypsy Davey" need search no further than Nick Tosches, "Orpheus, Gypsies, and Redneck Rock 'n' Roll," in *Country: The Twisted Roots of Rock 'n' Roll* (New York: Da Capo, 1996), 4–21. Through the filter of Orpheus offered by Tosches, similarities between the ballad and Caspary's *Laura* become apparent, with Mark playing the role of Gypsy Davey and Waldo the cuckold: "'Have you ever analyzed that particular form of romanticism which burgeons on the dead, the lost, the doomed? Mary of the Wild Moor and Sweet Alice With Hair So Brown, their heroines are always dead or tubercular, death is the leit-motif of all their love-songs. A most convenient rationale for the thriftiness of their

passion toward living females. Mark's future unrolls as upon a screen.' Waldo's plump hand unrolled the future. 'I see him now, romanticizing frustration, asking poor cheated females to sigh with him over the dead love'" (Caspary, *Laura,* 199).

38. "From the outset, especially in her insistence on wearing the derby-jacket-shirt uniform of the Krupa orchestra instead of a frilly gown, she was signaling that she was no mere canary. (To drive home this point, she once even threatened to measure her Krupa bandmates' dicks on the tour bus—all 15 of them.) Not an easy path this, considering that she, like many other women fronting big bands of the day, got little sympathy—and at times outright hostility—from the testosterone-dominated bandstand" (Matthew C. Duersten, "The Moon Looks Down and Laughs: The Wonderful, Horrible Jazz Life of Anita O'Day," in *Da Capo Best Music Writing 2002,* ed. Jonathan Lethem and Paul Bresnick [New York: Da Capo, 2002], 300). See also Will Friedwald, *Jazz Singing* (New York: Da Capo, 1996), 68–90.

39. Review of *The Hard Way* (Warner Bros., 1942), *Variety* (Daily), Sept. 21, 1942.

40. The PCA was not particularly impressed with the novel's subject matter: "This is a low-toned, sordid picture of a slice of American life in which the activities of criminals are dramatized to the tune of brutality, excessive drinking, industrial greed and improper care of industrial casualties; raw vulgarity, crudity, adultery, illicit sex, child-abandonment, drunkenness with a flavor of Negro-vs-white association; insanity, suggested marital infidelity, etc." All of that makes one wonder what was hidden behind the final "etc." PCA file, AMPAS.

41. Dorothy Chamberlain and Robert Wilson, eds., *In the Spirit of Jazz: The Otis Ferguson Reader* (New York: Da Capo, 1997), 111. According to Spaeth, "The Man I Love" (1924) was Gershwin's "best song." He is right, I think. Spaeth continues,

> The melodic pattern of this remarkable number is derived from the traditional "blue ending" which jazz bands of the day frequently added to a final chord, running from the fifth interval of the scale to the minor seventh and back again. The sound of that progression is quite familiar to anyone who has ever heard it, and its constant repetition in the melody of "The Man I Love" amazingly avoids monotony by the variety of the harmonies and the charm of Ira Gershwin's words. A descending chromatic scale acts as a countermelody and plays a prominent part in the harmonic scheme. Songs of this type are so far in advance of conventional popular music, particularly of the old fashioned kind, that comparisons are practically impossible.

From Spaeth, *A History of Popular Music in America,* 443.

42. Lupino's singing was ghosted by Peg La Centra, who also did the same for Hayward in *Smash-Up.* La Centra appears as a cocktail bar piano player and singer in *Humoresque* (Warner Bros., 1946), which, in one very wonderful

scene, has a character played by Joan Crawford singing along to her songs of sadness and heartbreak.

43. Lizabeth Scott replays this role in *Dark City* (Paramount, 1950); Charlton Heston takes the part of the damaged male.

44. Linda Mizejewski, *Ziegfeld Girl: Image and Icon in Culture and Cinema* (Durham, N.C.: Duke University Press, 1999), 122.

45. Ibid., 123.

46. Ibid., 120.

47. See Donald Bogle, *Dorothy Dandridge: A Biography* (New York: Boulevard Books, 1998), 477–83, for more on the film's production history and its links to the life histories of Dandridge and Billie Holliday.

Chapter 5: The City Stripped Bare

1. On the politics of folk music in the 1930s, see Robert Cantwell, *When We Were Good: The Folk Revival* (Cambridge, Mass.: Harvard University Press), 1996. For a history of the Popular Front, see Michael Denning, *The Cultural Front* (London: Verso, 1996).

2. Anatole Litvak, the director of *Blues in the Night,* also had a hand in the similarly themed melodramatic nonsense *City for Conquest* (Warner Bros., 1940), in which Eddie Kenny (Arthur Kennedy), brother of Danny Kenny (Jimmy Cagney), truck driver and boxer, stares out of a window à la *Blues in the Night* and gives voice to his dream of writing a "symphony of New York, the song of the magic isle, city for conquest. A full symphony with all its proud passionate beauty and all of its sordid ugliness." No doubt Gershwin's "Rhapsody in Blue" provided the model.

3. The singing Negro prisoner was a trope that was also featured in fiction of the period: "Our cell—it was more like a room—was in a small corridor set apart for the women prisoners' quarters. Down the hall I could hear them calling to each other and chatting back and forth from their cells. Somewhere a colored woman was singing a mournful dirge about 'That Bad Stackalee.' The verses were endless. The point of the song seemed to be that the Negro bully, Stackalee, had been killed with a 'big forty-four gun over a damned old Stetson hat.' In the most harrowing tones at the end of every verse the singer moaned the sad refrain, 'That ba-a-d Stackalee.'" The singing of the thirty or forty verses of Stackalee "invariably restores the laughing good humor and child-like confidence of the wronged one." Indeed. Jack Black, *You Can't Win* (1926; London: AK Press, 2000), 42.

4. Gabbard, *Jammin' at the Margins,* 110–15.

5. See Ferguson's piece on Benny Goodman, "The Spirit of Jazz." The quotation is from "A Breakfast Dance in Harlem," in *In the Spirit of Jazz,* ed. Chamberlain and Wilson, 68–73, 58–62.

6. In the same year of the film's release, 1941, Otis Ferguson wrote: "It is

pretty clear around New York that jazz has gone back to its obscure and un-profitable limbo again. And not only in New York at that, for whose are the top bands in the country? Glenn Miller, with a watered down version of what Benny Goodman's idea was when he started it six years ago; Guy Lombardo, with a scrupulously edited version of nothing at all; Kay Kyser, a zany practically innocent of all musical knowledge" ("Jazz at Random," in *In the Spirit of Jazz,* 108).

7. From the story summary produced by Warner Bros. for the PCA, *Blues in the Night* PCA file, AMPAS.

8. However, see, for example, Ferguson's critical detonation of the argot of jazz hipsters: "Man . . . You're Jiving Me Crazy," in *In the Spirit of Jazz,* 47–49.

9. Colin McArthur, "*Crossfire* and the Anglo-American Critical Tradition," in *Coming to Terms with Hollywood: BFI Dossier #11,* ed. Jim Cook and Alan Lovell (London: British Film Institute, 1981), 77–83. Steve Neale, *Genre and Hollywood* (London: Routledge, 2000), 115, 174, 180.

10. Robert J. Corber, *Homosexuality in Cold War America* (Durham, N.C.: Duke University Press, 1997), 86.

11. Saverio Giovacchini, *Hollywood Modernism: Film and Politics in the Age of the New Deal* (Philadelphia: Temple University Press, 2001), 195–98.

12. James Naremore, *More than Night: Film Noir in Its Contexts* (Berkeley: University of California Press, 1998), 115.

13. Giovacchini, *Hollywood Modernism,* 196.

14. Richard Brooks, *The Brick Foxhole* (Garden City, N.Y.: Sun Dial Press, 1945), 30.

15. Naremore, *More than Night,* 115–16.

16. Ibid., 118.

17. Brooks, *The Brick Foxhole,* 91.

18. For a short authoritative history of the 1930s and 1940s jazz revivalists, see Alyn Shipton, *A New History of Jazz* (London: Continuum, 2001), 607–31.

19. Short autobiographies of Gabler, Ertegun, and Hammond are collected in Arnold Shaw, *The Street That Never Slept: New York's Fabled 52nd St.* (New York: Coward, McCann, and Geoghegan, 1971).

20. Joseph Mitchell, *My Ears Are Bent* (New York: Pantheon Books, 2001), 125. For a 1939 account of record collecting, that strange disabling malaise that especially effects young male intellectuals, see Stephen W. Smith, "Collecting Hot," in *Jazzmen,* ed. Frederic Ramsey Jr. and Charles Edward Smith (London: Jazz Book Club, 1958), 287–300.

21. Dan Morganstern, notes accompanying the CD set *Hot Jazz on Blue Note* (Smithsonian Institute Press/Capital Records, 1996), 15.

22. Michael Denning, *The Cultural Front* (London: Verso, 1996), 458.

23. Ibid., 458–59.

24. A short history of the label is included in the essential compact disc box set *The Good Time Jazz Story* (Fantasy, 1995). Other essential collections of hot

jazz include *The Commodore Story* (BMG, CMD 24002, 1997), the anthology *Hot Jazz on Blue Note* (Smithsonian Institution/Capital Records, CDP 7243 8 35811 2, 1996), and *The Complete Hot Record Society Sessions* (Mosaic, MD6-187, 2002).

25. Paul Buhle and Dave Wagner, *A Very Dangerous Citizen: Abraham Lincoln Polonsky and the Hollywood Left* (Berkeley: University of California Press, 2001), 113, 109.

26. *Hollywood Reporter,* Aug. 13, 1947.

27. *Variety,* Aug. 13, 1947.

28. *Variety* (Daily), Aug. 13, 1947.

29. Jonathan Rosenbaum, *Placing Movies: The Practice of Film Criticism* (Berkeley: University of California Press, 1995), 73.

30. Buhle and Wagner, *A Very Dangerous Citizen,* 108–17. Thom Andersen, "Red Hollywood," in *Literature and the Visual Arts in Contemporary Society,* ed. Suzanne Ferguson and Barbara Groseclose (Columbus: Ohio State University Press, 1985), 141–96.

31. Buhle and Wagner, *A Very Dangerous Citizen.* Robert Rossen's contribution to *Body and Soul* has been consistently undermined by supporters of Polonsky, yet this was hardly new territory for the director. As a screenwriter, he was responsible for some of Warner Bros. most interesting films of the late 1930s, notably *Marked Woman, Sea Wolf, Roaring Twenties,* and *A Walk in the Sun.* His directorial debut, *Johnny O'Clock* (Columbia, 1947), is much more than a hack genre piece, as many critics have suggested; an astute and sympathetic reading is given by Brian Neve, *Film and Politics in America: A Social Tradition* (London: Routledge, 1992), 140–41.

32. *Body and Soul* PCA file, AMPAS.

33. Buhle and Wagner, *A Very Dangerous Citizen,* 101.

34. Mitchell, *My Ears Are Bent,* 8.

35. See cuttings in the *Body and Soul* PCA file, AMPAS.

36. Arnold Shaw, *The Street That Never Slept: New York's Fabled 52nd St.* (New York: Coward, McCann and Geoghegan, 1971), 200–201. For more rigorous analysis of Coleman's recording, see Scott DeVeaux, *The Birth of BeBop—a Social and Musical History* (London: Picador, 1999), and Alyn Shipton, *A New History of Jazz* (New York: Continuum, 2001), 415–17.

37. Andersen, "Red Hollywood," 141–96.

38. Robert Warshow, *The Immediate Experience: Movies, Comics, Theatre, and Other Aspects of Popular Culture* (Cambridge, Mass.: Harvard University Press, 2001), 3–18. For an account of postwar liberal critics' confrontation with mass culture, see Saverio Giovacchini, *Hollywood Modernism: Film and Politics in the Age of the New Deal* (Philadelphia: Temple University Press, 2001), 178–81, 216–18.

39. David Reid and Jayne L. Walker, "Strange Pursuit: Cornell Woolrich and the Abandoned City of the Forties," in *Shades of Noir,* ed. Joan Copjec (London: Verso, 1993), 61.

40. "Opinion" by V. G. Hart, Nov. 4, 1933, PCA file, AMPAS. The eponymous and economically independent heroine of Vera Caspary's 1942 novel *Laura* is described in similar terms: "Would you prescribe a nunnery for a woman of her temperament? She had a man's job and a man's worries. Knitting wasn't one of her talents" (Caspary, *Laura*, 40).

41. Reid and Walker, "Strange Pursuit," 74.

42. Ibid., 90.

43. Will Straw, "Urban Confidential: The Lurid City of the 1950s," in *The Cinematic City*, ed. David B. Clarke (London: Routledge, 1997), 111.

44. Ibid., 113.

45. This definition is provided by jazz club operator Ralph Watkins in Shaw, *The Street That Never Slept*, 215.

46. *Variety* (Daily), June 4, 1953, Legion of Decency report in PCA file, AMPAS.

47. Reid and Walker, "Strange Pursuit," 86.

48. Straw, "Urban Confidential," 120. This is also the subtext of Edward Dmytryk's extraordinary *The Sniper* (Columbia, 1952), another abandoned-city narrative with dead women at its center. The story concerns a young misogynistic psychopath that stalks and kills women. His first victim is Jean Darr (Marie Windsor), a nightclub pianist.

49. The reviewer for *Variety* thought the film represented "something of a retreat from the now traditional semi-documentary treatment of this sort of theme" (June 22, 1949).

50. Allen, *Horrible Prettiness*, 235.

51. Shaw, *The Street That Never Slept*, 335–41. The link between jazz and stripping formed the core of the long-playing album *Blues for a Stripper and Other Exciting Sounds*, composed and conducted by Mundell Lowe (Charlie Parker Record Corp., 1962): "Multi-talented Mundell Lowe has the uncanny ability of blending utter sophistication with a front row seat in a burlesque house and coming out with a swinging blue mood. . . . How does one summarize 'Blues For A Stripper'?—It's a 'gas.'"

52. Allen, *Horrible Prettiness*, 251.

53. Ibid., 252–51, 255.

54. Ibid., 256.

55. *The Phenix City Story* uses a similar all-white jazz combo for its opening burlesque scene, as much as the lesbian bar manager, the gambling and drinking, the removal of the singer's long black glove, and the first blast of rhythm and blues and Dixieland (a unique hybrid in American film as far as I can tell) confirms the Poppy Bar as the center of the city's corrupt and vice-ridden heart.

56. For a lengthy analysis of how American film used and abused Armstrong, see Gabbard, *Jammin' at the Margins*, 204–38.

57. Mickey Spillane, *The Long Wait* (London: Corgi, 1960), 128. In *Screaming Mimi*, burlesque dancer Yolanda (Anita Ekberg) is both victim of a knife attack and a killer of burlesque dancers.

58. Cited in Bernard Gendron, *Between Montmartre and the Mudd Club: Popular Music and the Avant-Garde* (Chicago: University of Chicago Press, 2002), 374.

59. In this context, it is worth looking again at the surrealist Jacques-Andre Boiffard's photograph of Renée Jacobi (1930), which suggests she is a corpse in a mortuary, and to consider Luc Sante's comments on crime photography: "In looking at a crime photo we know we are looking at an image of radical disjunction before we are consciously aware of its narrative content. But then crime retails death, or at best loss, so that even before spectators with no personal stake in the matter it is charged. It is surrealism with a knife" (introduction to *New York Noir: Crime Photos from the Daily News Archive,* ed. William Hannigan [New York: Rizzoli, 1999], 8).

60. D. H. Clarke, *A Lady Named Lou* (New York: Avon, n.d.; reprint Vanguard Press, 1941), cover and frontmatter.

61. Jean Baudrillard, *Symbolic Exchange and Death* (London: Sage, 1993), 101.

62. David Grubb, *The Night of the Hunter* (London: Simon Schuster, 1988), 25.

63. Allen, *Horrible Prettiness,* 244.

64. See Len Rothe, *The Queens of Burlesque: Vintage Photographs from the 1940s and 1950s* (Atglen, Pa.: Schiffer Publishing, 1997). For every nom de plume taken from untamed nature—Blaze Fury or Tempest Storm—there were dozens of dancers who simply lifted their stage names "Direct from Hollywood." Za-Za Amour—"The Bouncing Parisian"—whose name suggested Ms. Gabor, had an image that presented a more gaudy glamour. If Gilda never did any of those things as played by Rita Hayworth, the burlesque queen named after her character suggests she did it all and more. Rita Grable manages to combine the names of two of Hollywood's sex goddesses and the allure of neither. Scarlett O'Hara made a dress from velvet drapes but her burlesque namesake used net curtains. Ann Perri was billed as the "Parisian Jane Russell," but her cheesecake was cut at a Chicago photographic studio called Garbo's. Like the prostitutes who appear as Hollywood stars in James Ellroy's *L.A. Confidential* (1994), these burlesque queens claim a glamour that is not rightfully theirs. In the process, they diminish whatever aura of the "real" the stars they impersonate have accrued. They reveal the artifice of glamour across the divide—trumpery articles one and all.

65. Roland Barthes, "Striptease," in *Mythologies* (London: Vintage, 1993), 85–86.

66. Mickey Spillane, *The Long Wait* (London: Corgi, 1960), 26.

67. Joseph Breen to J. E. Baker, Republic Productions, Nov. 12, 1952, about concerns with the script for *City That Never Sleeps.*

68. Peter Stanfield, *Hollywood, Westerns, and the 1930s: The Lost Trail* (Exeter: University of Exeter Press, 2001), 173–80.

69. *Variety,* June 4, 1953, and *Motion Picture Daily,* June 11, 1953.

70. *Variety,* June 1, 1953, and *Hollywood Reporter,* June 4, 1953.

71. Joseph Mitchell, *My Ears Are Bent* (New York: Pantheon Books, 2001), 55.

72. *Le Surrealisme* published a survey on "Le Strip Tease," Meme no. 4 1958 edition. Benoit Landieres.

73. The tabloid and the press book for *Shock Corridor* are held in the open collection of the Margaret Herrick Library, AMPAS.

74. *Variety,* July 1, 1963; *Hollywood Reporter,* July 1, 1963; *Los Angeles Times,* Sept. 10, 1963; *Cue,* Sept. 14, 1963; *Film Quarterly* (Winter 1963–64); *Cinema,* Aug. 1963; *Herald Tribune* quoted in J. Hoberman, "Crazy for You," *Village Voice,* Feb. 17, 1998. Unless otherwise noted, all reviews are culled from the *Shock Corridor* cutting file, AMPAS.

75. Letter to J. C. Macgregor Scott, Esq., Warner Pathe Film Dist. Ltd., London (Nov. 11, 1963), *Shock Corridor* PCA file, AMPAS.

76. *Film Daily,* July 3, 1963.

77. *Film Quarterly* (Winter 1963–64).

78. "Soap Opera Prostitution," *Cosmopolitan,* June 1964.

79. *Variety,* July 1, 1963.

80. Manny Farber, *Negative Space* (New York: Da Capo, 1998): 3–11.

81. Peter Stanfield, "'Film Noir Like You've Never Seen': Jim Thompson Adaptations and Cycles of Neo Noir," in *Genre and Contemporary Hollywood,* ed. Steve Neale (London: British Film Institute, 2002).

82. Lawrence W. Levine, "Jazz and American Culture," in *The Unpredictable Past: Explorations in American Cultural History* (New York: Oxford University Press, 1993), 172–88.

Conclusion

1. W. T. Lhamon Jr., *Deliberate Speed: The Origins of a Cultural Style in the American 1950s* (Cambridge, Mass.: Harvard University Press, 2002), xxv.

2. Ibid., 86.

3. Ibid., 38. Brian Ward's *Just My Soul Responding: Rhythm and Blues, Black Consciousness, and Race Relations* (London: UCL Press, 1998) is an exemplary history of the post–World War II penetration of black culture into white consciousness and gives historical weight to Lhamon's argument. Moreover, it also tirelessly documents the link between the civil rights movement and black popular music.

4. Will Straw, "Urban Confidential: The Lurid City of the 1950s," in *The Cinematic City,* ed. David B. Clarke (London: Routledge, 1997), 111.

5. Nicholas Lemann, *The Promised Land: The Great Black Migration and How It Changed America* (London: MacMillan, 1991), 6.

6. Richard Maltby, "'Nobody Knows Everything': Post-classical Historiographies and Consolidated Entertainment," in *Contemporary Hollywood Cinema*, ed. Steve Neale and Murray Smith (London: Routledge, 1998), 21–44.

7. Ibid.

8. Douglas Gomery, *Shared Pleasures: A History of Movie Presentation in the United States* (London: British Film Institute, 1992), 169.

9. Elliott Currie, *Reckoning: Drugs, the Cities, and the American Future* (New York: Hill and Wang, 1994).

10. Dave Marsh, *Fortunate Son: The Best of Dave Marsh* (New York: Random House, 1985), 268–74.

Index

Peter Stanfield is a senior lecturer in film studies at the University of Kent at Canterbury. He is the author of *Hollywood, Westerns, and the 1930s: The Lost Trail* and *Horse Opera: The Strange History of the Singing Cowboy* and the coeditor (with Esther Sonnet and Lee Grieveson) of *Mob Culture: Hidden Histories of the American Gangster Film.* He is currently writing a book on the films of Anthony Mann, Samuel Fuller, Don Siegel, Robert Aldrich, and Audie Murphy.

The University of Illinois Press
is a founding member of the
Association of American University Presses.

———————————————————————

Composed in 9.5/13 ITC Stone Serif
with ITC Stone Informal and Bellevue display
by Jim Proefrock
at the University of Illinois Press
Designed by Dennis Roberts
Manufactured by Sheridan Books, Inc.

University of Illinois Press
1325 South Oak Street
Champaign, IL 61820-6903
www.press.uillinois.edu